THE FALL OF THE PRISON

The Fall of the Prison

Biblical Perspectives on Prison Abolition

Lee Griffith

William B. Eerdmans Publishing Company
Grand Rapids, Michigan

Copyright © 1993 by Wm. B. Eerdmans Publishing Co.
255 Jefferson Ave. S.E., Grand Rapids, Mich. 49503
All rights reserved

Printed in the United States of America

Library of Congress Cataloging-in-Publication Data

Griffith, Lee, 1948-
The fall of the prison: biblical perspectives on prison abolition
/Lee Griffith.
p.   cm.
Includes bibliographical references and index.
ISBN 0-8028-0670-8
1. Justice, Administration of — Biblical teaching.
2. Christianity and justice.   3. Church work with prisoners.
I. Title.
BS680.J8G75 1993
261.8'336 — dc20   93-8363
                                                     CIP

Unless otherwise indicated, all Scripture references in this book are taken from the
New American Standard Bible, © 1960, 1962, 1963, 1968, 1971, 1972, 1973, 1975,
1977 by The Lockman Foundation. Used by permission.

Portions of this book have appeared in slightly different form in the pages of
Sojourners magazine (P.O. Box 29272, Washington, D.C., 20017) and Brethren Life
and Thought. The author and publisher wish to thank these sources for permission
to use this material.

For Gary R. Kline,
who sang songs and harvested food from the garden
while I only harvested words

Contents

Foreword

A s in our health-care system, there is a growing crisis in structures that maintain prisons. The astronomical costs of "caring for" prisoners and adding to and building more modern "security" stockades constitutes an increasingly intolerable drain on our human and financial resources. At the same time, there remains a common gap between public opinion and informed prophetic voices; between those who believe tougher laws and longer incarceration will reduce crime and those who believe that the symptom of criminality will be alleviated only when we attack the illnesses of racism, unemployment, and gross injustices; between those who regard a large portion of our population as dispensable and those who regard each person as one for whom Christ died on the cross of Calvary.

The reference to the cross reveals my conviction about readers who may be the most intrigued and edified by this book. Those who share existential and educated concerns about the criminal justice system may appreciate substantive biblical and theological foundations for their prejudices and involvement. Those who feel grounded in the Christian tradition may be challenged by discussions of the illusion of rehabilitation and deterrence. Some of us will be called to examine the degree to which we belong to the cult of retribution. Some of us may be surprised by the historical overviews of prisons in the Bible and the church.

Like me, you may be both attracted to and scandalized by the proposal to banish prisons. I think of how scandalous the abolitionist movement to eliminate slavery must have been for the majority of nineteenth-century Americans. Subsequently, however, a strong case has been made for the abolition of slavery at the same time that we continue to be plagued with manifestations of racism and oppression. In the twentieth century, those who have participated in abolitionist movements to eliminate war have been regarded as fools or at best naive. Yet there is growing consciousness that we will be able to survive on this planet only if we can concretely live out this vision. Wherever you may stand on such issues, I appeal to you to be open to radical proposals, for basic changes will not come without biblical visions that pull us forward. Personally, I became more open to abolitionist proposals when I saw how incarcerated teenagers often develop an intense hatred for society and receive an education in criminal activity from their first experience in cages. I began to think that we might all be safer without jails and prisons.

As one who participated in a bail bond project with Lee Griffith when he was a seminarian, I can testify to his credentials. As a student and campus pastor, he has been an avid connoisseur of biblical and theological literature. As an activist on behalf of peace and justice, he has been a prisoner, visited prisoners, and demonstrated great compassion for victims of injustice in or out of jail. If you read carefully, you will also discern his deep concerns for victims of crime due partly to his own harrowing, life-threatening experiences with burglars.

Whatever your perspective, I hope that we all may be inspired to greater obedience to the biblical admonition to visit those in prison and to participate in our Lord's mission "to proclaim release to the captives."

Dale W. Brown
Professor, Christian Theology
Bethany Theological Seminary,
Oak Brook, Illinois

Preface

Somewhere apart from the pompous hierarchy of established religion and the profitable onslaught of religious proselytizing, a call for exodus can be heard today. It is a call for believers to join in a journey out of Christendom. The call comes in different forms from various quarters. It can be heard in the liberation theology and base communities of Latin America and in the struggle against apartheid in South Africa. In North America, the call is heard through black theology and feminist theology and the growing consciousness of liberation theology in the gay and lesbian community. The call is incarnated in the intentional Christian communities that seek to resist militarism and feed the hungry and house the homeless. Even if one differs with these movements on specific points of theology or social analysis, it is still possible to hear and heed the call. It is a call to radicalism in the literal sense of *radix*, returning to the root and foundation. The call for exodus from Christendom is an effort to put aside ecclesiastical concessions to power and respectability in order to look anew at the root gospel of Jesus of Nazareth.

So the call to journey out of Christendom is simultaneously a call to return to biblical faith. The people involved in this journey out and back have some powerful lessons to teach us about the manner in which we have read the Bible — or, more precisely, the manner in which we have permitted the dominant values of Western culture to govern our reading of Scripture. A revealing example is provided by the gay men and lesbians who have discovered that the condemnation and exclusion they have experienced in the church are based on an eisegesis of about ten verses in Scripture. Meanwhile, there are literally hundreds of biblical verses condemning opulence, yet the wealthy aren't excluded from the church; they're asked to build new Sunday school wings. Contrary to the claims of biblical support for patriarchy, feminists have discovered anew the way in which Jesus viewed women as partners in ministry as he renounced the civil and religious laws that served to legitimate male dominance. The people of South Africa have discovered that racism and economic exploitation are not foreordained by God and Romans 13. Oppressed people of the "Third World" have discovered that the Exodus story of the liberation of God's people is their story.

But how can we judge whether these fresh readings of Scripture are any less culturally conditioned than the orthodoxy of Christendom? Have the battered and excluded people managed to create a tabula rasa in their minds and spirits so that they can receive the unadulterated Word of God? In fact, they have not succeeded in doing that, nor should that be the criterion for entering into biblical study or theology. The very existence of the field of hermeneutics indicates that any pretense to total objectivity is illusory. Karl Barth had cause to encourage us to study the Bible and the newspaper side by side. He recognized that we must understand the context in which Scripture is read just as surely as that in which it was written. Those who stand outside the alliance of church and state and culture have significant lessons to share about how to read the Bible: if we think that the gospel permits us to wield weapons and pull triggers, we need to go back and read again. If we think that the gospel encourages our bigotries and segregations, we need to go back and read again. If we think that the gospel promises us wealth while others freeze and starve, we need to go back and read again. And if we think that the gospel enjoins us to imprison and cage our sisters and brothers in the name of order and justice and all things good, we need to go back and read again.

This book is an attempt to go back and read again the gospel as it pertains to prisoners and prisons. But as I read again, I have not set aside the newspapers. The context for this study is late twentieth-century America, a society that has more prisons and more judicially sanctioned executions and (despite it all) more crime than virtually any other nation on our planet. In view of my contention that biblical perspectives on prisoners are relevant to the many prisoners who surround us now, this may appear to some to be a book of advocacy rather than detached scholarship. While I confess to not aiming for detachment, I hope that I have managed nonetheless to be responsible in my references to and applications of theology, history, exegesis, and sociology. Insofar as advocacy is present, I hope that I have managed to advocate something more than just my own druthers. My own druthers are more in accord with the American dream of material comfort and security than I sometimes care to admit. In contrast, the path of discipleship is the way of the cross. In the words of Dostoyevsky's Father Zossima, "love in action is a harsh and dreadful thing compared to love in dreams."

I have intentionally adopted the approach in this study of seeking to allow Scripture to demythologize our current penal system. In the first chapter I prepare the ground by confronting some of the ways in which historical theologies have cast doubt on the gospel's relevance to concrete social and political situations. In the second chapter I present an overview of the prison in America today and of the various penal ideologies that have been promoted in defense of the efficacy of incarceration. By way of contrast, in the third chapter I examine biblical perspectives on prisoners and prisons. How has the church responded to the biblical understandings? In Chapter 4 I make an effort to trace some of the long history of the interactions between church communities and penal institutions, a history that alternately tells of a church community imprisoned and a church busily imprisoning people in its own dungeons. In the fifth chapter I write about applied theology in an effort to explore the concrete ethical implications of the biblical understandings of prisoners and prisons.

Regarding these concrete ethical implications, it should be noted that there is a dialectical tension inherent in the question of precisely who is being addressed by Jesus' call to discipleship. On the one hand, it is first a call to the church. The faithful response from the community of believers is to take up our cross and follow. We are not called to impose the cross upon others. We are not called to devise rules or to make demands about how others should follow or about what others "ought to do." And we are certainly not called to legislate a theocracy in which others are forced to assume the risks and the joys of discipleship whether they have heard the call or not (as if such were possible). On the other hand, there can be no doubt that Jesus is Lord of all creation or that the kingdom of God is already present in our midst. The church is commissioned to share that Good News with all nations (Matt. 28:19) and to speak truth to power. Discipleship is not to be privatized within the church; rather, it is to serve as a witness to all creation that death is defeated and that God has chosen life on our behalf.

The biblical word on prisons and caring for both prisoners and victims of crime clearly has radical implications for the discipleship of the church and the church's witness to the nations. In this study I try to show how this biblical word is in fact a proclamation of freedom for the prisoners (Luke 4:18). This news is fully Good News. But as with all of the gospel, the church hears and responds to this Good News in the context of our world, which is situated between the "already" and the "not yet" of God's kingdom. The idea of throwing open the prison doors is frightening. The effort to respond nonviolently to crime is risky. The attempt to meet the needs of victims of crime entails sacrifice. In other words, there is a cross to be borne. It is those of us in the community of believers who are called to bear this cross.

As I write about "applied theology" and the ethical implications of the biblical proclamation, you will note that, with some few exceptions in the final chapter, I have very little to say about legislative proposals or lobbying efforts or pragmatic plans regarding "what the government ought to do." My concern is to speak more of the attempt to witness to prison abolition through discipleship than of the effort (whether vain or not) to impose it through the legislation of institutional change. The difference is not insubstantial. The call to discipleship might lead individuals or communities of faith to refrain from calling on the power of the police, courts, and prisons. But is it desirable or even possible to legislate that our neighbors must respond similarly? The prison itself is the tool of such compulsion.

Please do not misunderstand. My point here is not to pass judgment on the discipleship of those who engage in political campaigns for legislative and institutional change. Among other people who could be cited, Martin Luther King, Jr., provided a remarkable witness to the path of discipleship while also serving as a skilled agent of institutional change. But King himself resisted any theocratic impulse which would pretend that our task is to build the kingdom of God or to legislate faithfulness. If political activity in the pursuit of institutional change is motivated by biblical faith, those who are involved in it have to be especially careful to ensure that the call to discipleship that the church has heard does not become a pretext for imposing sacrifices and risks on other people. Again, the call is to "take up your cross and follow," not to force the cross upon others.

But then does the community of believers have nothing to say to the governing authorities or to the nations? On the contrary, the church has been blessed with the mission to proclaim the entirety of the Good News not only to individuals but to the governing authorities and institutions and principalities and powers as well. As I stress in Chapter 3, however, God's justice is established through persuasion rather than through coercion, through the Suffering Servant rather than through the force of arms or the force of legal apparatus. It is by joining in this persuasion and by being willing to share in this suffering that the community of discipleship is able to bear prophetic witness to prison abolition.

Yes, the church has Good News to announce to the governing authorities and to everyone else as well: freedom for the prisoners. But the truth of the announcement does not await our effectuating a theocracy in which prisons are razed because we have coerced all people into taking the risks and making the sacrifices that might be required. The truth of the Good News lies in the kingdom of God that has already been established in our midst and in the freedom that God grants to believers to live now in the very real presence of that kingdom. Prisons will not be abolished when this or that governing authority declares it to be so. Rather, prisons will cease to exist when the community of believers faithfully lives according to that freedom which Jesus has already declared. Jesus has deprived the prison of its power. The walls are weaker than we imagine. The prison does not fall because of the coercion of the governing powers but because of the persuasion and the example of the Suffering Servant.

Along with all of the other weaknesses that will become only too apparent, I must confess to two glaring shortcomings in this study. I am guilty of having precious few references in this book to the peoples of Asia, Africa, and Latin America. This is not to suggest that the oppression of incarceration is absent from these lands. Historically, however, the story of collusion between penology and theology begins in western Asia and Europe. Thankfully, it was not until later that the people of other continents met the colonizers armed with crosses and swords. Nonetheless, I must confess to following the story most closely as it proceeds from Europe to North America. I can make excuses about being confined to the English language and about the sparsity of books and articles in English on the church and the development of prisons in Africa, Asia, and Latin America, but possessing fluency only in English is itself a sign of ethnocentrism. Of that I am guilty. And I am also guilty of relying on the many traditional histories and resources written about and by men. A few remarkable women emerge in this study, but I feel certain that their numbers and our learning are diminished by sexism.

Allow me to note that there are two major instances in which I reluctantly resort to the traditional language of the church:

1. The traditional designation of the division of Christian Scriptures into "Old" and "New" Testaments may reflect accuracy regarding chronology of authorship of the various books collected in each division, but far too often the titles of the testaments have said less about dates than about the church's attitude toward Judaism. Through history, the brutal anti-Semitism of the church has been fueled to no small degree by a theological contention that the "Old" Testament has been superseded by a new revelation that the Jews reject. In more than a few instances, the naming of the testaments has betrayed a belief in a new covenant that relegates Jews to the status of "former people of God." Such anti-Semitism also excludes Jesus from the community of God's people, for whatever else one might say about who Jesus was and is, Jesus is a Jew. It is noteworthy that one of Jesus' proclamations with a special significance for this study is in fact a quotation from the prophet Isaiah: "I have come to proclaim release for the prisoners." Testaments old and new commingle as Jesus preaches on the implications of his Jewish faith in the God who sent him to all people. Of course, I write from my own faith as it has been shaped by gospel and by experience in the church community. I resort to the traditional designations of Old and New Testaments because, at least for the time being, other possible alternatives risk offering only awkward phrasings that are subject to misunderstanding or (much worse) linguistic acrobatics that succeed in nothing so much as engendering a patronizing attitude toward the Jewish community. To speak of the Hebrew and Greek Testaments would be awkward and (given Aramaic) not altogether accurate. To speak of Tanach (the Bible of Judaism) and the New Testament hardly escapes the dilemma of the current designations. For the time being, I will rely on the traditional language of the testaments while praying that I manage to avoid some of the other manifestations of anti-Semitism so often fostered by our church community.

2. The reality that has traditionally been called "the kingdom of God" has more than passing significance in this study. Again, it is with some reluctance that I use this traditional phrase. The problem lies in the zeal with which some believers have affirmed that the ruler of this kingdom — the "King" — is a male deity. Biblically, the "gender" of God is less of a certainty than the zeal of ecclesiastical patriarchy might suggest. The Bible presents God as the comforting Mother (Isa. 66:12-13), as the Mother drawing her young close under her wings (Ruth 2:12; Matt. 23:37; Luke 13:34), as the Woman searching for the lost coin (Luke 15:8-10). Why waste time in a feud over so anthropomorphic a notion as the "gender" of God? The point has significance because of those all-too-frequent instances in which some within the church have sought to enlist a masculine deity in the service of maintaining male dominance and excluding women from full partnership in ministry. We have cause to beware of gods who are too easily summoned to speak a blessing over existing power arrangements. Like golden calves, such gods may be indebted to their creators. Biblically, the reality called the kingdom of God is certainly not a comfort to the powers that be. I continue to use this traditional phrase in this study, however, because of the effective manner in which the expression points to the radical political and social implications of God's promise and God's work in the world. The Bible is filled with political language that theologians have too often tamed through a spiritualizing process. Words such as *Lord* and *redemption* and *covenant* can be traced to political origins. Through the history of theology, some words have been so thoroughly reworked that we barely remember, for example, that the word *Savior* was once an honorific title applied to Roman emperors who had provided for the security and the material well-being of their subjects. There is danger that translating kingdom-of-God language into some alternative form such as "God's new reality" would serve only to detract from the recognition of the radical implications of God's revelation for *all* aspects of life. It is my hope that references to the kingdom of God will not serve further to entrench presumptions about a male deity. Apart from writing about the kingdom of God and directly quoting words written by others, I hope that I have been successful in my efforts to refrain from depicting God as male.

Over the years, I think that I have acquired some understanding of what others mean when they speak of being "pursued" by a certain calling. In my own experience, there have been times when unplanned (and occasionally unwelcome) circumstances have landed me in the company of prisoners and in the company of those who have been victimized by crime. If I had not been pursued by those circumstances and experiences, I doubt that I would have embarked on this study. So I am thankful.

I am thankful to the members of the DuPage County Bail Fund, a group with which I was privileged to work while I was in seminary. It was with the Bail Fund that I first learned that people behind prison walls are made of the same stuff as the rest of us; in jail or out, we are all capable of the most gentle caring or the most horrendous violence. I learned too that those who can offer genuine service to prisoners might come from the ranks of real estate brokers or insurance agents as well as from the ranks of the counterculture.

I am thankful for the several communities of which I have been a member: the Community for Creative Nonviolence in Washington, D.C.; Jonah House and Advaita House in Baltimore; Apodidomi in Elmira, New York. Some of these communities have provided hospitality for people released from prison and for people awaiting trial. All of these communities have sought to practice nonviolent alternatives to reliance on the judicial system. Even in the occasional presence of fists and knives and guns, some sisters and brothers in these communities have given powerful witness to the fact that there are alternatives to merely standing idly by on the one hand or matching guns with guns on the other.

While I cannot endorse incarceration, I am thankful nonetheless to the various judges who have sent me to jail. Had I not had some time behind bars, I suspect this book might be different in some particulars. But I make no pretense to having suffered the full wrath of the penal system. My sojourns in jail were usually brief and usually in the company of peace activists. I am certain that the treatment accorded us by judges and jailers was considerably gentler than that meted out to the vast majority of prisoners who cannot avail themselves of the benefits that the system normally bestows on those with social connections, middle-class status, and white skin.

And, with some reluctance, I am thankful to two brothers who broke into our community house in Baltimore in 1976. I have been victimized by crime in other instances, but never in such a frightening manner. The intruders brandished a gun, and their twenty-minute visit to our home included a debate about whether they should kill us. I will always remember the love and courage of two other community members, Phil Berrigan and Liz McAlister; they could have chosen to escape through the back door and leave me alone to cope with the armed intruders, but they chose to stay. I will also always remember the terror of those twenty minutes. Again, I make no pretense to having suffered the full consequences of crime, but after that night in 1976, I understood in a new way the urgent need to care for all of the victims of crime and the survivors of crime. I also understood in a new way that what I am writing about is not merely a matter of theory. Among less serious matters, this is also an inquiry into the relevance of the gospel at the juncture of life and death.

And I am thankful for the lessons and cautions implicit in the story of Elmira, New York, the area in which I have lived for a decade. Historically, the good and gentle people of Elmira have provided a home for the first fully accredited women's college in America, for the iconoclastic preaching of Thomas Beecher, and for the no less iconoclastic writing of Mark Twain. But Elmira has also served as home to unwilling guests. While Civil War raged to the south, Confederate soldiers froze to death in the prison camp at Elmira. The late nineteenth-century work of Zebulon Brockway and the building of America's first "reformatory" in Elmira set the stage for the transformation of this upstate community into a prison town. In addition to its city lockup and county jail, Elmira is home to state prisons both to the north and to the south. With the recent completion of the second state prison, Elmira's unemployment rate moved from one of the highest in New York to one of the lowest. Such an easy fix can spawn addiction; some in the area are putting forth proposals for a third state prison. The experience of Elmira serves to illustrate the fact that prisons are business — big business.

I gratefully acknowledge the assistance of those who have helped in the completion of this study. The Committee for Ministry in Higher Education of the Presbytery of Geneva, Presbyterian Church (USA), and the Council of Churches of Chemung County were generous in sponsoring a sabbatical from my work with Campus Ministry at Elmira College. The members of the Campus Ministry Advisory Committee facilitated and encouraged my sabbatical endeavors, while Kurt Katzmar ably continued and expanded the work of Campus Ministry during my absence.

Over the years, the comments, questions, agreements, and disagreements of students and faculty at Elmira College have served (often unbeknownst to them) to further this study. I am thankful for the skilled and friendly library assistance provided by Liz Wavle, head of technical services at Elmira College Library; as I sought help with research in academic journals, Liz was profoundly patient with my computer illiteracy. I am especially indebted to Dale Brown, T. A. Straayer, Steve Davis, Olivier Szlos, and Fred Turner for their willingness to read this manuscript and offer helpful suggestions. At the same time, it should be noted that blame for shortcomings must be assigned to me alone. Finally, I appreciate the ways in which the Schnippert clan and other friends tried to ensure that, despite the work, I didn't forget to play.

I am doubtless not alone among authors in some of the laments that I have felt: I wish I had more time to linger on that point; I would so much like to explore that detour; I wish my words would not come together so badly. But there comes a point with both our words and our deeds that we must let them go to fly or fall where they will.

Chapter I

Prisons and the Relevance of the Gospel

Remember Jesus Christ, risen from the dead, descendant of David, according to my gospel, for which I suffer hardship even to imprisonment as a criminal; but the word of God is not imprisoned.

2 Timothy 2:8-9

The gospel is profoundly scandalous, and until we hear at least a whisper of its scandal, we risk not hearing any part of it. Oh, certainly we can hear the recitation of religious scriptures intoned from pulpits and from religious broadcasting stations and in the blessings before meals and in the invocations before marching off to battle. Religion is something that we preach. It hits us in the ears endlessly until it makes perfect sense. But the gospel is Good News that Jesus preaches. It hits us in the guts and it makes no sense at all. Rather than offering any simple "Jesus is the Answer" slogans and formulas, the gospel points to a Jesus who assails all of our answers and our rules and our pretenses to religiosity. The gospel is scandalous — profoundly so.

The scandalous nature of the gospel is partially evident in the difficulty that some believers have in establishing precisely how or when or where it is that gospel ethics have relevance. Much of American Christendom already counts the gospel as having limited relevance internationally. There are not many among us who would call for turning an American cheek to a Russian first strike. Pragmatism would seem to

1

insist that our love of international neighbors be tempered by considerations such as trade balance, geopolitical strategy, and ideological stripe. And so some maintain that the gospel is not intended to be relevant for relationships between nations but only for interpersonal relationships.

Yet interpersonally, what are we taught? It is our learned and habitual response to rely on those civil institutions that have been concocted to buffer us from the seamier side of our neighbors. Almost by instinct, if someone commits a crime against us, if someone wrongs us or steals from us or threatens us with violence, we call the police and let the courts decide the justice of the matter. Some Christians who have scruples against keeping weapons in bedside drawers have no qualms about calling the police to wield the gun on their behalf. In an age of rampant crime, admonitions to do good to those who persecute us seem both impractical and dangerous. Indeed, turning the other cheek to common criminals seems even more absurd than loving foreign enemies.

Is it perhaps the case, then, that the gospel is not meant to apply to all interpersonal relationships but only to those within the covenanted community of believers? Maybe the admonitions of the Sermon on the Mount are fully applicable only in relationships among sisters and brothers in the church community. No, that too fails to provide an explanation of where it is that the gospel has its relevance, for in fact, be it a burden or a blessing, the majority of people in the Western world are professing Christians — and, whether we like it or not, so are the majority of lawbreakers.

So if the Good News is of only limited relevance to our life-style internationally and socially and interpersonally, even within the community of believers, where then does it have full authority and relevance? Is it in some other world, among the heavenly gathering of the elect? Is it in some theoretical Zion populated only by the righteous — there where the thought would not occur to love enemies because it would be a land without enemies, without persecutors, without sin? No, it would be in precisely such a fantasyland that the gospel would be most irrelevant. The gospel is meant to be proclaimed in and to a world populated by sinners as well as saints, hate as well as love, sorrow as well as joy. The Word of God is not imprisoned in heaven.

Is it unfair, however, to include American Christians among those who hedge on the relevance of the gospel? After all, it is with a zeal that could match the great revivals of the past that modern evangelists call for a restoration of prayer to public schools and a restoration of the sanctity of the nuclear family (Matt. 6:6 and 12:46-50 notwithstanding). Presidents declare Years of the Bible, call for days of repentance, and sit down to prayer breakfasts. Have the faithful not begun to challenge sex in the media and evolution in the textbooks? And now that godless Communism is on the run and the Supreme Court has ruled that nativity scenes may safely rest on public property, are these not signs that America is "turning back to the Bible"?

It is more likely that these are signs that America is turning back to a centuries-old view of itself as a nation with a manifest destiny and a special role in fulfilling God's plan for all of humanity. Early on, separation from the timeworn ways of Europe encouraged many Americans to understand their nation as the "new Adam," a pristine creation that had managed to recapture the innocence of the days before the fall. A related view is that of America as the "new Israel," the new people of God. In this new, specifically American covenant with God, the mission is to carry the light of a particular understanding of freedom to the gentile (i.e., non-American) world.[1] Some have even been so bold as to identify America with Jesus (John Quincy Adams: "Is it not that, in the chain of human events, the birthday of the nation is indissolubly linked with the birthday of the Savior?") or with the second coming of Christ (Theodore Roosevelt: "We stand at Armageddon and we battle for the Lord").[2] Such intimate relationship between nation and religion is reminiscent of the ancient marriage between state and god. In Greece and later in Rome, each political unit (*polis*, city) had a god, and worship of the civic god was considered vital to the welfare and security of the

1. For an examination of the way in which the "new Adam" motif has found expression in American literature, see R. W. B. Lewis, *The American Adam: Innocence, Tragedy, and Tradition in the Nineteenth Century* (Chicago: University of Chicago Press, 1955). America as "new Israel" is one of the views explored by Robert N. Bellah in his renowned essay "Civil Religion in America." In this view, notes Bellah, "Europe is Egypt; America, the promised land. God has led his people to establish a new sort of social order that shall be a light unto all the nations" ("Civil Religion in America," in *American Civil Religion*, ed. Russell E. Richey and Donald G. Jones [New York: Harper & Row, 1974], p. 29).

2. Both quotations are cited by George Armstrong Kelly in *Politics and Religious Consciousness in America* (New Brunswick, N.J.: Transaction Books, 1984), p. 134. Some have noted that Roosevelt's apocalyptic imagery reappeared in Ronald Reagan's early characterizations of the Soviet Union as an "evil empire."

community.[3] There is a distinct kinship between the civic religion of the *polis* and the contemporary agenda of American political religion. The appeal to "put God back into the classroom" (as if the whereabouts of God could be dictated by juridical decisions) is either an effort to appease a civic deity or an attempt to advance a political platform under the guise of piety.

The belief that America has a divinely covenanted role in history also entails a singular approach to reading Scripture. It is the product of an effort, in the words of William Stringfellow, "to construe the Bible Americanly."[4] The hermeneutical assumption is that the gospel would never conflict with the national self-interest. The national exegesis requires that the command to love our enemies must not preclude killing them, that the poor who are blessed are the "deserving" poor who stay off the public dole and never lapse in their appreciation for the work ethic, that stealing is something done by criminals in violation of private property and not by wealthy nations or acquisitive corporations in violation of the rights of the dispossessed, and that "liberty for the captives" is proclaimed to those suffering captivity to sin or to those living under Communist domination but that it emphatically is *not* proclaimed to common criminals in American prisons. In such a fashion, Christ is accommodated to our culture and the gospel is tamed.[5]

In addition to serving the national self-interest, the peculiarly American reading of the Bible serves to mitigate some of the scandal of the gospel preached by Jesus. A significant part of the scandal — indeed, absurdity — of this Jesus lies in his refusal to recognize that we have everything under control without him. Economically, we provide for the gainful employment of most of our people, and through social services we even provide for our poor. Along with the bread, there are circuses and

3. For a discussion of "political religion," see Jürgen Moltmann, "The Cross and Civil Religion," in *Religion and Political Society,* by Jürgen Moltmann et al. (New York: Harper & Row, 1974), pp. 21-24.

4. Stringfellow, *An Ethic for Christians and Other Aliens in a Strange Land* (Waco, Tex.: Word Books, 1973), p. 13.

5. While there was a period during which fundamentalists directed criticism of cultural accommodation against liberals, events suggest that the fundamentalists' critique was itself derived from a cultural commitment. H. Richard Niebuhr provided a helpful reminder that no group, radicals and Marxists included, can claim immunity to cultural accommodation. See Niebuhr, *Christ and Culture* (New York: Harper, 1951), pp. 101-15.

entertainments aplenty. We have provided for military defense against our foreign enemies and judicial defense against those who threaten our domestic tranquillity. For those of religious bent, opportunities for observances are ample. We recognize the occasional need for economic, cultural, religious, or political reform, but overall we are satisfied with the kingdom that we have created. It is precisely at this point that Jesus announces the inauguration of the kingdom of God. In the face of our pragmatism ("If it ain't broke, don't fix it"), such an announcement is clearly absurd. Why would Jesus even presume to think that we would be interested in another kingdom when the one we've got has served us so nicely? Over the years, many have agreed that such "Good News" needs to be tamed or at least understood in a way that renders it less absurd.

The Temporal Presence of the Kingdom[6]

The one central feature that pervaded all of Jesus' ministry was his proclamation of the inauguration of God's kingdom. When divorced from this central feature, the other aspects of his ministry that some believers regard as more awe-inspiring are actually rather commonplace by comparison. There were other itinerant preachers and miracle workers roaming the countryside of the Near East. In addition to the wonder workers of Judaism, healers were associated with the cults of Egyptian, Mesopotamian, Greek, and Roman deities. The Roman Emperor Vespasian also happened to be a healer; he is said to have restored sight to a blind man by applying spittle to his eyes and to have cured a crippled hand by (oddly enough) stepping on it.[7] Jesus' arrest and execution for posing a threat to established political and religious power was far from unprecedented. Josephus and others testify to the frequency with which the state resorted to crucifixion in the turmoil of Roman-occupied Palestine.[8] Even

6. As I indicate in the preface, my use of "kingdom" language is not intended to lend support to anthropomorphic notions of a male deity. For a helpful study on the need for caution in theological language, see Brian Wren, *What Language Shall I Borrow? God-Talk in Worship: A Male Response to Feminist Theology* (New York: Crossroad, 1989).

7. See Howard Clark Kee, *Miracle in the Early Christian World: A Study in Sociohistorical Method* (New Haven: Yale University Press, 1983), p. 75.

8. Among the many other accounts of execution, Flavius Josephus describes the crucifixion of 2,000 people as the result of one rebellious incident. See *The Antiquities of the Jews* 7.10; and *The Wars of the Jews* 2.5.

the accounts of resurrection are not unique to Jesus. Other resurrections appear within Christian tradition (including the brief mention of the resurrection of "many" in Matt. 27:52) and without (e.g., the resurrection of Apollonius of Tyana, a disciple of Pythagoras). Christian apologists might contend that the miracles and resurrections associated with Jesus were authentic while wonders worked by others were mere trickery, but as Lessing noted, the "great, broad ditch" of history tends to relativize any contemporary assessments of either authenticity or hoax.

In fact, many biblical scholars and theologians have noted that the chasm of history also dooms any effort to reconstruct a factually accurate biography of Jesus. Those presuming to engage in any definitive life-of-Jesus investigation were dealt a serious setback by the 1906 publication of Albert Schweitzer's *Von Reimarus zu Wrede.* According to Schweitzer, the would-be biographers of Jesus proffered less historical reconstruction than evidence that "each successive epoch of theology found its own thoughts in Jesus."[9] It would be inaccurate, however, to suggest that Schweitzer dismissed the possibility of saying anything substantial about the Jesus of history. Indeed, Schweitzer is largely responsible for the current consensus that the ministry and teaching of Jesus is pervaded by radical eschatology. No matter what else might be said about Jesus' sermons, miracles, crucifixion, and resurrection, all of these must be understood, said Schweitzer, in the context of Jesus' own milieu of first-century Jewish apocalypticism.

Contemporaneous with and following close upon the work of Schweitzer, the schools of literary, form, and redaction criticism continued to indicate more about what *cannot* be attributed to the historical Jesus than about what *can* be attributed with any degree of assurance.[10]

9. Schweitzer, *The Quest of the Historical Jesus: A Critical Study of Its Progress from Reimarus to Wrede,* trans. W. Montgomery (1910; reprint, New York: Macmillan, 1968), p. 4. Schweitzer's observation is confirmed by Jaroslav Pelikan in his study of the historically changing depictions of Jesus, *Jesus through the Centuries: His Place in the History of Culture* (New Haven: Yale University Press, 1985).

10. With these comments, I am not attempting nor intending to renounce biblical criticism as such. In helping to establish the *Sitz im Leben* of biblical writings, criticism offers a needed corrective to simplistic literalism. At its best, criticism respects the text as a potential source of truth and not just mere fact. At its worst, however, biblical criticism has been known to dissect and obscure the text. Insightful comments on criticism at its best and worst are offered by Northrop Frye in his introduction to *The Great Code: The Bible and Literature* (New York: Harcourt Brace Jovanovich, 1982).

Biblical critics hold that most Jesus traditions and genuine sayings of Jesus have been thoroughly reworked by biblical writers and redactors to serve the apologetic, liturgical, evangelical, theological, and other purposes of the primitive Christian community. Some biblical critics take their methodological skepticism to the extreme of claiming that the sayings that can most probably be linked to the historical Jesus are those that could prove embarrassing to the church community. Even with such a restrictive criterion, however, the kingdom of God still emerges as central for Jesus. One might well imagine a redactor being discomfited over a saying such as Mark 9:1: "Truly I say to you, there are some of those who are standing here who shall not taste of death until they see the kingdom of God after it has come with power."

Granting the central role of eschatology in the New Testament and in the ministry of the historical Jesus, what was it that Jesus was saying about the kingdom of God? Was he saying that the reign of God was near at hand in a chronological sense? If so, was there anything that distinguished his message from that of John the Baptist or other Jewish apocalyptic preachers? After all, the nearness of God's reign had been proclaimed by many since the days of the great prophets of Israel. Is it possible that Jesus was making an additional claim? Was Jesus maintaining that the kingdom of God had somehow already begun in his own ministry? If he was making this claim, it seems fair to pose the extrabiblical question of why the postresurrection world seems so little changed or redeemed or sanctified. Is it possible that, in sharp contrast to the Jewish apocalyptic context in which he preached, Jesus was actually announcing the inauguration of a kingdom that resided primarily in the interior spiritual or psychological lives of individuals and that the fate of the larger community in a social or political sense was really quite irrelevant to his mission? Finally, whether he was inaugurating or merely announcing the imminence of God's reign, what are the concrete ethical implications of Jesus' eschatological message?

From early in church history, theologians and church leaders have understood the need to struggle with some of these questions. Statements such as the one attributed to Jesus in Luke 17:21 ("behold, the kingdom of God is in your midst") have led some to conclude that Jesus was announcing that God's reign had somehow invaded temporal existence. But if God's reign had entered history, where was it? In his *City of God*, Augustine of Hippo was among the first to suggest that the kingdom of God is in fact the church. Certainly the church qualifies as having constituted a new historical reality that came into existence following the resurrection of Jesus. But Augustine had battled enough heretics in his day to realize that the kingdom of God could not be equated with the church simplistically. Likewise, there was enough hypocrisy in the church of the fifth century to put the lie to the assertion that gospel ethics were fully normative and authoritative within it. Augustine freely acknowledged that the visible church had some members who lived according to the standards of the world, but he asserted that within the church visible there was another, invisible church composed of people who lived by gospel standards. The kingdom of God was actually present, said Augustine, among the elect who constituted this invisible body of faithful believers within the larger, visible church.

If Augustine seemed occasionally to abandon his distinction between church visible and invisible and refer to the hierarchical church as the kingdom of God, all pretense to such distinctions was forsaken among later ecclesiastics. Claiming to possess sacraments with salvific power, the church eventually claimed to possess the kingdom as well. Even Thomas Aquinas used language that equated the church with the kingdom of God.[11] This equation only served to intensify the dilemma over the relevance of Jesus' ethical exhortations, however. While one might assume that gospel ethics would be fully authoritative within "the kingdom" (i.e., the church), theologians and church leaders held that matters were not so simple.

Both Augustine and Aquinas argued that Romans 13 binds Christians to obedience to the governing authorities of the state and that, while the general gospel admonition is to refrain from shedding blood, there are instances in which warfare may be justifiable. Under the "just war" theory articulated first by Augustine and then restated by Aquinas, Christians are freed to fight for just causes if called upon to do so by the governing authorities. Augustine and Aquinas both seem to have been aware that their positions could be understood as showing deference to the claims of political kingdoms over and above the call to discipleship in God's kingdom. Augustine sought to resolve that tension somewhat by referring to

11. See, e.g., "On the Episcopal Power," book 4, chap. 76, in *On the Truth of the Catholic Faith: Summa Contra Gentiles*, trans. Charles J. O'Neil (Garden City, N.Y.: Doubleday, 1957), pp. 290-92.

those instances in the Old Testament when warfare was apparently declared by God; thus, Christian participation in just war might sometimes be understood as a response to God's call rather than obedience to the claims of political kingdoms. Aquinas sought to resolve the tension further by arguing that there are some within the church who are still obliged to refrain from bloodshed in all instances: "Although to wage a just war is meritorious, nevertheless it is wrong for clerics because they are deputed to works of higher merit."[12]

What had begun with Augustine's effort to identify the kingdom of God with the elect of the invisible church resulted in the medieval claim that kingdom ethics are fully relevant only for those within the church who are highly visible — namely, the ecclesiastical hierarchy. What started as an effort to explain where and how the kingdom of God is present in history resulted in a curtailment of the temporal relevance of that kingdom. The medieval church could assert its claim to be the locus of the kingdom not because it was a community seeking to follow in the way of the cross but because the meaning of the cross had been encapsulated in sacraments of body and blood, not because it was a community that loved enemies but because priests refrained from killing them, not because it was a community that had renounced material acquisitiveness but because nuns and monks had taken vows of poverty.

Of course, official declarations of dual standards for the "religious" and the "laity" cannot be viewed as corresponding to actual practice within these two groups. In medieval and other times, there have been countless stories of the faithful witness of saintly laypeople. And not all clerics have found it possible or necessary to be meticulous in their observance of the standards that ostensibly set them apart. Officially, however, the double standard for religious and laity continues in much of modern Christendom. In many regions of the world, clerics are still held exempt from the call to arms in times of war. And many of these same clerics are called to speak a blessing over the warrior Christians who are still held exempt from gospel admonitions to put away the sword. Such a double standard is not peculiar to Christendom. Many religions of the world have found cause to rethink the wisdom of their

---

12. Aquinas, quoted by Robin Gill in *A Textbook of Christian Ethics* (Edinburgh: T. & T. Clark, 1985), p. 324.

own spiritual leaders. When the way of Gautama Buddha or the way of Mahavira was reckoned too demanding for life in the mundane world, less rigorous precepts were devised for the laity.[13] So too with the way of Jesus.

The evolution of double standards for religious and laity among Christians has contributed to the view that God's reign has limited temporal relevance. Seeking to live according to gospel ethics somehow entailed less risk for those who were safely tucked away behind church doors or cloistered walls. There was a growing sense that the message of Jesus was unrealistic for life in "advanced" civilization. This was already true in the time of Augustine and later Aquinas, but it has become much more common among people of the modern era. Can it not be said that we are wiser in the ways of the world than was Jesus? In fact, is there not a certain quaint character to biblical ethics? The call to give away a second coat (Luke 3:11) is a fine gesture for an age when clothing was scarce, but is there not a sense in which that merely highlights how distant Jesus is from our own age of plentiful resources? He had less to protect. Fine to talk about turning the other cheek to all manner of assailants, but his tune might have changed if he had had a family to protect. In his folksy, peasant culture of first-century Palestine, how can we expect that Jesus would have understood the crime and horrors of our own age? Back then, there were not as many people who would take advantage of you, so it was easier to speak of love toward those who posed a threat. Back then, one could be idealistic without having to suffer. consequences. Unless, of course, one considers the consequence of the cross.

Gaps in the historical record prevent us from knowing whether the crime rate in first-century Palestine was comparable to that in our own society, but the biblical and extrabiblical accounts of beatings, robberies, murders, and crucifixions convey the impression that Jesus' setting did not conform to idyllic notions of silent nights in peaceful hamlets. People of every historical epoch believe that there are special circumstances that prevent them from living faithfully according to the

13. This process is certainly not exclusive to Buddhism and Jainism, but, with Jainism especially, there are some interesting parallels to the process of institutionalization and cultural accommodation in Christianity. See David S. Noss and John B. Noss, *Man's Religions*, 7th ed. (New York: Macmillan, 1984), pp. 94-104.

standards and principles they claim to value. Of course we value peace, but there are the special circumstances of terrorists or communists who require us to be prepared for war. Of course we value freedom, but there are the special circumstances of maniacal murderers that require us to build more and more prisons. Some regretfully plead the necessity of setting aside certain ideals in order to meet practical needs in a dangerous world. For example, some men speak of their willingness to turn the other cheek but then cite a higher calling to safeguard the well-being of wives and children (no matter the sexist "damsel in distress" implications of such a claim).

Living our lives and making our ethical decisions according to such special circumstances means in actuality that our values and ethics are controlled by the lowest common denominator. In essence and in fact, we are being controlled by terrorists and maniacal murderers because they are the people who we claim are forcing us to abandon the high principles by which we would otherwise abide. At best, it is little more than a convenient fiction to claim to hold certain values that are rarely applicable in fact because of special circumstances. At worst, it is a dishonest approach to life. I would quickly note here that I am not saying any of this in order to make some oblique endorsement of works righteousness or personal purity. No one can claim a life that has been free from the betrayal of people or values. Confession and *metanoia* are appropriate to such betrayal. But if there are a priori calculations about those circumstances in which the principles we hold do not apply, then questions must arise about whether we in fact hold those principles at all. What point is there in professing an intent to turn the other cheek except in times of threat? In the nature of it, a slapped cheek always implies a threat. Of course, we are free to allow those who threaten us to determine our response, but then we should acknowledge from the outset that we are allowing our ethical decisions to be determined by terrorists and maniacs and thieves. And likewise, we must allow thieves the freedom to act according to the ways in which they may feel threatened by lack of money for food or drugs or other "needs" or the ways in which political terrorists may feel threatened by superpowers or the ways in which maniacal murderers may feel threatened by the spirits that haunt their minds and order them to act as they do. After all, we are a world full of people in "special circumstances" that may lead us to do things we would not do in the best of all possible worlds.

It is into his world and our world of special circumstances that Jesus announces the inauguration of the kingdom of God. There is no longer a need to be governed by the lowest common denominator, for God's reign has already begun. Enemies are to be loved in this world now and not later in some theoretical best of all possible worlds. The call to discipleship is to live now *as if* the world were fully governed by love and peace and justice, for in *fact* God's reign of love has already begun. There can be no more of waiting for better times in which to practice discipleship. The future is now because the kingdom is now.

While an earlier age formulated the contention that God's reign is authoritative only within particular spheres of the church, some twentieth-century theologians have mounted additional challenges to the temporal relevance of gospel ethics. They have suggested that Jesus' pronouncements on the kingdom indicate that he expected an imminent end to human history as we know it and that he offered his ethical teachings with the assumption that they would be normative for only a short interval. Later I want to take a closer look at whether eschatological thought always presumes an imminent end to human history, but at this point we should take a closer look at the perspectives of Albert Schweitzer and Rudolf Bultmann, two prominent twentieth-century theologians who believed that Jesus preached just such an "end of the world" message.

Albert Schweitzer helped shape the modern consensus that eschatology was central to the message of the historical Jesus. He maintained that at his baptism, Jesus received a revelation that he was destined to be the Messiah. Through an examination of various sayings attributed to Jesus (e.g., Mark 9:1), Schweitzer concluded that Jesus expected an imminent eschatological event — an event that in fact never took place. After he went up to Jerusalem and asserted his messianic claim, Jesus was crucified and nothing happened; God did not usher in the kingdom as Jesus had expected. Schweitzer seemed little concerned that Jesus was mistaken on such a fundamental point. Schweitzer merely suggested that the foundation of Christianity is a "spiritual force" that flows from Jesus, a force that "can neither be shaken nor confirmed by historical discovery."[14] What are the ethical implications of Jesus' failed eschatological hopes? Schweitzer argued that they should lead us to understand

14. Schweitzer, *The Quest of the Historical Jesus*, p. 399.

Jesus' parenetic sayings not as exhortations concerning a way of living in the mundane world but rather as the heart of an "interim ethic." They were not meant to provide guidance for the long haul; they were ethical instructions for life during the short interval until apocalypse. The interim nature of the ethic, according to Schweitzer, explains why Jesus' exhortations are essentially world-denying and impractical.

It is helpful to remember that Schweitzer was reacting against the liberal theological presumptions of his own day, some of which maintained that humanity was evolving toward the kingdom of God or that people were capable of building the kingdom. Coming on the eve of World War I, Schweitzer's counterassertions constituted a healthy reaction to the sorts of theological notions that identified God's reign with mere political schemes. But it was also a severe reaction that risked divorcing ethics from theology.[15] Schweitzer's perspectives on Jesus have faced serious questions. If what we know for certain about the historical Jesus has to do with his proclamation of the kingdom of God, how can the fate of that central proclamation be of so little consequence to our own theology and faith? If Jesus' eschatological proclamations were based on mistaken expectations, why not allow him the dignity of failure rather than presuming to rescue through reinterpretation some elements of his thought that might still serve our religious needs?

Precisely such reinterpretation of New Testament eschatology figured prominently in the theology of Rudolf Bultmann. Bultmann held that our understanding of Scripture is clouded by the fact that biblical writings presuppose a cosmology that is foreign to our modern worldview. He proposed an approach of "demythologizing" Scripture so that modern people might be confronted with the true claims of biblical faith rather than stumbling over mythological accounts of supernatural occurrences. According to Bultmann, Jesus' proclamations

---

15. It should be noted that, despite some of the possible implications of his own theological work, Schweitzer did not divorce ethics from faith in his own personal life. Both his work in service to others and his reflections on "reverence for life" give him deserved status as a moral leader of the twentieth century. This remains true despite questions about how much his work in Africa may have been influenced by colonial preoccupations with "the white man's burden." Less favorable views of Schweitzer can be found in books such as Gerald McKnight's *Verdict on Schweitzer: The Man behind the Legend of Lambaréné* (New York: John Day, 1964).

regarding the kingdom of God fell within the purview of that which stood in need of demythologizing: "The mythical eschatology is untenable for the simple reason that the parousia of Christ never took place as the New Testament expected. History did not come to an end, and, as every schoolboy knows, it will continue to run its course."[16] Bultmann maintained that we can best understand Jesus' eschatology by removing the mythological husk and recognizing it as a call to decide for God and against the world. Every instant, every "now," is a "crisis of decision" that may be each individual's last chance to decide in favor of God. The crisis of decision has ethical implications in that each individual is called to love of neighbor, but Bultmann resisted any inclination to understand Jesus' teachings legalistically. Precisely what was meant by "love of neighbor," said Bultmann, would become clear in each concrete moment of decision.

It must be counted as odd that the reinterpretation of such a cataclysmic pronouncement (according to Bultmann, the end of history) should have to do with mere individualized decision making. Bultmann is not alone in his resort to what Ched Myers calls "the hermeneutics of privatism":

> Fundamentalists and modern existentialists may be philosophically antagonistic, but they share in an essential commitment to approaching the text with concerns about the individual's search for, respectively, "holiness" and "authentic existence." Conversion is a fundamentally individual affair. The "personal Savior" of American evangelicalism is domesticated, no longer Lord of the world but of our hearts, into which we invite him. Contemporary theology's preoccupation with the ravages of *Angst* and the search for personal wholeness is similarly caught up. . . . Both reflect the modern tendency to flee from an increasingly uncertain conflict-ridden history to the refuge of self-absorption.[17]

While there is no denying the importance of the scholarly contributions of either Schweitzer or Bultmann, it is also clear that their

---

16. Bultmann, "New Testament and Mythology," in *Kerygma and Myth*, ed. Hans Werner Bartsch (New York: Harper & Row, 1961), p. 5.

17. Myers, *Binding the Strong Man: A Political Reading of Mark's Story of Jesus* (Maryknoll, N.Y.: Orbis Books, 1988), p. 9.

respective positions had the effect of taming or relativizing any ethical implications of Jesus' eschatological proclamations. Whether the implications of kingdom ethics are suspect because of their interim nature or because they are clouded by mythological cosmology, the relativizing impact is the same. The manner in which Bultmann "demythologized" eschatology was obviously influenced by existentialism. More than a few critics have wondered whether Bultmann has not actually *re*mythologized the message of Jesus so that he appears more of a twentieth-century European philosopher than a first-century Jewish preacher. Some have observed that Bultmann apparently lacked familiarity with intertestamental Judaism and that he understood Hellenism to be the primary context for all of primitive Christianity.[18] It is certainly accurate to say that some biblical writers (notable among them, Paul) were seeking to interpret the gospel for a Hellenistic audience, but the reason such interpretation was even necessary had to do with the fact that the historical context for the message of Jesus was decidedly *not* Hellenism. If the one certain historical fact that we can know about the message of Jesus is that it centered on a proclamation of the kingdom of God, then we have a responsibility to try first to understand that eschatology in its own context of first-century Judaism rather than twentieth-century existentialism or mysticism or premillennialism or any of the other possible schemes that may or may not provide interesting hermeneutical perspectives.

There was, of course, a rich variety of theological perspectives among first-century Jews in both Israel and the Diaspora. Eschatology was a comparatively minor theme for some schools and traditions. There was a wisdom tradition linked to the second-century-B.C.E. writings of Jesus ben Sira and the Greek translations of those writings made by his grandson. Philo of Alexandria was representative of the philosophical schools that sought to bring the Torah into dialogue with Plato or Aristotle or the Stoics or other philosophies of the Hellenistic world. Drawing upon the Torah for practical moral guidance, the leaders of the rabbinic tradition came to prominence after the destruction of the

---

18. For a helpful summary of Bultmann's treatment of eschatology and the response of his critics, see Richard H. Hiers, Jr., "Pivotal Reactions to the Eschatological Interpretations: Rudolf Bultmann and C. H. Dodd," in *The Kingdom of God in Twentieth-Century Interpretation*, ed. Wendell Willis (Peabody, Mass.: Hendrickson, 1987), pp. 15-33.

Temple in Jerusalem in 70 C.E.[19] More than in these other traditions, however, the context for understanding Jesus' message about the kingdom of God is to be found in the strong currents of first-century Jewish apocalypticism.[20]

While it is not possible within the scope of this study to give detailed attention to Jewish apocalypticism, a brief exploration of some major themes may prove helpful for understanding New Testament eschatology and the message of Jesus.[21] It is first helpful to establish that certain elements that have been proposed as features of apocalypticism are in fact not necessarily associated with it. Contrary to implications in the positions of both Bultmann and Schweitzer, apocalypticism does not inevitably predict or foresee an end to all of human history. While the Greek root of the word *eschatology* can mean "last" in a chronological sense, it also has the sense of "ultimate," as in Revelation 1:17: "I am the first and the last."[22] With reference to the kingdom of God, the vision often encountered in apocalyptic writings is one of God's reign invading and radically altering history rather than ending or obliterating it.

And, it must be emphasized, it is *history* that is invaded. Early on, Christians were sensitized to the fact that their "kingdom" language was

19. For a summary of these and other perspectives, see Wayne A. Meeks, *The Moral World of the First Christians*, Library of Early Christianity, vol. 6, ed. Wayne A. Meeks (Philadelphia: Westminster Press, 1986), pp. 68-91.

20. While I use the terms *eschatology* and *apocalypticism* interchangeably, some have sought to make a sharp distinction between them, sometimes for the questionable purpose of trying to differentiate between the message of Jesus and "more radical" apocalypticism. See the discussion by Carl E. Braaten in chap. 1 of *Christ and Counter-Christ: Apocalyptic Themes in Theology and Culture* (Philadelphia: Fortress Press, 1972).

21. Those interested in reading extrabiblical eschatological writings are encouraged to explore some of the books of the Apocrypha, the Dead Sea Scrolls, and Jewish pseudepigrapha. An excellent source for the latter is *The Old Testament Pseudepigrapha*, 2 vols., ed. James H. Charlesworth (Garden City, N.Y.: Doubleday, 1983). A secondary source of enduring value is D. S. Russell's *The Method and Message of Jewish Apocalyptic*, Old Testament Library (Philadelphia: Westminster Press, 1964). On postbiblical apocalyptic movements, see Norman Cohn, *The Pursuit of the Millennium: Revolutionary Millenarians and Mystical Anarchists of the Middle Ages* (New York: Oxford University Press, 1970).

22. See Walter Bauer, *A Greek-English Lexicon of the New Testament and Other Early Christian Literature*, trans. and ed. William F. Arndt and F. Wilbur Gingrich (Chicago: University of Chicago Press, 1957), pp. 313-14.

exactly the same language used to refer to the Roman Empire. In an effort to reassure the political powers that no threat was intended, some second-century Christians such as Hegesippus began to characterize the kingdom of God as "neither of the world nor earthly, but heavenly and angelic."[23] This notion of the kingdom as another world where "souls" go after death is totally foreign to the way Jesus presents it. Drawing on the dualistic understanding of soul as separate from body in Egyptian and Greek religions, the Gnostics were among the first to develop a cosmology that viewed the kingdom of God as a realm of refuge for disembodied souls.[24] There are biblical references to life after death, but that is not the focus of the kingdom of God. Nor should we assume that biblical references to the "kingdom of heaven" refer to an other-worldly realm. Linguistic taboos against uttering the name of God often led biblical writers to substitute euphemistic language when referring to God.[25] Matthew was especially likely to substitute "heaven" language for "God" language. In fact, the "kingdom of heaven" and the "kingdom of God" are synonymous.

The Jewish apocalyptic vision was not one of souls fleeing from the earth but rather of injustice and iniquity being banished from the earth (1 Enoch 10:16; 2 Esdras 16:52). The reign of God was to be established not just over the hearts and spirits of individuals but over the nation of Israel. Through Israel, all nations were to be drawn under God's reign of justice and peace. God's establishment of the kingdom was most often understood as a temporal event with clear social, political, and ethical significance.[26] Indeed, the apocalyptic vision has most

---

23. Hegesippus, quoted by Everett Ferguson in "The Kingdom of God in Early Patristic Literature," in *The Kingdom of God in Twentieth-Century Interpretation*, p. 204.

24. See, e.g., "The Exegesis on the Soul," trans. William C. Robinson, Jr., in *The Nag Hammadi Library*, 3d ed., ed. James M. Robinson (New York: Harper & Row, 1988), pp. 192-98.

25. See G. B. Caird, *The Language and Imagery of the Bible* (Philadelphia: Westminster Press, 1980), pp. 43, 72-75.

26. In defense of Schweitzer, it should be noted that he did much of his writing on eschatology without the benefit of discoveries such as the 1947 uncovering and 1956 publication of the Dead Sea Scrolls of the Essene community at Qumran. While the writings of this community reveal that their thought was thoroughly imbued with eschatological expectation, they did not foresee an end to history. They awaited the coming of both the "Messiah of Aaron" and the "Messiah of Israel," but they anticipated the temporal continuation of their community even after the coming of these messianic

frequently arisen in a context of economic and political oppression, and Jewish apocalypticism anticipated that the Babylonians and the Greeks and the Romans and any other would-be rulers would *not* be the governing authorities precisely because God would be.

If Jewish apocalypticism envisions God's reign invading time, new questions arise regarding Jesus' message. Even if Jesus was not predicting the end of history, the problem remains the same. Is it not still the case that Jesus was crucified and nothing happened? If his purpose was not to end history but to inaugurate a temporal kingdom, where is this kingdom? And if it is a kingdom of justice and peace, can anyone seriously claim that there has been more of either justice or peace in the past two millennia? So this is the impasse: Jesus' proclamation of the kingdom of God seems absurd outside of the context of first-century Jewish apocalypticism, but when we view the gospel from within that context, it seems equally absurd.

While there is a need to respect historical context, it seems likely that part of the appearance of absurdity and part of the very real scandal of Jesus' proclamation of the kingdom of God has been similar for people of all times. Among other challenges, the biblical records of Jesus' teachings on the kingdom totally violate our common understandings of space, time, and practicality.

1. *Space.* We ordinarily think of a nation or kingdom as having clear parameters. The ruler has authority within certain boundaries or among a certain group of people. Similarly, it was the expectation of Jewish apocalyptic writers that the kingdom of God would be established through the liberation of Israel, and then God's reign would encompass other nations. The Gospels give no indication that Jesus envisioned the kingdom in geographical terms, however. Rather than laying out the borders of a realm, Jesus was comparing the kingdom with a mustard seed (Matt. 13:31; Mark 4:31; Luke 13:19) or a treasure hidden in a field (Matt. 13:44). Nor did he associate the kingdom with people of special piety or religious allegiance; to the contrary, he spoke

---

figures. In the new order, holiness would be established and any questions concerning the law would be resolved. Until that time, the community lived by the "Manual of Discipline." Schweitzer's concept of a world-denying "interim ethic" actually describes the Manual of Discipline better than it describes the teachings of Jesus. See J. M. Allegro, *The Dead Sea Scrolls: A Reappraisal,* 2d ed. (Baltimore: Penguin, 1964), pp. 167-72.

of it encompassing those of ill-repute (Luke 7:36-50) and heretical belief (10:25-37).

It must quickly be added that the point is *not* that Jesus was reacting against peculiarly Jewish notions about the kingdom. We can at least credit Jewish apocalyptic writers with having understood that the kingdom of God would eventually encompass all nations. The more rigid borders are drawn by Hegesippus and later Christians who sought to contain the kingdom within heaven or within ecclesiastical boundaries so that political authorities would not feel threatened.

The portrait that emerges from the Gospels is one of Jesus declaring the advent of God's reign without respect to geographical borders or ethnic or religious groups. Insofar as God's reign is incarnated wherever the will of God is followed and fulfilled, the decisive question is not "Where is the presence of the kingdom?" but rather "Who is the presence of the kingdom?" The answer of the Gospels is clear: Jesus is the presence of the kingdom.

2. *Time.* Outside the realm of theoretical physics, our sense of time is often as rigidly organized as our understanding of space. In speaking of the arrival of, say, a letter, we say that it either arrived in the past or it is arriving now or it will arrive at some future point. Our sense of time is partially influenced by language; for example, the English language stresses punctiliar time, whereas other languages make greater allowance for continuous action. Nonetheless, categories of past, present, and future still constitute our general framework for understanding time. The Jewish apocalypticists believed there would be no mistaking the presence of the kingdom. Either Israel would be liberated from oppression or this liberation would still be off in the future.

More than a few biblical scholars have noted that the conception of time in the Gospels does not conform to our linear understandings.[27]

27. On biblical conceptions of time, including the important distinction between *kairos* and *chronos,* see Oscar Cullmann, *Christ and Time: The Primitive Christian Conception of Time and History,* rev. ed., trans. Floyd V. Filson (Philadelphia: Westminster Press, 1964). For a treatment of the "already" and the "not yet" in the eschatological message of Jesus, see W. G. Kümmel, *The Theology of the New Testament according to Its Major Witnesses: Jesus — Paul — John,* trans. John E. Steely (New York: Abingdon Press, 1973). The dialectical implications of the "already" and "not yet" are played out in stunning fashion in the theology of Karl Barth. I heartily recommend your dipping into *Church Dogmatics* at any point, but on the dialectics of what is already completed and what remains to come and the way in which each is summed up in the other, see

In the Gospel accounts of Jesus, there are clear indications that the kingdom is fully present (e.g., Luke 17:21) and that it is coming in the future. Clearly, this is not merely a matter of different theologies for different Gospel writers. Indeed, in a single chapter of Luke, the author cites Jesus' proclamation of the kingdom's presence (11:20) and Jesus' instructions for the disciples to pray for the kingdom's coming (11:2). Unless one maintains that Luke was totally oblivious to the implications of his references to time, there is an unmistakable message that the kingdom is both present and future.

The references to the kingdom as both present and future should not give rise, however, to evolutionary schemes suggesting that God's reign is gradually expanding or (even worse) that humanity is engaged in a process of building the kingdom. As W. G. Kümmel notes regarding the parables comparing the kingdom with yeast (Matt. 13:33) or seeds (Mark 4:26-29), the emphasis is on the harvest that comes without the intervention of human bakers or farmers.[28] The presence of the kingdom and the hope for the future are not based on any Social Gospel ideas of "the immense latent perfectibility in human nature."[29] Rather, the kingdom is to be understood as God's gift. The kingdom is in the future insofar as it looks forward to that day when all people and principalities and powers will recognize God's reign of justice and peace. The kingdom is present insofar as the future proleptically invades the present and establishes God's reign as authoritative now. The kingdom is present because Jesus has already won the decisive victory.

3. *Practicality*. Even more than our conceptions of space and time, our understandings of pragmatism and practicality and effectiveness are challenged by the gospel proclamation that Jesus' decisive victory is won by way of the cross. That is simply not the way kingdoms and reichs

---

Karl Barth, *The Doctrine of Reconciliation*, vol. 4, part 2, of *Church Dogmatics*, trans. Geoffrey W. Bromiley and Thomas F. Torrance (Edinburgh: T. & T. Clark, 1958). Some of the ethical implications of dialectical eschatology are explored in Jürgen Moltmann's classic work *Theology of Hope: On the Ground and the Implications of a Christian Eschatology* (New York: Harper & Row, 1967).

28. Kümmel, *The Theology of the New Testament according to Its Major Witnesses*, pp. 38-39.

29. Walter Rauschenbusch, *Christianity and the Social Crisis*, ed. Robert D. Cross (New York: Harper & Row, 1964), p. 422. This book was originally published in 1907, near the prime of the Social Gospel movement.

and empires are supposed to be established. In the context of first-century apocalypticism and revolutionary zeal, it seemed like a defeat rather than a victory. Here was a parody of power politics: a king on a cross, a servant as lord, a royal family composed of the poor and hungry. It is a radically "upside-down kingdom."[30] While those zealous for revolution expected the liberating king to be enthroned by force, here was a ruler enthroned through suffering. Even in the Revelation of John, the most apocalyptic of New Testament writings, it is clear that the victory is won through love and suffering. As G. B. Caird notes,

> John . . . is fond of a resonant title for God, 'the Omnipotent', which he uses nine times. But he repeatedly makes it clear that in using it he is recasting the concept of omnipotence, which he understands not as unlimited coercion but as unlimited persuasion. He hears a voice proclaim the victory of the Lion of Judah, but what he sees is 'a lamb with the marks of slaughter upon him' (Rev. 5:5-6); and it is by the blood of the sacrificed Lamb that the conquering martyrs win their victory, which is the only victory of God (12:11).[31]

Once again, the point is *not* that first-century Jews were incapable of recognizing Jesus' victory and the presence of the kingdom. If the resurrection means that death is conquered, then it is in fact Christendom that preaches the defeat of Jesus whenever churches allow for efficacious killing in a "just war." It is Christendom that renounces the presence of God's reign whenever churches embrace the social respectability of the well-heeled while ignoring God's royal family of the poor and dispossessed. More than a judgment on people of other religions, the presence of God's kingdom stands as a judgment against Christendom itself.

But how can God's reign be relevant (let alone authoritative) for people living in the midst of the complexities of our technological era? We do not live in some boundless kingdom but in nation-states altogether willing to spill blood in order to maintain the integrity of their geographical borders. We do not live in some realm where it makes sense to speak of events as both "already" and "not yet"; we live in a computer age in which time is money and is meted out in nanoseconds.

---

30. For an excellent description of how profound the parody is, see Donald B. Kraybill, *The Upside-Down Kingdom* (Scottdale, Pa.: Herald Press, 1978).

31. Caird, *Language and Imagery of the Bible*, pp. 51-52.

And above all, we live in a place and time that puts a premium on pragmatism and efficiency. We know what is necessary, we know what will work, and we live our lives accordingly.

Necessity is the fundamental ethic of the technological kingdom. We have nuclear weapons not because we believe the capacity to incinerate cities to be good in and of itself but because they are necessary. We have prisons not because we believe the caging of human beings to be good in and of itself but because they are necessary. The scandal of the gospel and the effrontery of God's reign can be summed up in this: Jesus fails to respect what we believe to be necessary.

If we approach the gospel with a priori assumptions that we will find nothing that contradicts what is generally accepted as expedient or even necessary, then in certain settings the gospel will endorse cannibalism. In different places and at various times, cannibalism has seemed both expedient and necessary. If we live according to contemporary standards of what is necessary, we must be willing to confess the possibility that we ourselves may have a penchant for savagery. Indeed, the savagery of cannibalism seems gentle next to our nuclear capacities.[32]

Rather than endorsing standards of necessity, Jesus proclaims the freedom to live in the presence of God's kingdom. Jesus does not issue a call to legalism, to a new set of rules; he issues a call to see the world in a new light, a call to discipleship in a new kingdom. This Good News is ethically relevant and authoritative not because of legalism but because, in the words of Eduard Schweizer, "discipleship is the only form in which faith in Jesus can exist."[33] God's invasion of history through Jesus means that there can be no question of believers being concerned with only ethereal and atemporal matters having to do with "the soul." The incarnation means that we need to speak of the temporal presence of the kingdom of God.

Directly to the point of this study, in what sense can we speak of the relevance of the Jubilee and of Jesus' proclamation of liberty for the prisoners? Is it possible that when we rely on the so-called "criminal justice system," when we reach for the phone to call the police and

32. For an insightful critique of the ethics of necessity, see the first chapter of Jacques Ellul's *Ethics of Freedom*, trans. and ed. Geoffrey W. Bromiley (Grand Rapids: William B. Eerdmans, 1976).

33. Schweizer, quoted by Ched Myers in *Binding the Strong Man*, p. 11.

someone is arrested as a result, we are at the same time questioning the relevance of the gospel? Even though talking of response to lawlessness and violence has become standard fare in political discourse, is it possible that response to crime is not just a political issue but a question of faith? In seeking to answer these questions, the point is not to try to understand the Bible socially and politically. The point is to try to understand our political and social life biblically.

Traditional Appeals to Romans 13
and Theologies of Two Kingdoms

Even if we grant the temporal relevance of God's reign and even if we are not civil religionists, don't we still have cause to wonder whether the proclamation of "liberty for the captives" should be understood as applicable in a real, physical sense for offenders in real prisons? After all, in texts such as Romans 13:1-7, doesn't the Bible itself tend to contradict such an understanding? Regarding Romans 13, is it not the case that this Pauline text accords a position of honor to the state, especially with regard to the state's right to deal with offenders as it sees fit? In fact, is it not possible that criminal offenders are the ones to whom Paul refers when he writes that the governing authorities are a terror to evil behavior, not good? Among others, Anabaptists have had a tendency to explicate Romans 13 in such a way that it applies specifically to the state's juridical but not military affairs.[34] Perhaps a subtle danger with this traditional Anabaptist understanding is that, in the process of offering a laudable witness for peace by speaking out against participation in the military establishment of the state, there has been a simultaneous blessing (whether intentional or not) of the domestic military — police, jails, and prisons.

Regarding Romans 13, it must first be noted that this text is not the only nor the first nor the last nor even the typical biblical word on the state. A biblical view of political authority and the state must also take into account Genesis (which tells us that all of creation is fallen), Exodus (which identifies God as the one who liberates the oppressed from tyranny), 1 Samuel (which tells us that to choose a king is to reject

---

34. See, e.g., the work by the Mennonite scholar John Howard Yoder entitled *The Politics of Jesus* (Grand Rapids: William B. Eerdmans, 1972), pp. 205-7.

God), 2 Kings (which portrays the idolatrous and murderous "bad kings" as the most politically successful kings, the best administrators, the winners at war, and portrays the compassionate and faithful "good kings" as the least politically successful, the losers of war and wealth),[35] Daniel (which points out that political power demands to be worshiped), the classical prophets (in which incumbent political authority is denounced as faithless), Matthew (in which we read of political authorities massacring babies in pursuit of deicide and in which the temptations account identifies Satan as being in possession of the kingdoms of the world), John and the synoptic Gospels (in which we find the governing authorities killing the Christ and, like Pilate, incapable of recognizing truth), Acts (in which the state is identified as the jailer and persecutor of virtually all of the apostles), Corinthians and Ephesians and other writings by Paul himself (in which he refers to magistrates as "unwise" and "unrighteous"), and Revelation (in which the state is identified as the beast). Altogether, Scripture offers something less than a ringing endorsement of incumbent political authorities or particular governments or even the abstract "idea" of the state and political power.

So then, does Romans 13 stand in contrast or contradiction to other biblical words on the state? Certainly Scripture contains a rich variety of perspectives, and those who would seek to convert the rough, biblical terrain into a smooth unity often seem to be performing some dangerous contortionism. But even granting such variety, we need to beware of declaring Paul an apologist for state power. In fact, Romans 13:1-7 marks a radical departure from the prevailing religious and political sentiment of the Roman Empire, and the same might be said for some of the other New Testament texts that have traditionally been understood as bestowing divine blessing upon the state (e.g., 1 Pet. 2:17). In a day when the common rule was to worship the emperor, the call of these texts merely to "honor the emperor" and "be subject to the governing authorities" might have been considered more than a little anarchistic. Subjects were expected to pray *to* the emperor, not just *for* him.

While some have tried to make the case that Romans 13:1-7 is an interpolation, these efforts have been unconvincing. These verses make

---

35. This view of politics in 2 Kings is elucidated by Jacques Ellul, *The Politics of God and the Politics of Man*, trans. and ed. Geoffrey W. Bromiley (Grand Rapids: William B. Eerdmans, 1972).

textual sense standing where they do between Paul's admonition to Roman Christians in chapter 12 to "bless those who persecute you" and avoid being "conformed to this world" and the eschatological tone of Paul's writing in the last verses of chapter 13. Oscar Cullmann, Clinton Morrison, and others have examined Pauline cosmology and the ways in which it relates to his eschatological understanding of the principalities and powers.[36] According to Paul, the principalities and powers of the spirit world correspond to the governing authorities *(exousiai)*, and he stressed Jesus' victory over the principalities and powers as a central theme of the eschatological event. How is this victory to be anchored historically? Again, the question of time emerges. Has this victory already taken place, is it now being worked out, or will it be accomplished in a future apocalyptic event? The question is foreign to Paul. He thinks in terms of an eschatological dialectic that should not be dissolved.[37] Jesus *has been* and *is now* victorious over the principalities and powers, and he *will be* revealed as Lord, invading and turning around the tyrannical pretensions of all powers.

When viewed in its ethical (Rom. 12; 13:8-10) and eschatological (Rom. 13:11-14) contexts, Romans 13 may be understood as granting the freedom to be subject to the governing authorities insofar as that subjection is a witness to the eschatological — that is, the ultimate — lordship of Jesus. And it is, in fact, freedom that is granted. Too often, Romans 13 is viewed as law, not gospel, but the text itself actually draws us into the freedom that is inherent in gospel. "Render to all what is due them: tax to whom tax is due." In freedom, the believer is called upon to determine what tax is due to whom and for what, or even if perhaps what is most overdue is a refusal of taxes for the next round of military adventurism that might threaten not only enemies and neigh-

36. See Morrison, *The Powers That Be: Earthly Rulers and Demonic Powers in Romans 13.1-7*, Studies in Biblical Theology, no. 29 (Naperville, Ill.: Alec R. Allenson, 1960).

37. This dialectic is noted by Ernst Käsemann in "Justification and Salvation History in the Epistle to the Romans," in *Perspectives on Paul* (Philadelphia: Fortress Press, 1971), pp. 67-68. Unfortunately, however, Käsemann does not discern an eschatological tone in the first verses of Romans 13. In one of his later writings, Käsemann seems in danger of surgically divorcing 13:1-7 from 13:11-14. He writes of 13:1-7, "we do not find any specifically eschatological or christological motivation" (*Commentary on Romans*, trans. and ed. Geoffrey W. Bromiley [Grand Rapids: William B. Eerdmans, 1980], p. 351).

bors but all of God's creation. The text draws us into freedom not only in the determination of what is "due" but also in the appeal to conscience: "be in subjection, not only because of wrath, but also for conscience' sake." *Conscience (syneidesis)* is a word that appears only rarely in the biblical text.[38] In Romans 13, "conscience" appears as a reminder that believers are to be subject to a governing authority to the extent that that authority is in fact "a minister of God for good"; it is then that the subjection, chosen in freedom and conscience, might serve as a witness to the victory of Jesus over the principalities and powers.

We must not deny the relevance of Romans 13, but neither should we deny the relevance of other biblical texts that speak to our relationship to the state.[39] Theologians who have always stressed the ethical relevance of Romans 13 and the eschatological relevance of Revelation 13 might profit by also learning to reverse those perspectives,[40] for in

---

38. C. A. Pierce notes that *syneidesis* does not appear in the Septuagint at all. The word is used six times in those writings that are generally considered to be authentic Pauline epistles (*Conscience in the New Testament*, Studies in Biblical Theology, no. 15 [London: SCM Press, Ltd., 1955]).

39. The "German Christian" movement under Hitler was notorious for its preoccupation with Romans 13 as *the* summary of the divinely ordained purposes of the state. The German Christian position was laid out in a document called "The Rengsdorf Theses," which asserted that "State and Church are orders both willed by God. Consequently they cannot prove to be in conflict. If, however, this should happen, then an encroachment from one side or the other has occurred. The Church owes obedience to the State in all temporal matters. The State has to guarantee to the Church scope to carry out its commission."

Karl Barth responded with an opposing view: "Not divine orders but the human realities of Church and State must and will always find themselves in conflict in history dominated by sin. *Wherein* the obedience in temporal matters which the Church owes the State consists, and *what* scope the State has to guarantee to the Church for carrying out its commission, are questions that have to be asked ever again by both sides giving heed to God's Word. Whoever today thinks he is finally able to settle the relationship between Church and State on the basis of general considerations apart from listening to the living Word is already actually thinking of an authoritarian State."

Both statements are quoted by Arthur C. Cochrane in *The Church's Confession under Hitler* (Philadelphia: Westminster Press, 1962), p. 122.

40. A similar point is made by William Stringfellow in *Conscience and Obedience: The Politics of Romans 13 and Revelation 13 in Light of the Second Coming* (Waco, Tex.: Word Books, 1978), pp. 46-48. For a further discussion of Romans 13, see also Jacques Ellul, "Anarchism and Christianity," in *Katallagete* 7 (Fall 1980): 14-24. For a more recent and quite helpful study by Ellul, see *Anarchy and Christianity*, trans. Geoffrey W. Bromiley (Grand Rapids: William B. Eerdmans, 1991).

fact a biblical ethic is inherently an eschatological ethic. And Anabaptists who have traditionally viewed Romans 13 with an eye to "thou shalt not kill" might profit by also viewing it with an eye to "release for the captives." The Word of God is not imprisoned by the state.

But is such a fundamental questioning of the power of the state indicative of a "two kingdoms" theology? It is necessary to be specific when speaking of two-kingdoms theology, because there are many different manifestations of it. There is a sociopolitical dualism accompanying Augustine's *City of God* thesis and an ethical dualism inherent in Reinhold Niebuhr's distinction between individual and social morality.[41] Historically, however, Martin Luther's two-kingdoms model has been most prevalent. After observing that "we must divide the children of Adam and all mankind into two classes, the first belonging to the kingdom of God, the second to the kingdom of the world," Luther reflects on the political meaning of such a division:

> Certainly it is true that Christians, so far as they themselves are concerned, are subject neither to law nor sword, and have need of neither. But take heed and first fill the world with real Christians before you attempt to rule it in a Christian and evangelical manner. This you will never accomplish; for the world and the masses are and always will be un-Christian, even if they are all baptized and Christian in name.[42]

The point seems to be that Christians can and should participate in the political kingdoms, but biblical ethics are of another realm. Luther would not retaliate against his neighbor, but princes could and should retaliate against rebellious peasants, and believers should be full participants in the retaliation.

There is a different, Anabaptist version of two-kingdoms theology. Ironically, some Anabaptists have conceded Luther's main point that there are two separate and distinct realms, each with its own set of ethical perspectives. And so, some Anabaptists might grant the right of

---

41. See Niebuhr, *Moral Man and Immoral Society: A Study in Ethics and Politics* (New York: Scribner's, 1960).

42. Luther, "Temporal Authority: To What Extent It Should Be Obeyed," in *Luther: Selected Political Writings*, ed. J. M. Porter (Philadelphia: Fortress Press, 1974), p. 56.

the political kingdoms to imprison offenders or even to conduct warfare (sinful though it may be) while maintaining that in order to maintain faithfulness to the kingdom of God, believers must remain uninvolved with the political kingdoms.

Of the Anabaptist and Lutheran perspectives on two-kingdoms theology, Luther's version seems to offer a particularly severe challenge to the ethical relevance of the gospel. But even of Anabaptists it must be asked if biblical people may in fact concede that there is a separate realm that is governed by the principalities and powers in any final sense. And if it does not exist in a final sense chronologically, can it be said to exist in any ultimate sense now? In the "already" and "not yet" of the kingdom that Jesus inaugurates, there may exist a *coincidentia oppositorum*, but only in the sense that God's reign is overcoming the old rule of the principalities which have already suffered their decisive defeat.

Ultimately, there are not two kingdoms but one — the kingdom of God. If it is established among us now only as a mustard seed, it is among us nonetheless, turning around the tyrannical pretensions of all, principalities and powers included. "Freedom to the captives" is not proclaimed in some other world but in our world. The matter finally comes down to a peculiar question: Are there prisons in the kingdom of God? And if there are no prisoners there and then, how can we support the imprisonment of people here and now? For in fact, the kingdom of God is among us here and now.

Chapter II

Prisons and the Social Order

*And the merchants of the earth weep and mourn . . . , be-
cause no one buys their cargoes any more; cargoes of gold
and silver . . . and cargoes of horses and chariots and slaves
and human lives.*

Revelation 18:11-13

Locking people in cages is such an accepted practice in contemporary
society that we are likely to be met with no small incredulity if we
ask, "Why do we have prisons?" The answer to the question will likely
refer to the need to protect society through deterrence of crime or the
need to reject immoral or antisocial behavior through retribution or
(rarer these days) the need to treat or "rehabilitate" offenders. The
answer will also likely allude to this or that individual who is considered
to be *the* example of "the criminal mind" — Richard Speck, Charles
Manson, David Berkowitz, Ted Bundy, or some other pathological individual who has committed the most recent atrocity to spark public
indignation.

Prior to the 1980s, authoritarian regimes in South Africa and
the Soviet Union led the world as the governments most likely to
imprison their own citizens. Today, that dubious distinction is held
by the United States.[1] One out of every 250 Americans is in jail or

---

1. "Talk of the Town," *New Yorker,* 13 April 1992, p. 27.

prison.[2] But it is incorrect to assume that these people are "criminals" even in the judicial definition of the word. Many of those incarcerated in the United States today are people awaiting trial — people who are in jail not because they have been convicted of a crime but because they are not rich enough to pay the bail. Even when a prisoner has been convicted of a crime, however, the pronouncement of the court does not constitute evidence that he or she is any more "dangerous" than the rest of us.

The definition of crime is a relative matter that changes with the whims of legislative bodies.[3] Homosexuality, polygamy, and prostitution are crimes in some nations, states, and cities but not others. Murder is typically considered a crime — unless the perpetrator acted in self-defense or by reason of insanity or "in the line of duty" as a member of a police force or military body. Indeed, soldiers might be criminally liable for *refusal* to kill on order. It is considered criminal behavior to lie under oath, but otherwise lying is lawful for everyone from presidents to common folk. It is illegal to speak about classified documents and it is illegal *not* to speak before grand juries — unless the speaking would involve self-incrimination, in which case it becomes legal not to speak — unless one has been granted immunity from prosecution, in which case it once again becomes illegal not to speak. In short, everything from killing (or the refusal to kill) to speaking (or the refusal to speak) is or is not a crime depending on the widest range of circumstances. So divorced is civil law from moral reflection that we barely blink when presidents somberly intone that we've just got to stop violence in America, while as a nation we spend thousands of dollars a minute building bombs.

Criminal law has ostensibly served any number of purposes throughout history. In ancient history, the enforcement of laws and the

2. According to Bob McNamara in a report on the CBS Evening News broadcast 11 December 1989. The U.S. prison population doubled during the 1980s; more than one million Americans are now being held in jails and prisons.

3. Many fall prey to the unfortunate assumption that civil law can be easily identified with morality or divine law. For a discussion of this issue, see Jacques Ellul, *The Theological Foundation of Law,* trans. Marguerite Wieser (New York: Seabury Press, 1969). On the historical divergence of legal systems from ethics and justice, see Herman Bianchi, "Tsedeka-Justice," *Review for Philosophy and Religion,* September 1973, pp. 306-18.

imposition of sanctions was understood as activity performed at the behest of the gods. Of course, kings and potentates were very early viewed as instruments for both recording the legislative will of the gods and inflicting the divine wrath upon violators. The state was conveniently situated to assume all divine functions as the gods faded into obscurity. It is far from certain that the various states have been any more noble in their formulations of criminal statutes than were the most ornery of tribal gods. If slavery or concentration camps suit the purposes of the state, law books and judicial precedent will provide these institutions with the appropriate underpinnings. The development of the prison system in colonial Tanganyika (now Tanzania) provides one example of the manner in which criminal law serves different purposes in various settings. The people of Tanganyika were accustomed to working for the provision of their own needs, but their unwillingness to provide the additional labor needed to work the colonial plantations profitably led Europeans (first Germans and later the British) to characterize them as "lazy natives." Through the imposition of a series of taxes, Tanganyikans were compelled to leave their own agricultural endeavors in order to work for wages. A prison system was developed to deal with those who failed to pay the taxes, and the prisoners were in turn set to work building the roads that served the colonial plantations.[4] For those who are convinced that there is a "need" for prisons, it is disconcerting to realize that the need may sometimes be so blatantly manufactured.

Even if the definition of crime is a relative matter, is there not still a sense in which prisons can be said to protect society? Almost every year we hear frightening reports from Washington about increases in crime rates. In response, federal, state, and local governments allocate more money for more police and more guns and more prisons, and the result is that the following year the crime rates are worse than the year before. If the purpose of prisons is to protect people by curbing crime, it is strange that in our supposedly pragmatic society so few people stumble on the observation that prisons do not work. After all, every scream of the siren spells another failure for prisons. And equally important, if one of the goals of a system of justice is to provide comfort and assistance for the

4. David Williams, "The Role of Prisons in Tanzania: An Historical Perspective," *Crime and Social Justice: Issues in Criminology,* Summer 1980, pp. 27-38.

victims of crime, prisons contribute nothing toward attaining that goal. Yet, the American prison system has been expanding dramatically, and the rate at which people are imprisoned continues to climb. There are occasional calls for prison reform but rarely any fundamental questioning of the system itself or of the very practice of caging people. What accounts for this apparent immunity from criticism?

A number of factors contribute to the free ride for the prison system, a significant one being the fact that many Americans have little regard for the system's victims, not only because they have been labeled as criminals but also because they are usually poor and black or brown. More attention will be paid later to the scapegoating phenomenon, but it is also worth noting that the entrenchment of the prison system has been facilitated by (1) the influence of powerful financial and bureaucratic interests, (2) the view of imprisonment as an ethically neutral "technique," and (3) the secrecy and invisibility under which prisons are run and by which they escape public scrutiny.

1. Prisons are big business. Considered together, jails and prisons in America have more employees and control more capital than most of the country's largest corporations. With some states devoting almost ten percent of their entire state budget to "corrections,"[5] there are clearly vested financial interests at work. As with other big industries, intense lobbying efforts are carried on by prison administrators, unions of prison employees, professional associations, and others who might stand to gain from the construction of new prisons or the allocation of additional funds. In addition to budget concerns, the lobbyists are frequently engaged in campaigns for or against specific legislation and programs and, when the lobbyists are Department of Corrections personnel, their efforts are totally subsidized by public funds. Just as we pay for Pentagon officials to lobby for this or that weapons system, we also pay for prison officials to lobby against reform programs.[6]

5. Such is the case in California, e.g.; see Clare Regan, "Harris Cites Need for Change in Sanctions," *Justicia* (Newsletter of Genesee Ecumenical Ministries Judicial Process Commission, Rochester, N.Y.), May 1988, p. 2.

6. The practice continues today on a scale that might well match the experience in 1971 in California when the Department of Corrections launched a publicly financed campaign against each of the 175 prison reform bills that came before the state legislature in that year. See Fay Honey Knopp et al., *Instead of Prisons: A Handbook for Abolitionists* (Syracuse: Prison Research Education Action Project, 1976), p. 194.

Typically, the lobbying efforts of prison officials are handsomely rewarded with yearly budget increases, a trend that is almost certain to continue. Many local jails and state prisons are in a situation comparable to the federal prison system, which is overcrowded by fifty percent and has a prisoner population increasing at the rate of fifteen percent annually.[7] The inhuman conditions bred by overcrowding win some strange allies to the prison industry's pitch for more money as humanitarians and prison reformers plead with legislators to alleviate misery by allocating more funds. And yet additional funding is rarely used to relieve crowding or provide decent food or better conditions for prisoners; the extra money is usually used to hire more administrators or guards or to buy more security equipment or new stainless steel prisons, which are often scheduled to be overcrowded even before construction is finished. In the words of Jessica Mitford, "far from benefiting those at the bottom," extra funding for prisons "floats or is propelled up to the top." Mitford quotes a public relations man from the American Correctional Association as he encouraged prison officials to welcome the presence of do-gooders: "We shouldn't be afraid of them. We should let them in the prisons, because they can become our best lobbyists for funds. Although they may still go on squawking about all the things they don't like, they are invaluable in getting appropriations out of the legislature."[8]

After pouring billions of dollars into thousands of jails and prisons, Americans do not seem prepared to abandon the investment. Nonetheless, there is something outrageous about a system that can base its appeal for more funds on its own failure. The law enforcement agencies designed to combat and prevent crime and the prison system designed to take offenders out of circulation and to deter crime need more funding because crime is being neither prevented nor deterred. "No other public organization gets away with this tactic," notes Kevin Wright.

> If welfare stated publicly that it was unable to help those in need, or the fire department claimed it could not fight fires, the political

---

7. *Justícia*, April 1988, p. 6.

8. Mitford, *Kind and Usual Punishment: The Prison Business* (New York: Alfred A. Knopf, 1973), p. 170. Although the statistics in Mitford's book are now somewhat dated, her perspective on the bureaucratic morass of the penal system stands as a valuable contribution.

backlash would be intense, and there would be an investigation, cuts in the budget, major shifts in personnel, and perhaps even elimination of the agency. But the criminal-justice system uniquely utilizes fear. Its failures are qualified by explanations: the courts handcuff the police with procedural safeguards, the system does well with the resources available but the volume of criminal activity exceeds its ability, new methods or programs hold the answer to the problem. Since few alternatives are available to citizens, they cling to the assurances of the system. Most Americans have no direct and personal interest in welfare, so its failure is met with resignation, but because fear of crime is so intense the public is willing to invest further in the potential of law enforcement.[9]

But the investment takes a toll. According to a National Institute of Justice study, "For every person who goes to prison, two people don't go to college. For every day a person stays in jail, twenty children eat starch instead of protein."[10]

2. The National Rifle Association campaign to win support for the assertion that "guns don't kill people" is well geared to the presumptions of our technological society. Techniques and means and tools are presumed to be ethically neutral. The prevailing technological sentiment holds that the only judgments that can be brought to bear on various techniques concern whether they are efficient and/or necessary — determinations that are best made by those with technical expertise in a certain field. Difficulties arise, however, with an abstract concept such as "justice," which often eludes efforts at definition, let alone quantification and measurement with regards to efficiency. And so, many Americans have arrived at an understanding of justice that closely corresponds to the definition offered by totalitarian regimes: justice is that which provides for security and order; justice is served when those who disrupt order and security are apprehended and penalized. That can be measured.[11]

9. Wright, *The Great American Crime Myth* (New York: Praeger, 1987), pp. 97-98.

10. The National Institute of Justice study by Joan Mullen and others is cited by Elliott Currie in *Confronting Crime: An American Challenge* (New York: Pantheon Books, 1985), p. 90.

11. On the triumph of technical ideology in jurisprudence, see Jacques Ellul, *The Technological Society*, trans. John Wilkinson (New York: Vintage Books, 1964), pp. 291-300.

One salient feature of our technological era is the manner in which people in virtually every field of human endeavor are beginning to claim for themselves the privileges that accrue to technical expertise. A growing phalanx of paralegals, lawyers, correctional officers, investigators, judges, criminologists, law enforcement officers, probation officials, parole boards, and others claim such expertise in the field of "justice." The introduction of each new technique calls for an influx of experts. DNA "fingerprinting," for example, necessitates the addition of specialists in crime laboratories.[12] Increasingly, the involvement of people who are not experts in the field is seen as an intrusion. From a technical perspective, plea bargains are valuable because they increase the efficiency of the system and also because the diminishing number of jury trials limits the intrusion of laypeople into the realm of experts.

This technological ethos has helped to insulate the prison system from criticism because many have come to regard imprisonment as an ethically neutral technique and the prison as merely one of several tools available in a technologically sophisticated assault on crime. From the perspective of technique, if prisons do not appear to have contributed to rehabilitating offenders or lowering crime rates, the problem does not lie with the neutral means (caging people) but rather with the need for additional precision and expertise in the application of the technique. We are told that this tool (the prison) could be made to work if only sentences were longer or shorter or determinate or indeterminate or if we adopted this or that educational program or work release project or if we trained guards to use proper psychology or to administer proper drugs. The question rarely arises about whether in fact the prison itself is morally and socially tolerable. Few people pause to wonder whether the dehumanizing impact of prisons contributes to more criminality, violence, and misery than it prevents.

3. Of course, how can you criticize what you cannot see? Whatever or whoever it is that prison administrators administer and correctional officers correct is hidden away from public view. Increasingly, even the buildings themselves are out of sight. In Elmira, New York, for example, the nineteenth-century reformatory (now a state prison) was indeli-

---

12. See Stephen G. Michaud, "DNA Detectives: Genetic 'Fingerprinting' May Herald a Revolution in Law Enforcement," *New York Times Magazine,* 6 November 1988, pp. 70ff.

cately situated next to a major thoroughfare. While local residents grow accustomed to the sight, it is mildly disconcerting for visitors in the area to drive by the thick-walled fortress surrounded by guard towers and an occasional stretch of razor wire. During the holiday season, the effect is mitigated somewhat by gaily lit greetings sprawled across a sizable portion of the prison's front yard: "We wish you a Merry Christmas." Precisely who the wishers are is unclear. The new state prison to the south of Elmira is more carefully tucked away from public view.

But if the prisons themselves are frequently out of sight, so much more so the goings-on inside. When they feel it necessary to do so, prison officials can plead "security" as the reason for maintaining the secrecy and invisibility of the institution, but they rarely need to do so. As a society, we seem content to have prisoners remain out of sight and out of mind. Questions arise about the degree to which the removal of prisoners from visibility is part of a larger compulsion to render all "problem people" invisible through institutionalization (the emotionally disturbed to psychiatric hospitals, the elderly to nursing homes) or ghettoization (the Native Americans to "reservations," the poor to urban slums and rural hollows). Philip Slater is accurate in his observation that our culture is beset by a pattern of thought which he calls

> the Toilet Assumption — the notion that unwanted matter, unwanted difficulties, unwanted complexities and obstacles will disappear if they are removed from our immediate field of vision. . . .
>
> When these discarded problems rise to the surface again — a riot, a protest, an exposé in the mass media — we react as if a sewer had backed up. We are shocked, disgusted, and angered, and immediately call for the emergency plumber (the special commission, the crash program) to ensure that the problem is once again removed from consciousness.[13]

But if the prison is removed from public consciousness and visibility, the prisoners themselves remain perpetually visible to their keepers. Relentless surveillance is a primary control mechanism in the prison. The vital role of surveillance in facilitating domination has been noted by many, but its utility in penal institutions was best elucidated two hundred

---

13. Slater, *The Pursuit of Loneliness: American Culture at the Breaking Point* (Boston: Beacon Press, 1970), p. 15.

years ago in Jeremy Bentham's *Panopticon*. Noting that the dark recesses of the dungeon permitted surreptitious behavior and bred resistance to control, Bentham proposed to bring light and visual access to prison cells. In his architectural proposal, cells would be arranged in circular tiers with a guard tower in the center. A barred window to the back of each cell would permit light to enter through and render each prisoner fully visible to those in the central tower, but a series of blinds would prevent the observers in the tower from being visible to those being observed. Each prisoner would have no way of knowing if he or she were being observed at any particular moment, but the impact would be the same as if every prisoner were being observed at every moment. The most effective and efficient types of controls are not those which are imposed and enforced from without but those which are internalized and self-sustaining. The aim of the Panopticon was to facilitate the internalization of perpetual surveillance. Each prisoner was to become both the agent and the subject of his or her own domination.[14]

Bentham's Panopticon was never built, but aspects of it have been incarnated in a plethora of jails and prisons. The impact of architecture in establishing various options for restraint, isolation, surveillance, and other forms of domination led the nineteenth-century Boston Prison Discipline Society to pronounce architecture a science by which "great moral changes can be more easily produced."[15] The moral changes envisioned involve internalizing surveillance and domination to the extent that the individual's interior life itself becomes a correctional facility so secure that there is no need for exterior architecture. Anthony Burgess provides a crude but revelatory caricature of the ultimate goal of corrections in *A Clockwork Orange*: the very thought of "doing wrong" should induce nausea. The mechanisms of control can remain the same even if the cultural and societal definitions of "doing wrong" are subject to alteration.

Prisoners are walled in by the architecture, but punitive and correctional ideologies are not. Among others, Michel Foucault has noted "the way in which a form of punitive system . . . covers the entirety of

14. Michel Foucault offers helpful commentary on the internalization of control in a chapter on "Panopticism" in *Discipline and Punish: The Birth of the Prison*, trans. Alan Sheridan (New York: Vintage Books, 1979), pp. 195-228.

15. Cited by David J. Rothman in *The Discovery of the Asylum: Social Order and Disorder in the New Republic* (Boston: Little, Brown, 1971), p. 83.

a society."[16] Some leaders and theorists of the nineteenth-century prison reform movement were remarkably candid about their convictions that prisons should provide models for individual conduct and social organization. More often than not, these leaders and theorists were Christians. The Reverend James B. Finley, chaplain of the Ohio penitentiary, was not alone in his stated belief: "Could we all be put on prison fare, for the space of two or three generations, the world would ultimately be the better for it." We would see the triumph of Christianity, said Finley, "should society change places with the prisoners, so far as habits are concerned, taking to itself the regularity, and temperance, and sobriety of a good prison."[17]

Indeed, Bentham himself noted that, in addition to prisons, the Panopticon principles were equally applicable to "mad-houses," factories, hospitals, and schools.[18] Had he lived in a later era, he might well have extended his list to include other locales such as shopping centers and banks equipped with security cameras and city streets illumined by high-powered vapor lamps. Had he lived later still, he might have recognized that surveillance need not rely on so primitive a faculty as vision; sometimes a computer can work both more efficiently and less intrusively. Chaplain Finley's wish that "society change places with prisoners" may be nearer than even he would have dared to hope.

Even people who have no concerns whatsoever regarding the impact of prisons on prisoners might have cause to wonder about the impact of the presence of these inherently authoritarian, total institutions on the rest of society. To what extent can an ostensibly "free" people coexist with growing numbers of institutions of domination and restraint? As we express a growing need to cage others, are we simultaneously confessing a willingness to cage more effectively something within ourselves? American society already seems possessed of a surfeit of willing obedience to authority and admiration for conformity.[19] As

16. Foucault, *Power/Knowledge: Selected Interviews and Other Writings, 1972-1977,* ed. Colin Gordon (New York: Pantheon Books, 1980), p. 68.

17. Finley, quoted by Rothman in *Discovery of the Asylum,* pp. 84-85.

18. See Dario Melossi and Massimo Pavarini, *The Prison and the Factory: Origins of the Penitentiary System,* trans. Glynis Cousin (Totowa, N.J.: Barnes & Noble, 1981), pp. 41-42.

19. On this, see Stanley Milgram's alarming study of social psychology *Obedience to Authority: An Experimental View* (New York: Harper & Row, 1974).

Herbert Marcuse observed, freedom in a given society must be measured by the actual scope and variety of the ways in which people act and think and speak rather than by the range of options that are theoretically available to them.[20] A society of conformists is not free even if the members of that society are theoretically at liberty to depart from conformity. To what extent have we become a caged society? To what extent do we willingly submit to increasing external surveillance? Are we so effectively under the sway of an internalized surveillance that we are sickened at even the thought of "doing wrong" (i.e., not conforming)? To what extent have schools or media or workplaces or churches borrowed lessons from "correctional" institutions? To what extent have we been "corrected"?

Some people give voice to a certain vindictive sentiment that offenders should be sent to prison *for* punishment and not just *as* punishment. They maintain that mere confinement in (to borrow the popular parlance) "a country club prison" constitutes no punishment at all. They want to see suffering meted out in the form of hard labor, scant rations, and other harsh conditions. As they see it, genuine punishment begins only when additional hardships are added to the incarceration. What does it say about the condition of the human spirit when barbed wire fences and cages for people can be viewed as trifling matters?

What accounts for the prison's immunity from criticism? One of the more frightening possibilities is that the penal fascination with confinement and control is seeping through the prison walls.

The Illusion of Rehabilitation

Some of the greatest atrocities in history have been performed in the name of fixing something. It cannot be denied that there was plenty that needed fixing in eighteenth-century European penology. What were touted as enlightened systems of jurisprudence frequently resorted to punishments of torturous brutality. In reaction to public whippings, burnings, and hangings, a reform movement slowly gathered and found its voice in the writings of a Milanese lawyer named Cesare Beccaria.

20. Marcuse, *One-Dimensional Man: Studies in the Ideology of Advanced Industrial Society* (Boston: Beacon Press, 1964), pp. 7-8.

Initially published in 1764, Beccaria's *On Crimes and Punishments* went through several printings and received wide circulation throughout Europe. Beccaria's opposition to the death penalty influenced several monarchs and legislative bodies to circumscribe more carefully those offenses that were judged to merit execution and to make the executions themselves less of a public spectacle. The reforms were not met with universal acclaim. In response to a proposal to close the public gallows at Tyburn, Dr. Johnson complained to Boswell, "The age is running mad after innovations, even Tyburn is not safe. Executions are intended to draw spectators. If they don't, they don't answer their purpose."[21]

In fact, Johnson and Beccaria would have agreed that punishments need to answer a purpose; moreover, they would have agreed on the nature of some of the purposes to be served. To be fair to Beccaria, his opposition to capital punishment was doubtless motivated by humanitarian sentiments, but his arguments were utilitarian. While there were earlier variations on the expression, it was in Beccaria's writings that Jeremy Bentham first encountered the phrase "the greatest happiness shared by the greatest number."[22] Beccaria's basic position was that, rather than dwelling on retaliation for past crimes, punishment should be utilized to correct the offender and to deter future crime. Anything more than that was wasteful brutality; anything less was ineptitude. Beccaria was describing in other words what modern utilitarian penologists have come to call "rehabilitation" and "deterrence."

Prison as "rehabilitation unit" or "correctional facility" is the technological society's secularized version of the earlier reformatory or penitentiary. An earlier era reckoned that something was awry with an offender's soul or spiritual life and that a change had to be effected through penitential solitude or religious indoctrination. The more recent version reckons that something is awry with an offender's mind or psychological and social adjustment, and a change has to be effected through counseling or vocational training or behavioral conditioning or (at the basest level) drugs. A shift in language accompanies the

21. Johnson, quoted by Daniel P. Mannix in *The History of Torture* (New York: Dell, 1964), p. 137. It should be noted that there was also significant clerical opposition to Beccaria's reform proposals. See Susan Jacoby, *Wild Justice: The Evolution of Revenge* (New York: Harper & Row, 1983), p. 368n.14.

22. Beccaria, *On Crimes and Punishments*, trans. Henry Paolucci (Indianapolis: Bobbs-Merrill, 1963), p. 8.

treatment model of imprisonment: prisoners become "residents" or "clients," guards become "correctional officers," solitary confinement cells become "adjustment units," and so on.

At the very basis of the rehabilitation ideology is a disease paradigm. It is not a new notion that prisoners are somehow sick; the idea even antedates Samuel Butler's 1872 satire *Erewhon*. Historically, the popular association between criminality and illness was partially fostered by the identical treatment of lawbreakers and the sick: they were both confined and isolated from the rest of society. Sociologists and historians have explored the manner in which the development of penal practices is partially indebted to lessons learned from leper colonies, insane asylums, and quarantines in times of plague. During the 1630-1633 plague in Florence, for example, the Public Health Magistracy was fully empowered to apprehend and confine in hospitals those who were under suspicion of illness.[23]

But "rehabilitative" imprisonment draws on the disease paradigm in ways other than just the mechanisms of confinement. Victor Hugo's depiction of Jean Valjean notwithstanding, prisoners are usually thought to be morally culpable in ways that the rest of us are not. Similarly, the sick of ages remote and recent have often been viewed as having been struck down by physical maladies as the result of sins hidden or obvious. Looking back on the cholera epidemic that struck the United States in 1832, the hindsight of medical knowledge renders it understandable that the first people to fall victim to the disease were the poor and the newly arrived immigrants who were herded together in the less kempt sections of America's nascent cities. There amid the garbage and the open sewers that ran by the sides of the roads, cholera did its work. But how the preachers did rant and rave! Even when the cholera spread to the wealthier sections of towns, the source of God's displeasure was still associated with the immoral poor and heterodox foreigners who had initially visited the disease on the community. The ferocity of the judgments leveled against those who first contracted cholera was very nearly matched by the denunciations in the 1980s of gay men and intravenous drug users suffering with Acquired Immune Deficiency Syndrome.

---

23. Giulia Calvi, *Histories of a Plague Year: The Social and the Imaginary in Baroque Florence*, trans. Dario Biocca and Bryant T. Ragan, Jr. (Berkeley and Los Angeles: University of California Press, 1989), pp. 155-96.

There are undoubtedly some serial killers and repeat offender rapists and other lawbreakers (as well as law-abiders) who are under the sway of pathologies. Even if one were to join with Thomas Szasz in maintaining that "mental illness" is a fictive social invention,[24] physical brain damage is no fiction, and there are occasional instances in which acts of horrendous violence have been traced back to a root source in such physical ailment. In such rare instances, it is certainly reasonable to hope that offenders would receive the medical treatment to which all people should be entitled. If brain damage renders an individual incapable of consenting to medical treatment, the standard procedures of medical ethics suggest that consent for treatment be sought from next of kin or guardians. This medical model of procuring treatment for those who are unable to give consent certainly carries its own potential for abuse. But it is quite another matter to suggest that the medical and penal models should be merged. While some offenders may be acting under the sway of physical afflictions that could be alleviated with proper medical care, it is quite another matter to assert that all offenders are "sick" or to join biological determinists in the belief that criminality can be attributed to genetic predisposition.

Professional psychiatric testing has failed to establish that there is any higher rate of "psychoses" among convicted felons than among the general population.[25] The criminogenic gene has yet to be found. As Stephen Jay Gould notes regarding biological determinism, bad biology is often enlisted in support of bad politics.[26] Even so, it would be inaccurate to ascribe evil intent to all who believe that offenders must be treated and rehabilitated. Indeed, some who subscribe to the rehabilitation ideology believe that society will take a kinder view of prisoners if it can somehow be established that illness or genetic predisposition or behavioral maladjustment is at the source of criminality. Of course, it is a case that is fundamentally impossible to make. One would have to establish that prostitution results from genetic or behavioral predisposition to criminality in some cultures but not in others where prostitution is legalized. Or one would need to establish that there are

24. Szasz, *The Myth of Mental Illness: Foundations of a Theory of Personal Conduct*, rev. ed. (New York: Harper & Row, 1974).

25. Knopp and her coauthors cite studies to this effect in *Instead of Prisons*, p. 29.

26. Gould, *An Urchin in the Storm: Essays about Books and Ideas* (New York: W. W. Norton, 1987), pp. 145-54.

genes or illnesses specific to thievery or specific to prostitution or specific to violence but, for example, that "violence illness" is only present in individuals whose violence is legislatively prohibited. No matter how generous the intent of those who wish to treat and rehabilitate prisoners, the definition of crime is culturally too fluid to permit of any notions that criminal offenses are caused by maladies that merit treatment. Besides which, public reaction to epidemics past and present indicates that, rather than being viewed as an occasion for empathy and understanding, illness is frequently perceived as a sign of moral culpability. And since the treatment of disease is often viewed as a "battle" against an "invader,"[27] it is far from certain that prisoners who are ostensibly being rehabilitated are treated any better than those who are simply being punished.

The U.S. Supreme Court has rarely proven to be a friend of prisoners' rights,[28] but a special sense of foreboding might well accompany the 27 February 1990 ruling that prison officials may force prisoners to take powerful antipsychotic drugs against their will. The point here is not to cast aspersions on the intent of the Court. It may well be that the justices intended their ruling to safeguard the well-being of those prisoners whose actions are blatantly self-destructive, but the ruling reaffirms the fact that the custody exercised by prison authorities is total and that penal and medical guardianship are merged. No matter the intent of the Court, history points to the inevitability of medical abuse when the power to treat is merged with the power to punish.

27. This militaristic view of disease is explored by Susan Sontag in *Illness as Metaphor* (New York: Farrar, Straus & Giroux, 1988), pp. 72-87.

28. The need for "security" has typically been cited as the ground for denying prisoners rights, and the Supreme Court invariably heeds the cautions of prison officials regarding what constitutes a threat to security. When North Carolina prisoners sought to form a union to pursue improved working conditions and to serve as a channel for their grievances, a lower court ruled the union permissible on the grounds that prison officials failed to offer evidence that it would pose any threat to security. But in the 1977 *Jones v. North Carolina Prisoners' Union* case, the Supreme Court reversed the decision because, in the words of Justice Rehnquist, prison officials "have not been conclusively shown to be wrong." In other words, prisoners had the burden of proving the negative, that the union would not threaten security. In the 1987 *O'Lane v. Shabazz* ruling, security was again cited as the reason for denying some Muslim prisoners the right to attend Jumu'ah worship services. These and other cases are cited by Fred Cohen in "The Law of Prisoners' Rights: An Overview," *Criminal Law Bulletin* 24 (July-August 1988): 321-49.

Of course, the practice of administering assorted drugs and experimental therapies to willing and unwilling prisoners is not new. After experimenting on hogs, Italian psychiatrist Ugo Cerletti is credited with the introduction of electro-convulsive therapy into psychiatry with his 1938 shocking of a prisoner who was screaming in agony during "treatment."[29] While the Nazis were conducting medical experiments on involuntary subjects during World War II, American prisoners were being offered money and promises of early release to volunteer to be infected with malaria and treated with experimental therapies. In 1952, the American Medical Association's house of delegates denounced the use of prisoners in medical experiments; the concern expressed by the AMA was not that prisoners might be unduly influenced to participate, nor that the experiments might be a threat to prisoner health, but rather that "heinous" criminals might use the experiments to gain undeserved privileges.[30]

The 1990 Supreme Court ruling stipulates that drugs should be forcibly administered to prisoners only in those instances when it has been determined that the drugs are in the best medical interests of the prisoners or when prisoners constitute a danger to themselves or others. The atrociously high rate of suicide in American prisons tends to indicate that prison personnel have not been particularly well-trained in determining when prisoners constitute a danger to themselves.[31] There is little doubt that a nursing home or a hospital or a school with a suicide rate approximating that of the average prison would be besieged with public investigations. Concerning what might be in the best interests of prisoners medically, it is placing a severe burden on prison doctors to expect that they will not be influenced by the observations of guards that this or that prisoner has been "acting up." Independent research

29. See *The History of Shock Treatment*, ed. Leonard Roy Frank (San Francisco: Leonard Roy Frank, 1978), pp. 8-9. This book also cites the 1940 court-ordered "cure" of a homosexual prisoner through drug-induced convulsions (p. 16). In 1971, electroshock was administered 433 times to prisoners at a single institution, the prison medical facility at Vacaville, California (p. 87).

30. "Prisoners as Research Subjects," Staff Paper of National Commission for the Protection of Human Subjects of Biomedical and Behavioral Research, in *Crime and Justice*, vol. 3: *The Criminal under Restraint*, 2d ed., ed. Leon Radzinowicz and Marvin Wolfgang (New York: Basic Books, 1977), pp. 312-31.

31. On suicide rates in jails and prisons, see Knopp et al., *Instead of Prisons*, p. 193n.108 and accompanying material.

into the use of drugs on prisoners in California in the 1970s found that the paralytic drug Anectine, a derivative of the South American poison curare, was most frequently used on prisoners who were viewed as offensive or troublesome to the staff (e.g., Black Muslims or gay prisoners).[32] In certain doses, other drugs such as Prolixin are said to produce the effect of "incarceration within the incarceration."[33] But still other drugs are eagerly sought out by prisoners in search of a bit of euphoria to relieve the tedium; regarding the prescription of such drugs, one prison physician's assistant observed, "It was easier to say 'yes' than argue for twenty minutes to say 'no.'"[34] Such are the vagaries of medical treatment in prison.

There is no small similarity between the American model of incarceration as rehabilitation and the old Soviet practice of using mental hospitals for the imprisonment of wide-ranging categories of offenders and dissidents.[35] With the reforms instituted by Gorbachev and expanded by Yeltsin, the Russian use of psychiatric incarceration is declining, but there have been various other manifestations of the rehabilitative motif in the penology of communist governments. After the reunification of Vietnam, for example, prostitutes, thieves, and officials who had worked for the former regime in the south were among those sent to "re-education camps." As one might expect, different political systems are accompanied by different emphases on precisely what it is from which and to which a prisoner is being rehabilitated. The Vietnamese showed prisoners how they had been

32. Wayne Sage, "Crime and the Clockwork Lemon," in *In Prison: Writings and Poems about the Prison Experience,* ed. James E. Trupin (New York: New American Library, 1975), pp. 49-51.

33. Norman Mailer, *The Executioner's Song* (New York: Warner Books, 1979), p. 397.

34. Cited by John McCoy in *Concrete Mama: Prison Profiles from Wala Wala* (Columbia, Mo.: University of Missouri Press, 1981), p. 123.

35. This is not to suggest that the United States is free from the use of psychiatric incarceration. As Szasz suggests in *The Myth of Mental Illness,* the practice is rampant. Indeed, one expression of sexism in our society is the manner in which women have more often been sent to mental institutions on charges for which men have been sent to prison. See Knopp et al., *Instead of Prisons,* p. 193n.120 and accompanying material. The sexism cuts both ways. Some may see prison as the worse fate of the two, but commitments to psychiatric institutions have tended to be indeterminate in length, and therefore the actual time of psychiatric incarceration may be longer than a fixed prison sentence on comparable charges.

mistaken on ideological matters. As befits a capitalist society, rehabilitation of prisoners in the United States is often geared toward productivity and the development of good work habits and job skills. It must immediately be noted, however, that what is depicted as "job training" in American prisons is frequently no more than the exploitation of a literally captive labor pool. It is no mere coincidence that prisons cut expenditures for food service employees by providing prisoners "job training" to become cooks and bakers and cafeteria workers.[36] In view of the fact that the "trainees" might be paid a few cents an hour, the institutional savings are huge. Nothing is more akin to slavery in contemporary America. In fact, the thirteenth amendment to the U.S. Constitution ("Neither slavery nor involuntary servitude, except as a punishment for crime whereof the party shall have been duly convicted, shall exist within the United States, or any place subject to their jurisdiction") is revealing in its acknowledgment of the enslavement of offenders as the only constitutionally permissible form of slavery.

If it is jobs for which prisoners are being trained and prepared, the adherents of the rehabilitation ideology overlook the manner in which imprisonment stigmatizes people and leaves them less likely to find meaningful employment. The findings of researchers that "a record of conviction produces a durable if not permanent loss of status"[37] remains true despite the enactment of antidiscrimination laws in some states. Prisons can hardly make the claim that they prepare offenders for a return to society when imprisonment itself stigmatizes them so that they are sure to be rejected by society on return.

Indeed, the very process of stigmatizing someone as a "bad person" might actually be a powerful factor contributing to crime. Many notorious lawbreakers (to name just one, Gary Gilmore) share the experience of having been institutionalized in a prison or reform school at an early age and having been labeled as "incorrigible." Benedict Alper

36. A California study showed that only 12 percent of one group of released prisoners found work related to their vocational training in prison. Estimates are that percentages would be even lower elsewhere. See *Struggle for Justice: A Report on Crime and Punishment in America* (New York: Hill & Wang, 1971), p. 90.

37. Richard D. Schwartz and Jerome H. Skolnick, "Legal Stigma," in *Deviance: The Interactionist Perspective*, 2d ed., ed. Earl Rubington and Martin S. Weinberg (New York: Macmillan, 1973), p. 223.

has written about the experience of the members of a Brooklyn youth gang who went on occasional rampages of brawling and vandalizing. The police eventually apprehended all members of the gang except for one. The members of the gang who were arrested all went on to commit other offenses and to be sentenced to lengthy prison terms. The one gang member who was never arrested despite his early criminal behavior went on to earn a doctorate and to teach science in a university.[38] In his classic essay "The Dramatization of Evil," Frank Tannenbaum describes the process of stigmatizing the "bad person":

> The process of making the criminal . . . is a process of tagging, defining, identifying, segregating, describing, emphasizing, making conscious and self-conscious; it becomes a way of stimulating, suggesting, emphasizing and evoking the very traits that are complained of. If the theory of relation of response to stimulus has any meaning, the entire process of dealing with the young delinquent is mischievous in so far as it identifies him to himself or to the environment as a delinquent person.
>
> The person becomes the thing he is described as being. Nor does it seem to matter whether the valuation is made by those who would punish or by those who would reform.[39]

But the valuations of those who seek to reform and rehabilitate often carry special power. Rather than a fixed prison sentence, the rehabilitation ideology has often encouraged indeterminate sentences (e.g., ten to twenty years or twenty years to life), which give prison officials and parole boards more freedom to determine when it is that a prisoner has been sufficiently reformed. By implication, prisons exist not because certain crimes have been committed but rather because certain characters and personalities stand in need of remolding. In the words of one prisoner, "You are no longer judged for your act. Your act is merely a lever for the judging of your every aspect."[40]

38. Alper, *Prisons Inside-Out: Alternatives in Correctional Reform* (Cambridge, Mass.: Ballinger, 1974), pp. 146-47.

39. Tannenbaum, "The Dramatization of Evil," in *Deviance: The Interactionist Perspective*, pp. 214-15. This "self-fulfilling prophecy" is also noted by Sage in "Crime and the Clockwork Lemon," pp. 52-53.

40. "Notes from Isolation," in *Inside: Prison American Style*, ed. Robert J. Minton, Jr. (New York: Vintage Books, 1971), p. 145.

A game is played out as prisoners facing parole hearings scurry to enroll in programs and complete classes to convince those who will judge them that they have become "model prisoners." The question of whether being a "model prisoner" is even remotely related to being able to live a peaceful and fulfilled life beyond the prison walls is inconsequential to the whole process. The game requires that prisoners coming before parole boards will have collected certificates and diplomas "like Boy Scouts collected merit badges."[41] But the game is played with a stacked deck. Parole may be denied because a guard or prison official has placed an unfavorable report in a prisoner's file (and most such reports are not even seen by the prisoners) or because one or more members of the parole board may have unspecified feelings about a prisoner's appearance or attitude or race. Parole may even be denied "in the prisoner's own best interest" so that he or she may benefit from additional rehabilitation. C. S. Lewis was justifiably incensed by such a humanitarian guise for punishment:

> Of all tyrannies a tyranny sincerely exercised for the good of its victims may be the most oppressive. It may be better to live under robber barons than under omnipotent moral busybodies. The robber baron's cruelty may sometimes sleep, his cupidity may at some point be satiated; but those who torment us for our own good will torment us without end for they do so with the approval of their own conscience. They may be more likely to go to Heaven yet at the same time likelier to make a Hell of earth.[42]

To judge the rehabilitation model on the basis of its own utilitarian criteria requires an evaluation of effectiveness. Rates of recidivism among prisoners who have been "rehabilitated" do not bode well for the efficacy of penal reformatory work. After noting that the rehabilitation model may entail involuntary administration of therapies and drugs and may be accompanied by indeterminate sentences that can be longer than those faced by other prisoners, Norman Bishop observes that "this all might-just-be acceptable if treatment actually

41. McCoy, *Concrete Mama*, p. 179.

42. Lewis, "The Humanitarian Theory of Punishment," in *God in the Dock: Essays on Theology and Ethics*, ed. Walter Hooper (Grand Rapids: William B. Eerdmans, 1970), p. 292.

produced results, but the evidence for successful penal treatment is both meager and unreliable."[43] After reviewing hundreds of studies of programs involving hundreds of thousands of individuals, Robert Martinson concluded that these programs "give us very little reason to hope that we have in fact found a sure way of reducing recidivism through rehabilitation."[44]

From a biblical perspective, however, considerations regarding effectiveness are quite inconsequential compared to other questions that must be brought to bear on rehabilitation ideology — among them, questions of idolatry. The work of ostensibly reforming individual lives inevitably involves positing some ideal life to which offenders should be brought into compliance. To judge from rehabilitative efforts, the ideal life involves conformity to conventional patterns in dress and speech, places a high value on the work ethic and punctuality and materialism, and above all, incorporates meticulous obedience to authority. If the truth be told, it is into our own image of middle-class respectability that correctional personnel and social service workers seek to rehabilitate offenders. But if another truth be told, many of us would not qualify for parole.

The rehabilitation model of imprisonment involves a radically atomistic view of crime. In this view, crime is not perceived as having anything to do with the larger community but rather as resulting from the activity of bad individuals who need to be treated and reformed. *We* are not a problem; *they* are a problem. The solution to crime is to be rid (in one form or another) of those individuals whom J. Edgar Hoover called "vermin in human form," "public rats," and "scum from the boiling pot of the underworld."[45]

One of the difficulties with such a view is that crime is far more prevalent and normal than Mr. Hoover may have chosen to believe.[46] What is distinctly *ab*normal about people in prison is that they happened to be caught and prosecuted and imprisoned. Estimates are that

43. Bishop, "Aspects of European Penal Systems," in *Progress in Penal Reform*, ed. Louis Blom-Cooper (London: Oxford University Press, 1974), p. 97.

44. Martinson, "What Works? A Comparative Assessment," in *The Criminal under Restraint*, p. 27.

45. Hoover, quoted by Wright in *The Great American Crime Myth*, p. 89.

46. On the normality of crime, see sociologist Emile Durkheim's essay "Crime as a Normal Phenomenon," in *Crime and Justice*, vol. 1: *The Criminal in Society*, ed. Leon Radzinowicz and Marvin Wolfgang (New York: Basic Books, 1971), pp. 391ff.

about one out of sixty-seven serious offenses results in imprisonment. Kevin Wright summarizes the findings as follows:

> 1 out of 3 offenses are reported (1 chance in 3).
> 1 out of 5 reported offenses result in arrest (1 chance in 15).
> 1 out of 2 people arrested are formally charged (1 chance in 30).
> 9 out of 10 people charged are convicted (3 chances in 100).
> 1 out of 2 people convicted receive prison sentences (3 chances in 200 or 1 chance in 67).[47]

Indeed, in response to confidential surveys, some 90 percent of Americans surveyed confessed to having committed serious misdemeanors or felonies for which they might have been imprisoned had they been apprehended.[48] Corporate crime seems equally normal, with as many as 60 percent of America's largest corporations having been convicted of criminal violations.[49]

So why is it that imprisoned offenders are any more in need of rehabilitation or reform than the rest of us? Moreover, why should society limit its efforts at coercive rehabilitation to those who have violated certain legal strictures? Is it not possible (even likely) that a greater amount of productivity and public and private wealth have been lost to laziness and incompetence than to thievery? Who of us is not a candidate for rehabilitation? Who of us does not deserve the surveillance of Bentham's Panopticon?

Our response to lawbreakers is inevitably influenced by our view of human nature. The perennial question reasserts itself: Are people by nature basically good or evil? The response to that question by Martin Luther King, Jr. was both theologically and politically profound.[50] Drawing on insights from Jesus, Tolstoy, Gandhi, and others, King said that people are neither basically good nor basically evil; rather, we all have potential for either acts of grace-filled benevolence or works of horrendous malevolence. Therefore, our task, said King, is one of seeking

47. Wright, *The Great American Crime Myth*, p. 115.
48. Knopp et al., *Instead of Prisons*, pp. 190n.2, 192n.62.
49. Study cited by L. Harold DeWolf in *Crime and Justice in America: A Paradox of Conscience* (New York: Harper & Row, 1975), p. 12.
50. For a summary of King's view, see John J. Ansbro, *Martin Luther King, Jr.: The Making of a Mind* (Maryknoll, N.Y.: Orbis Books, 1982), pp. 87-90.

to appeal to the potential for good within others. King's observations on human nature provide a framework for maintaining the dialectical tension inherent in the biblical understandings of the creation and the fall. The biblical pronouncement that human beings are created in the image of God precludes a theological assertion that we are evil by nature. The reality of the radical fall from grace precludes a theological assertion that people are basically good. We are both and neither. We all stand in need of *metanoia* and total reform. If we have any illusions that such reform can be accomplished through caging, who will be the keepers and who the kept? And if our task is to appeal to the potential for good within others, can it seriously be claimed that prisons appeal to the potential for good within anybody?

The Illusion of Deterrence

As people gathered on Tyburn Hill, young pickpockets wended their way through the crowd. The artful brush or bump against another person is the primary skill required for a pickpocket to successfully ply the trade. "Accidental" jostling of someone can be carefully coordinated and timed so that he or she does not even feel the lifting of wallet or purse or jewelry. The pickpockets could have very profitable days on Tyburn Hill because large crowds would gather to watch the hangings — of pickpockets. The springing open of trapdoors and the snapping of young necks were precisely the types of awful distractions that made it easier to lift a purse here or a watch there. It slowly dawned on late eighteenth-century Britons that hanging pickpockets did precious little to deter pilfering.[51]

Along with the rehabilitation model, the ideology of deterrence is thoroughly steeped in utilitarian assumptions that we may (indeed, we should) inflict a modicum of pain or suffering now for the sake of decreasing the likelihood of greater suffering in the future. Reliance on a lesser evil may be necessary to avoid an evil that is really — well, evil. A peculiarity of utilitarianism is its gradation of evil and enthusiastic embrace of what are presumed to be the lesser manifestations. At times,

---

51. For historical references along these lines, see Mannix, *The History of Torture*, p. 129.

the gradation is accomplished through mere quantification. For example, if you know that one person is going to kill two people (an explanation of how one can have certain knowledge about such things is not provided by utilitarians), is it not far better that you should kill that one person than to permit two to die? If you know that half a million people will die in an invasion of the Japanese mainland, is it not far better to incinerate a hundred thousand people in Hiroshima and Nagasaki than to permit the invasion to proceed? Fundamentally, such utilitarianism is a way of doing ethics by body count. But even if one were to grant (which I do not) that the ethically "good" decisions are the ones best calculated to leave the most people standing, the calculations and the supposed foreknowledge of utilitarianism are shortsighted. The mathematical calculations shift, for example, if the person who kills one in order to save two is so changed by the experience that he or she goes on to kill again. And after Hiroshima, the shifting mathematics must account for those many who starved while the world went mad with a nuclear arms race and the million or so left dead as the result of non-nuclear wars by proxy in Southeast Asia and elsewhere.

In penology, utilitarianism has produced two theories of deterrence that are separate but not mutually exclusive. The theory of special or specific deterrence maintains that imprisoning or otherwise punishing an offender will deter that specific individual from future offense. In the theory of general deterrence, the utilitarian aim is not so much to deter the individual being punished as it is to deter the criminality within the rest of us. The theory of general deterrence maintains that the exemplary punishment of a few will dissuade many from committing crimes.

There is something about the theories of both specific and general deterrence that violates the sense of fairness in which our judicial system is theoretically grounded. One is innocent, we are told, until sufficient evidence of wrongdoing has been presented. Upon conviction, a framework for sentencing is provided by statutory guidelines that stipulate, for example, that it is no longer permissible to execute pickpockets. In theory at least, "the punishment fits the crime." The theory of deterrence takes the additional step of suggesting that punishment should fit some imaginary or potential crime in the future. With specific deterrence, an offender is sent to prison because of a crime she or he might commit in the future. With general deterrence, an offender does time because of a crime you or I might commit. The logic entailed in the penology of deterrence stands in such stark contradiction to our common notions of fairness that not a few commentators have been reminded of the twisted logic in Lewis Carroll's *Through the Looking-Glass:*

> The Queen said:
> "Here is the King's messenger. He is in prison now being punished and the trial does not even begin until next Wednesday, and of course the crime comes last of all."
> "But suppose he never commits the crime?" asked Alice.
> "That would be all the better, wouldn't it?" the Queen responded.
> Alice felt there was no denying that. "Of course it would be all the better," she said, "but it wouldn't be all the better his being punished."
> "You are wrong," said the Queen. "Were you ever punished?"
> "Only for faults," said Alice.
> "And you were all the better for it I know," the Queen said triumphantly.
> "Yes, but I had done the things I was punished for," said Alice. "That makes all the difference."
> "But if you hadn't done them," the Queen said, "that would have been better still, better, better and better!"
> Her voice went higher with each "better" until it got to quite a squeak.
> Alice thought, "There is a mistake somewhere."[52]

By suggesting that the purpose of punishment is to avoid crimes that have not yet been committed, deterrence theory raises questions about whether the same benefit could not be had by punishing people who are innocent of any criminal violations. If the public believed an individual to be guilty, would it not be possible to derive social benefit from the punishment of that person even if she or he were innocent?[53] Or what about preemptive action? Since the vast majority of offenders are young people between the ages of approximately fifteen and thirty-five, might there not be genuine deterrent value in the nineteenth-century proposal by Sir Edmund DuCane that young people with "marked criminal tendencies could either be locked up or kept under

52. See, e.g., *Struggle for Justice*, p. 67; and Knopp et al., *Instead of Prisons*, p. 111.
53. This quandary for utilitarian theory is noted by Joseph Grcic in *Moral Choices: Ethical Theories and Problems* (New York: West Publishing, 1989), p. 332.

supervision until they had passed, say, the age of forty"?[54] Lest it be reckoned that such proposals are primitive artifacts of a bygone age, there are similarities in the proposal by President Nixon's physician, Dr. Arnold Hutschnecker, that mass psychological testing be administered to children at the age of six so that those with violent criminal tendencies could be housed in special camps for treatment.[55]

By its very nature, the theory of specific deterrence involves a prediction of dangerousness and criminal tendencies. The theory holds that deterrent punishment must be inflicted on an individual who has been convicted of an offense because it is likely that that individual will commit another offense unless deterred from doing so. Yet, most predictions of dangerousness and criminality have proved notoriously inaccurate. When the U.S. Supreme Court ruled in 1966 in *Baxstrom v. Herold* that people could not be held for long periods in maximum security hospitals for the criminally insane unless they had been granted proper judicial review, the subsequent release of 967 people from incarceration in two New York hospitals was accompanied by dire predictions from mental health professionals that a violent crime wave would result. Four years later, only 26 of the 967 people released had been returned to hospitals for the criminally insane. More recent studies from "The Center for the Care and Treatment of Dangerous Persons" and the sudden mass release of offenders from Massachusetts youth training schools indicate that criminal tendencies defy prediction.[56]

In fact, the lowest rates of recidivism are among those offenders who are likely to elicit the greatest amount of public fear and outrage — people who have been convicted of violent offenses such as murder. Those who have been convicted of economic crimes have much higher rates of recidivism.[57] The low number of repeat offenders among those convicted of murder may be partially due to the fact that in this country most murderers know their victims (in fact, most murders are a case of one family member killing another), and the killings are frequently irrational acts of momentary rage or passion. Random acts of stranger-

---

54. DuCane, quoted by Peter Kropotkin, in *In Russian and French Prisons* (New York: Schocken Books, 1971), p. 354. Kropotkin's book was originally published in 1887.

55. See Mitford, *Kind and Usual Punishment*, p. 56.

56. See DeWolf, *Crime and Justice in America*, p. 220; and Knopp et al., *Instead of Prisons*, pp. 130-35.

57. DeWolf, *Crime and Justice in America*, p. 45.

to-stranger murder account for less than twenty percent of all murders.[58] In view of the much higher rates of recidivism for economic crimes than for crimes of violence, a consistently applied theory of specific deterrence would seem to require that shoplifting be dealt with more harshly than murder.

Regarding general deterrence, it appears unlikely that rational calculations concerning potential punishment could intervene to deter the irrationality of a murderous rage. Crimes of passion aside, many of us know firsthand that deterrence also has limited impact in more mundane situations. Many of us who are in meticulous compliance with speed limits when police cars are in view have few qualms about exceeding the limits by a few miles per hour when the police are out of sight. There seems to be more than a little validity to Karl Menninger's observation that what punishment deters is not crime but getting caught.[59]

Utilitarian schemes beg to be judged on the basis of their empirically demonstrated utility, and on that basis there is, in the words of Charles Colson, "no valid demonstration that the existence of prison deters crime."[60] The state of New York was forced to admit that imprisonment seemed to provide no deterrent; the state abandoned its mandatory sentence of life imprisonment for dealing in drugs after discovering that the stiff sentence resulted in nothing but a prison population and a drug problem that were both growing at an alarming rate.[61] As Texas more than doubled its prison population from 14,000 in 1970 to 31,000 in 1981, the state's homicide rate simultaneously increased by 41 percent.[62] The validity of deterrence theory is further challenged by the fact that the United States has one of the highest crime rates in the Western world while it is simultaneously "the most punitive nation in the modern western world" with a rate of incarceration more than

58. In 1976, stranger-to-stranger murders accounted for 18.4 percent of the total; in 1981, the percentage had dropped to 15.5. See Wright, *The Great American Crime Myth*, p. 24.

59. Menninger, *The Crime of Punishment* (New York: Viking Press, 1969), p. viii.

60. Colson, "Towards an Understanding of Imprisonment and Rehabilitation," in *Crime and the Responsible Community*, ed. John Stott and Nicholas Miller (Grand Rapids: William B. Eerdmans, 1980), p. 161.

61. Charles Colson and Daniel Van Ness, *Convicted: New Hope for Ending America's Crime Crisis* (Westchester, Ill.: Crossway Books, 1989), p. 111n.1.

62. Currie, *Confronting Crime*, p. 34.

double that of Canada, France, or England, six times that of Japan, and twelve times that of the Netherlands.[63] A comparative study of California, England, and Japan found that someone convicted of robbery had a 63 percent chance of being imprisoned in California versus a 48 percent chance in England and a 46 percent chance in Japan. Moreover, the person imprisoned for robbery in California spent an average of twice as much time in prison as those incarcerated for robbery in England. Still, California's robbery rate is over seventeen times that of England and twenty-eight times that of Japan.[64]

In fact, there is a growing body of evidence suggesting that, contrary to deterring offenses, prisons may actually play a role in causing crime. Several studies indicate that the shorter the sentence and the less time spent in jail or prison, the lower the rates of recidivism.[65] Leonard Orland writes that

> the empirical data on imprisonment and recidivism, although crude, are quite startling. They appear to suggest that if reduction of crime is the objective, the less we do to (or for) the offender after conviction, the more likely it is that he will not commit a new crime. Stated conversely, the data suggest that the longer we imprison the offender, the more likely it is that he will commit new crimes when released.[66]

Orland goes on to cite research indicating that fines have more deterrent effect than probation, probation more than prison, and minimum security prisons more than maximum security prisons. The findings suggesting that the less punitive the response the better hold true regardless of the seriousness of the offense and regardless of whether the offender being sentenced has a record of previous convictions. The evidence leads some to the conclusion that, by paying for increasing reliance on imprisonment, "the public is buying crime and doesn't know it."[67] The evidence also suggests that those who are seriously interested in deterrence of crime might do well to work for prison abolition.

63. Wright, *The Great American Crime Myth*, p. 125.

64. The study, by Kenneth Wolpin, is cited by Currie in *Confronting Crime*, pp. 30-31.

65. Several of these studies are cited by Martinson in "What Works?" pp. 15-16.

66. Orland, *Prisons: Houses of Darkness* (New York: Free Press, 1978), p. 37.

67. Ben H. Bagdikian and Leon Dash, *The Washington Post National Report: The Shame of the Prisons* (New York: Pocket Books, 1972), p. 33.

From a biblical perspective, however, the difficulties with the theory of punitive deterrence are far more serious than simple lack of effectiveness. Indeed, the cross stands as an indication that faithfulness need not (or perhaps even *will not*) be effective. The saints will be defeated (Dan. 7:21; Rev. 13:7). Assuming that we are able to choose actions that are good and faithful (no small assumption, says Paul in Rom. 7:15-19), there are no guarantees that such actions will be effective in terms of benefit for "the greatest number" or even in terms of self-preservation. Simply stated, effectiveness is not a criterion by which faithfulness can be judged.

But in an odd twist, utilitarianism makes no pretense of choosing good for the sake of effectiveness. Rather than choosing good, the utilitarian theory of deterrence involves the exact opposite: it involves intentionally choosing evil in the belief that such a choice will effectively precipitate good at some later point. In fact, there are utilitarians aplenty who will happily tell pacifists and those who are seeking to do works of justice and mercy that the attempt to refrain from doing evil is actually very harmful. Refusal to use violence against an attacker, say those of deterrence persuasion, is just encouraging future attacks against others. Giving free food to the hungry, say those with an eye to the greater good, is just encouraging laziness and dependence. While it is certainly true that pacifism should not be permitted to lapse into mere passivism, and while it is certainly true that acts of charity should not be substitutes for the pursuit of justice, it is quite another matter to suggest that either peace or justice can be won through evil means or that the well-intentioned infliction of sufficient quantities of agony will give birth to utopia.

The gospel message is not a utopian fantasy. Rather than issuing a call to build a utopia, Jesus announces that the kingdom of God is already present in our midst. The decisive victory is already won. Far more utopian is the utilitarian notion of needing to defer the good for the sake of a bigger and better reality. Far more utopian is the claim that, like peasants who starve for the sake of a Stalinist revolution, some must suffer evil for the sake of a larger good.

The notion of doing a little evil for good is essentially a Faustian pact with the devil. We are told that the ends (theoretically, lower crime rates) justify the means (inflicting pain and suffering). Of course, once one walks down that path, there is no end to the brutality that can be justified by visions utopian or otherwise. Is it not likely that Hitler thought his unsavory means were justified by ends the goodness of which would someday be apparent to everyone? As Faust discovered, pacts with the demonic do not come to a good end.

The theories of deterrence posit a view of life that is untenable from a biblical perspective. The theory of general deterrence suggests that people are merely means — that the punished person is a means by which the crimes of others can be deterred. The theories of both general and specific deterrence further betray a low valuation of human beings by supposing that we react to situations in a manner akin to Pavlov's dogs: our fear of punishment causes a reflex avoidance reaction. Gerald McHugh notes that this reductionist, pleasure/pain model of human behavior "is fundamentally non-Christian anthropology."[68]

McHugh also notes that Jesus persistently sets a "bad example" by deterrence standards.[69] How can sin be deterred when Jesus is always going around befriending sinners? Or how can the law be enforced when Jesus associates with lawbreakers and sometimes breaks the law himself? If a rallying cry for punitive deterrence is sought, it is not likely to be found in the teachings of one who urges us to "do good to those who hate you."

The Cult of Retribution

The persistence of punishment as a feature common to many (if not all) human societies and the zeal with which some societies inflict it would tend to indicate that there is something primordial about punitive behavior — perhaps not primordial in the sense of the primeval forest but certainly in the sense of the nursery. When parents punish children, no matter what other lessons they may assume are being inculcated, the primary lesson is about the nature and various justifications of punishment itself. The guises for punishment in child rearing have included blatant physical abuse as well as subtler impositions of a sense of shame.[70] In the United States, the use of corporal punishment has been

68. McHugh, *Christian Faith and Criminal Justice: Toward a Christian Response to Crime and Punishment* (New York: Paulist Press, 1978), p. 109.

69. McHugh, *Christian Faith and Criminal Justice*, p. 117.

70. On the possibility of correspondence and interaction between techniques of punishment in child rearing and punitive measures in penology, see Richard Sennett, *Authority* (New York: Vintage Books, 1981), pp. 89-97.

more prevalent than in many other societies. Indeed, Native Americans referred to European settlers as "the people who whip children."[71] Some criminologists have even wondered how much the prevalence of corporal punishment contributes to a rate of violent crime, which is much higher in America than in nations such as Sweden, where corporal punishment in secondary schools was outlawed in the 1920s and corporal punishment by anyone (parents included) was outlawed in 1979.[72] Whatever its other effects, punishment of children can sometimes be exercised in such a way as to communicate no message other than "might makes right." According to U.S. Supreme Court Justice Oliver Wendell Holmes, it is precisely this principle that is the sole foundation of law. The will of the sovereign is law, said Holmes, simply because of the "power to compel obedience or punish disobedience, and for no other reason."[73]

Few legal theorists have agreed with Holmes's position that brute force and the power to inflict punishment constitute the sole basis of law, but even fewer have been willing to renounce the use of punishment. In fact, claims of the value and validity of punishment have been reasserted by some who willingly admit that the punishment of offenders serves no rehabilitative or deterrent purpose. Immanuel Kant was among those who questioned the morality of utilizing punishment as a means to attain some other goal such as deterrence, but he nonetheless upheld the validity of punishment as a "categorical imperative," which he defined as an action that is "good in itself."[74] Kant renounced what he called "the serpent-windings of utilitarianism"[75] in favor of the

71. Karl Menninger, *Whatever Became of Sin?* (New York: Hawthorn Books, 1975), pp. 27-28.

72. Currie, *Confronting Crime*, p. 42. Currie also notes that, despite the American liking for "old-fashioned discipline" in our schools, the schools that utilize the harshest disciplinary measures also tend to be the ones with the highest rates of student violence (pp. 44-45). This does not establish a cause-and-effect relationship between the discipline and the student violence, but it does tend to indicate that punitive measures fail to provide a remedy.

73. Holmes, quoted by David Cowan Bayne in *Conscience, Obligation, and the Law: The Moral Binding Power of the Civil Law* (Chicago: Loyola University Press, 1966), p. 22.

74. *Kant Selections*, ed. Theodore M. Greene (New York: Scribner's, 1957), p. 298.

75. Kant, quoted by Graeme Newman in *The Punishment Response* (New York: J. B. Lippincott, 1978), p. 191.

simple principle of retribution — which is to say, he considered punishment a "just desert" for wrongdoing.

Within the Christian tradition, some proponents of retribution have gone so far as to suggest that when we dispense judicial punishment, we do so in God's stead. Drawn from Romans 13, such claims have come from Protestant as well as Catholic circles. The Protestant theologian Emil Brunner maintained that "properly understood, the human judge is merely a representative of God. He acts in the name of the divinely established order of the community. That is why the powers wield the sword . . . as holy servants of God, whether they know this God or not. What they do in the name of the state, they do, albeit unwittingly, by God's command."[76] Brunner's perspective on the "divinely established order" seems to have been shared by Pope Pius XII, who proclaimed in 1954 that every criminal act is directed not merely against things and people but against higher authority and "in the end always against the authority of God." It is that fact alone, said Pius, rather than any utilitarian motives, that makes every offender "deserving of punishment."[77] Of course, with such melding of God and state, there is little to prevent one from claiming that the Boston Tea Party was an act directed against God rather than George III and that Nazi judges were unwittingly performing God's will as they rounded up Jews and punished those few Christians who offered their attics as sanctuary. Most advocates of retribution are less sweeping in their convictions about the sanctity of punishment.

The roots of the penal ideology of retribution lie in the ancient practice of *lex talionis,* the law of retaliation or revenge. While many of the more recent advocates of retribution object to any identification of their thought with vengeance,[78] concepts of punishment as "just desert" can be traced to the ancient practice of victims or the surviving family, clan, or tribe of victims exercising revenge against offenders or their family or tribe. The biblical passage most frequently cited as justification for retribution is Exodus 21:23-25, which prescribes an "eye for eye, tooth for tooth"; the biblical passage most frequently ignored by advo-

76. Brunner, *Justice and the Social Order,* trans. Mary Hottinger (New York: Harper, 1945), p. 223.

77. Pius XII, quoted by Orland in *Prisons,* p. 42.

78. See, e.g., Brunner's objections in *Justice and the Social Order,* p. 222.

cates of retribution is Jesus' comments on the Exodus passage in Matthew 5:38-39 ("You have heard that it was said, 'An eye for an eye, and a tooth for a tooth.' But I say to you, do not resist him who is evil; but whoever slaps you on your right cheek, turn to him the other also"). In its origins, however, rather than exhorting people to acts of great vengeance, the *lex talionis* in Exodus actually prescribed limits to retaliation: an injured person may exact no more by way of retaliation than the injury that was suffered.

Through history, the practice of retribution has undergone a process of abstraction so that today the person who has been victimized or injured is formally irrelevant to the pursuit of punishment. Most frequently in the juridical process, the injured party is no longer a real person who has suffered loss but rather "the U.S." or "the People" or "the State of . . ." This process of abstraction has its origins in an earlier age when the monarch was understood to be the actual embodiment of the realm, and any violation against people or property within the realm was viewed as an attack upon the body of the king or queen. Both judges and prosecutors were representatives of the monarch. Retribution was sought not on behalf of the individuals who had been immediately victimized but rather on behalf of the monarch. The actual victim was viewed as only peripheral; the true victim was the king or queen, and any rights pertaining to the *lex talionis* belonged to no one else.[79] Thus began the development of abstractions and legal fictions still prevalent in jurisprudence today. Most often in criminal proceedings, "just deserts" are no longer sought on behalf of individuals who have actually suffered but rather on behalf of legal entities such as the society or the state.[80]

But the identification of who has been victimized is not the only element of the ideology of retribution that has undergone a process of

79. For a consideration of this and other consequences of the view of the monarch as the embodiment of the realm, see Ernst H. Kantorowicz, *The King's Two Bodies: A Study in Medieval Political Theology* (Princeton: Princeton University Press, 1957).

80. Claiming to be influenced by Darwinism, some legal theorists have been quite literal in their understandings of society as the "body" that is victimized by crime. In a late nineteenth-century article in the *International Journal of Ethics*, F. H. Bradley wrote that punishment arises from "the right and duty of the organism to suppress its undesirable growths" ("Some Remarks on Punishment," in *Ethical Choice: A Case Study Approach*, by Robert N. Beck and John B. Orr [New York: Free Press, 1970], p. 341).

abstraction. The meaning of "just deserts" has also been manipulated and calculated into abstraction, a process that has been influenced to no small degree by increasing reliance on prisons. The *lex talionis* in the Old Testament was quite concrete, and the retribution to be exacted was determined with direct reference to the injury that had been suffered. If property was damaged, the offender would forfeit an amount of wealth equivalent to the cost of the damage; if an eye was lost, the offender would lose an eye. While the idea of plucking out an offender's eye seems so inhumane that even those who ignore Matthew 5 would not be prepared to advocate the literal retribution of Exodus, the question rarely arises about whether our contemporary calculations of just deserts are any more humane. In the whole abstracted process, how is one to determine, for example, how much time behind bars is just desert for a theft of a hundred dollars? In a situation such as stealing, some Old Testament guidelines are far more humane and less abstract than the calculations of American jurisprudence. After all, if someone robs a bank, the robber did not cage the bank manager for ten years and take away his or her job, family, and friends.

In the bloody equations of life for life, some advocates of capital punishment may reckon that the punishment of death for murder constitutes the perfect just desert. But as Albert Camus explained,

> there is no equivalence. Many laws consider a premeditated crime more serious than a crime of pure violence. But what then is capital punishment but the most premeditated of murders, to which no criminal's deed, however calculated it may be, can be compared? For there to be equivalence, the death penalty would have to punish a criminal who had warned his victim of the date at which he would inflict a horrible death on him and who, from that moment onward, had confined him at his mercy for months. Such a monster is not encountered in private life.[81]

The calculated and premeditated nature of execution is an intentional and integral part of the punishment itself. Otherwise, why did the state of Utah seek medical treatment to save a condemned Gary Gilmore after a suicide attempt? The state saved his life so that the state could

---

81. Camus, "Reflections on the Guillotine," in *Resistance, Rebellion, and Death*, trans. Justin O'Brien (New York: Vintage Books, 1974), p. 199.

take it at the premeditated time and in the calculated circumstances that it deemed appropriate.

The example of Gilmore also illustrates the considerable subjectivity that enters into the determination of what constitutes just desert. Gilmore was killed, while Lt. William Calley received a milder sentence of ten years following his conviction for the murders of twenty-two Vietnamese. If advocates of retribution are to assert that punishments are justly deserved, how do they explain why ten defendants in Selective Service cases coming before one judge in the Southern District of New York deserved prison but none of the six defendants in similar cases coming before another judge in the same Court District deserved prison? And why does a businessman convicted of embezzling $100,000 deserve a suspended sentence, while an unemployed person convicted of shoplifting a $50 watch deserves a prison term?[82] Or why is state-imposed death not a just desert in New York State so long as there is a governor opposed to the death penalty, but death becomes quite just the moment a governor of different opinion takes office? The ideology of retribution must confront the reality that whether this or that punishment is "just" is determined by nothing so much as the eye of the beholder.

While there are numerous reasons to object to the ideologies of rehabilitation and deterrence, at least these utilitarian schemes permit of some external criteria by which their claims to validity might be measured and weighed. What are the criteria by which the practitioners of retribution bless assorted punishments with the designation of "just desert"? Is it merely the shifts in legal opinion or public opinion or the opinions of the wealthy and powerful? On what basis did Americans object to the punishment of Soviet dissidents when such punishment was once firmly supported by Soviet legal opinion? If the validity of various punishments is founded on nothing more than shifting opinions (even the opinions of "legal experts"), then should we not honestly label such punishments as the preferences of those in power rather than calling them retribution that offenders justly deserve? Contrary to the

82. These cases and other disparities are cited by Carl T. Rowan and David M. Mazie in "The Sentencing Process Does Not Work," in *Criminal Justice: Opposing Viewpoints*, ed. David L. Bender and Bruno Leone, Opposing Viewpoints Series (St. Paul: Greenhaven Press, 1981), pp. 33-35.

ideology of retribution, the nature of the punishments are determined not by the nature of the violations but by the shifting preferences of legislators or judges or public opinion. Just desert should be made of sterner stuff.

An additional problem with quite serious consequences is the juridical pretension that we can exact retribution in a manner akin to a childhood game. Children may try to win by being nasty or cruel but cry foul if their playmates do the same. Children may declare the game over when they appear to be winning and want to avoid any further play that could jeopardize the lead. In similar fashion, those who exact penal retribution believe that, having gained the upper hand, they should be able to declare the process at an end. Consideration is rarely given to the possibility that the punishment may only be fueling vicious circles of retribution and revenge. Jesus' admonition to turn the other cheek actually says, "the perpetual cycle of retaliation ends with me." In contrast, the ideology of retribution says, "we assert the right to retaliate, and the cycle must end with you, the offender." In other words, society expects the offender to live up to standards that the society freely confesses it cannot abide.

Some prisoners arrive at the point of recognizing the ways in which their actions may have victimized others and some prisoners go beyond that to make sincere efforts at restitution, but we are fooling ourselves if we believe that the vast majority of offenders perceive their own imprisonment as "just desert." Ninety-eight percent of all prisoners will eventually be back in the community,[83] and there is little doubt that some of them will be back with an eye to exacting their own retribution for what has been done to them. Indeed, the brutality of some prisoners during the Santa Fe prison uprising in 1981 and the brutality of some state officials at Attica in 1971 indicate that the wheels of retribution keep turning inside the prison.[84] It is fantasy to believe that the wheels necessarily stop turning for all prisoners when they are released. The words of convicted mass murderer Carl Panzram are chilling:

83. Alper, *Prisons Inside-Out,* p. 148.

84. The New York State Special Commission on Attica noted that, "With the exception of Indian massacres in the late 19th century, the State Police assault which ended the four-day prison uprising was the bloodiest one-day encounter between Americans since the Civil War" ("Bloody Attica," in *Social Crises: A Casebook,* ed. Robert Hybels [New York: Thomas Y. Crowell, 1974], p. 334).

If someone had a young tiger cub in a cage and then mistreated it until it got savage and bloodthirsty and then turned it loose to prey on the rest of the world, to go anywhere and kill anyone it wanted to, then there would be a hell of a roar from those in danger of the mad tiger. Everyone would believe that to be the wrong thing to do. But if some people do the same thing to other people, then the world is surprised, shocked and offended because they get robbed, raped and killed. Yet this is exactly what is being done every day in this country. They done it to me and then don't like it when I give them the same dose they gave me.[85]

Frank Rondel, a psychiatrist who once worked in Soledad Prison, describes the sort of prisoner who is filled with bitterness and rage as "a human personality that has been developed within the department of corrections."[86] Through such developments, the prison serves to keep the wheels of retaliation turning. But there is another way in which prison may contribute to calculated violence. In the words of a person released from San Quentin, "If I have to take a chance on going back into one of these institutions, I'm not going to stop and entertain conversation with a policeman. I'll kill him on the spot!"[87] While cal-

---

85. Panzram, quoted by Thomas E. Gaddis and James O. Long in *Killer: A Journal of Murder*, cited in *In Prison*, p. 155.

86. Rondel, quoted by Sage in "Crime and the Clockwork Lemon," p. 59.

Dr. Meredith Bombar, a social psychologist and friend of mine who has served as tenured associate professor of psychology at Elmira College, notes that it would be difficult intentionally to shape a more effective breeding ground for aggression than that which already exists in the average prison. In personal correspondence, Dr. Bombar writes, "When I teach Social Psychology class, I spend a week or so going over the social/learned causes of aggression (e.g., provocation, modeling, punishment, extreme frustration, roles and social norms calling for aggression, physical discomfort, crowding, the presence of guns and other objects associated with aggression, etc.). After the students have digested that, I ask them to imagine a horrible fantasy world which would put together all of these known social/environmental causes of aggression. What would it be? A typical prison."

It is not necessary here to dwell on an additional way in which prisons contribute to crime — the oft-cited role of prisons as "training schools" for crime. At times, prisons may prepare people for crime in a quite literal fashion. In his book *In Cold Blood*, Truman Capote tells of how the two people who brutally murdered a rural Kansas family got information about the family, the floor plan of their house, and the details of their daily routine from another person with whom they had been imprisoned at Kansas State Penitentiary.

87. Quoted by Sage in "Crime and the Clockwork Lemon," p. 60.

culations are being made about which punishments are just, the punishments may lead some offenders to calculations of their own about what they may "justly" do to avoid apprehension.

While it is clear that retribution can have a horrible impact on those who receive the "just deserts," attention must also be paid to the influence retribution has on the rest of us. When the spirit of retaliation is applauded in our judicial system, such a spirit is reinforced in other aspects of our lives. Far too often, this spirit of retaliation is manifested as petty vindictiveness in our interpersonal relationships — a vindictiveness that sometimes has catastrophic results. The point is illustrated in the alarming findings of a study of capital punishment by William Bowers and Glenn Pierce from Northeastern University's Center for Social Research.[88] After looking at murder rates in the months following executions in New York State over the period from 1907 to 1963 (availability of data figured into their choice of location and dates), Bowers and Pierce found that, on average, there were two additional murders in New York during the month after an execution. The researchers note that the figure of two additional murders may actually be low, because they only considered the month following and not the month of an execution. Bowers and Pierce attribute the additional murders to the brutalizing effect of executions. While capital punishment is presumed to communicate the message "Do not commit a murder or you will be punished," executions may actually communicate a different message: "It is necessary to kill bad people." The state is demonstrating that "bad people" deserve death, and individuals who respond to this message may be more inclined to take it upon themselves to kill people whom they consider to be deserving of retribution. A more recent, international study confirms the Bowers and Pierce thesis regarding the brutalizing effect of executions. Dane Archer and Rosemary Gartner found that most nations that abolished the death penalty experienced a decline in rates of homicide.[89] The brutalizing effect of capital punishment may account for the findings of a survey of condemned men in Bristol Prison in 1886; of 167 men sentenced to death, 164 had witnessed

88. Bowers and Pierce, "Deterrence or Brutalization: What Is the Effect of Executions?" *Crime and Delinquency* 26 (October 1980): 453ff.

89. Archer and Gartner, *Violence and Crime in Cross-National Perspective* (New Haven: Yale University Press, 1984), p. 136.

at least one execution prior to their own imprisonment.[90] As George Bernard Shaw wrote, "It is the deed that teaches, not the name we give it. Murder and capital punishment are not opposites that cancel one another, but similars that breed their kind."[91]

Whatever the form of retaliation, the process of exacting retribution inherently entails focusing all energy and attention on the offender. Just as the victim is lost in the maze of legal proceedings that are brought in the name of abstract victims, the real victim is also forgotten in the rush to retaliate against the offender. While the offender is given what the judge may calculate to be just deserts, the victim may be given nothing. Despite the enactment of victims' rights legislation in some states, most victims are still left without adequate financial and emotional support to help them cope with their losses. The ideology of retribution reinforces the practice of spending billions of dollars on chasing, prosecuting, and imprisoning offenders, while a mere pittance is spent on seeking to care for those who have suffered loss. Rather than seeking to diminish the suffering of the victim, retribution seeks to increase the suffering of the offender. Any ideology that demands the intentional increase of suffering rather than its diminution can hardly lay claim to the title "justice."

Yet, Christians are among the groups advocating the harshest forms of retribution and the most punitive treatment of offenders.[92] With what appears to be indifference to a gospel that beckons us to forgive seventy times seven, Christians often fall into the role of the sanctimonious brother of the prodigal son (Luke 15:11-32). In the account of the woman taken in adultery (John 8:1-11), Jesus acted in a way that prevented the imposition of the sentence that the law clearly demanded. But many Christians seem to believe that justice is denied unless all lawbreakers receive retaliatory punishment.

The notion that justice must entail the increase rather than the diminution of suffering is not derived from the biblical concept of justice but rather from the definition of justice inherited from Greco-Roman philosophy and jurisprudence. Like Oliver Wendell Holmes, some philos-

90. Camus, "Reflections on the Guillotine," p. 189.

91. Shaw, quoted by Ian Gray and Moira Stanley for Amnesty International U.S.A. in *A Punishment in Search of a Crime: Americans Speak Out against the Death Penalty* (New York: Avon Books, 1989), p. 5.

92. See Wright, *The Great American Crime Myth*, p. 72.

ophers have maintained that justice itself has a basis in brute force. The argument is made by the Sophist Thrasymachus in Plato's *Republic:* "I affirm that the just is nothing else than the advantage of the stronger."[93] That position is echoed in the eighteenth-century writing of Blaise Pascal:

> It is dangerous to tell people that the laws are not just, for they obey the laws only because they think they are just. For this reason people must be told to obey the laws because they are laws, just as they must obey the rulers not because they are just, but because they are rulers. If this is understood, any insurrection is forestalled. This is the true definition of justice.[94]

Neither Plato nor Aristotle endorsed such a definition. Plato maintained that justice must be based not only on the power but also on the "virtue" of the state. Both Plato and Aristotle taught that this virtue entailed consistently giving all people their "due," their "just desert."

The biblical concept of justice has nothing to do with either the power to compel obedience or the "virtue" of the state. The Bible envisions justice as quite simply that which is in accordance with the will of God.[95] Such justice cannot be abstracted into rules or confined in law books, because God's will is always revealed as judgment in particular situations.[96] But this judgment and justice of God has nothing in common with calculations about which punishments are due to whom. In fact, God's judgment is always followed by pardon.[97] In Chapter 3 I address the manner in which *tsedeka* (justice, righteousness) has as its goal not "just desert" but the restoration of covenanted community. God's justice is always an expression of the will to restore, and God accomplishes this by standing with the accused. As Jacques Ellul notes, God's justice is neither distributive nor retributive: "It is a substitutive justice."[98]

---

93. From book 1 of the *Republic*, in *Plato: The Collected Dialogues*, ed. Edith Hamilton and Huntington Cairns, Bollingen Series 71 (New York: Pantheon Books, 1961), p. 588.

94. From Pascal's *Pensées*, cited in a note by translator Marguerite Wieser in Ellul's *Theological Foundation of Law*, p. 85.

95. This understanding is elaborated by Ellul in *The Theological Foundation of Law*, pp. 46ff.

96. See Ellul, *The Theological Foundation of Law*, p. 48.

97. Ellul, *The Theological Foundation of Law*, p. 88.

98. Ellul, *The Theological Foundation of Law*, p. 43.

Rather than drawing on this biblical understanding of justice, Charles Colson and Daniel Van Ness appear to be utilizing the definitions of Greek philosophers when they observe that "if justice means getting one's due, then justice is denied when deserved punishment is not received."[99] It must be noted that Colson and Van Ness are making exemplary efforts to be of service to both prisoners and those who have been victimized by crime, but they stand with the rest of humanity (I more than most) who are spared the punishments we so richly deserve. In fact, justice cannot mean "getting one's due," because the God of justice shows love to the least deserving. The God of justice gives equal treatment to those who come late to the fields (Matt. 20:1-16). If we are wise, we will ask this God of justice to continue to embrace us in unmerited love rather than to give us just deserts.

Inside

The most realistic and factually accurate descriptions of prison life (and death) are found in works of fiction, especially fiction written by people who have been prisoners, such as Solzhenitsyn, Piñero, Bienek.[100] There is an unreal and surreal quality to life in a cage that cannot be captured by statistical or theoretical analyses by criminologists, psychologists, or sociologists. How but in fiction can one describe the surreal experience of existing in an environment where everything tells you that you no longer exist? If you had work or a career in the "outside" world, where is your work now?[101] If there was someone you loved, where is she or he now? Where are your parents or children? Any friends with whom you visited or streets on which you walked or newspapers you read or vistas you surveyed are nowhere to be found — not even the clothes you used to wear. The people, events, and things that help to shape a sense of identity are stripped away, and that "you"

99. Colson and Van Ness, *Convicted*, p. 63.

100. I refer to the gulag writings of Alexander Solzhenitsyn, Miguel Piñero's play *Short Eyes* (New York: Hill & Wang, 1975), and the amazingly bleak but life-affirming novel by Horst Bienek entitled *The Cell* (Santa Barbara: Unicorn Press, 1972).

101. Gresham M. Sykes notes that "the prisoner is supposed to live in poverty as a matter of public policy, an unwilling monk of the 20th century" (*The Society of Captives: A Study of a Maximum Security Prison* [New York: Atheneum, 1966], p. 4).

no longer exists.[102] What is stripped away is not only what had facilitated your crime or your anger or your "antisocial" behavior but also that which had engendered any sense of love or kindness or gentility. The stripping away is of such brutal abruptness and of such duration and takes place in such a callous environment that it is not surprising that some commit murder during or after imprisonment. What *is* surprising and a true testament to both grace and the human spirit is that some prisoners maintain or nurture a modicum of human kindness. It's not that prisons sometimes succeed; it's that sometimes in the midst of death, life abounds.

But prisoners are not the only immediate victims of the prison system. In ways both subtle and obvious, prison guards are also victimized. There are certainly instances in which guards are injured or killed in the performance of duties, but a far more common victimization consists in the emotional and spiritual toll exacted by working in a situation that is inherently structured as both authoritarian and adversarial. F. William Howton draws an appropriate analogy between the stress experienced by prison guards and that of soldiers in battle, with the important distinction that the battle never ends for the guards and, other than seeing that no one escapes, it is a battle with "not much rhyme or reason. He [or she] lacks a sense of cause, because there is no tangible objective and no way to calculate progress."[103] In addition to the stress, some studies suggest that prison guards face the special risk that their work may influence their attitudes and personalities in subtle and pernicious ways. In a study conducted by Philip Zimbardo, well-adjusted college students developed harsh and punitive attitudes after a brief period of playing the role of prison guards; indeed, the attitudes were so alarming that Zimbardo feared for the safety of some of the student "prisoners" and ended the study ahead of schedule.[104] Ad-

---

102. Barbara Deming writes that the act of putting a person in jail is "essentially the act of trying to wish that man [or woman] out of existence. From the moment of arrest one begins to feel against one's flesh the operation of this crude attempt at sorcery" ("Prison Notes," in *Seeds of Liberation*, ed. Paul Goodman [New York: George Braziller, 1964], p. 472).

103. Howton, *Functionaries,* Problems of American Society series (Chicago: Quadrangle Books, 1971), p. 225.

104. See Zimbardo, "The Psychological Power and Pathology of Imprisonment," in *Behavior Disorders: Perspectives and Trends,* 3d ed., ed. Ohmer Milton and Robert G. Wahler (New York: J. B. Lippincott, 1973), p. 153.

mittedly, real prison guards are trained to abide by procedures and to curb punitive instincts, but they are also likely to perceive more genuine threats than are role-playing guards interacting with pretend prisoners. Certainly there are decent people who are prison guards, and none of this is to suggest that they inevitably become punitive and authoritarian. The point is not that guards are bad people but that the prison system takes a toll on the keepers as well as the kept.

Over the years, I have been inside a score or more of jails and prisons, at times as a visitor, at times as a volunteer with literacy programs or bail projects, at times "doing time." Late in 1975, I was sentenced to a term in a large metropolitan jail in an east coast city.[105] I relate parts of the experience below, but not because I believe it is a "typical" prisoner's experience. On the one hand, my experience in 1975 was much milder than that of most prisoners, since my sentence was fairly brief and (I feel certain) I was insulated from the harsher aspects of the jail by the unsolicited deference accorded to my white skin and my social connections on the outside. On the other hand, the jail I entered was/is a real hellhole. It is undeniable that there are jails and prisons with "better" conditions. But I hasten to caution against any assumptions that the conditions described here are peculiar to this one institution or that the conditions in 1975 no longer exist today. In some places, I am sure that conditions are worse. As a society, we are much more adept at building new prisons than at tearing down old ones. A deteriorating office building is given the wrecking-ball; a deteriorating prison meets no such fate.

I was sentenced in the morning, a circumstance that was not altogether happy, since prisoners had to while away their post-sentencing hours in a large holding cell in the bowels of the courthouse pending transport to the city jail in the evening. Prior to being escorted into the holding tank, we were frisked and had to empty our pockets and surrender our belts. A few unopened packs of cigarettes and one or two books were all that prisoners were permitted to take into the city jail from the outside world, but even these were prohibited in the holding cell. Contents of pockets and belts and books were dumped into bags and marked for later transport. I was told that one of the books I had brought would not be allowed into the city jail anyhow; it so happens

---

105. The account that follows is based on journal notes I wrote at that time.

that the individual volumes of Karl Barth's *Church Dogmatics* constitute a threat — not, presumably, because of content but because they are of sufficient size and weight to serve as weapons.

Since there were (thankfully) no televisions in the holding cell, the only thing to watch was the holding cell itself as it filled up with people. Individually and sometimes in small groups, men would be ushered into the large tank. Somewhere up above, a gavel would bang and another one would appear. Lunchtime came and went without notice. The holding cell was furnished with one water fountain, two or three fully exposed toilet bowls, and seating for about fifty in the form of long, flat metal benches bolted into the floor. By late afternoon, about one hundred people filled the cell. As dedicated judges worked into the evening, dinner was served. Between the bars of the holding cell, each prisoner was handed two pieces of white bread with a slice of bologna stuck in the middle — small comfort for a vegetarian.

The time for transport arrived. Prisoners were warned to stand to the back of the cell until their names were called, but in fact, the crowded cell did not permit of much movement to back or front. As names were hollered between the bars, individuals would work their way through the crowd. The door swung open, a small group was led into an anteroom, and the door slammed shut again. The unnerving sound of slammed heavy doors is a constant feature of life for prisoners. In the anteroom, the surrealism mounted. Off to the side behind barred enclosures stood guards with weapons. In the anteroom itself, other guards worked with a Houdiniesque array of chains and cuffs and shackles. Some prisoners were handcuffed to each other, some had their ankles shackled together, some were handcuffed to chains that had been wrapped snug around their own waists, and still others received multiple chainings of ankles and waists and wrists. Clinking and clanging, we were led in small groups into other rooms and down hallways until we stepped into a courtyard surrounded by walls topped with barbed wire. The barbed wire was interrupted at one point by a small cage in which stood a guard who made sure that his weapon was visible. To the one side of the yard was a gate that opened to permit exit by the buses that transported us to city jail.

Some might think it odd that the first real fear I felt that day came not from the judge and the sentencing procedure, nor from my fellow prisoners, nor even from the guards with prominently displayed weapons. It came from the bus. It was a converted school bus in which all of the windows had been replaced by metal plates with the exception of a small window above the steering wheel. Inside, a large cage had been constructed down the length of the bus so that, once the gate in the front was closed and locked, the passengers were totally cut off from the driver and from the only exit. Even for those who lack the slightest twinge of claustrophobia, I suspect that the sensation is similar to that of a trapped animal. I was being carried from one cell to another while chained to another person as we both sat inside a cage constructed within a metal-plated bus. The layer upon layer of restraint bore the message, "Now you are ours." But more than wondering about whether this scenario was specifically devised to communicate a feeling of being trapped or whether it was necessitated by the "security needs" that serve as the excuse for many of the horrors in prison, I was struck by how dangerous the situation was. As the bus went careening down city streets at no small rate of speed, I knew that a fiery crash could mean death for all aboard. Here and in other areas of prison life, "security needs" take precedence over the safety of prisoners.

The journey ended after the bus had been driven down a steep incline and through what I imagined was a tunnel. We were underneath the city jail. We were unloaded and directed to climb a set of stairs, no small feat for those with shackled ankles. A door opened and we entered a large room where a sizable number of guards and prisoner trusties prepared to "process" us. The trusties are prisoners who, through "good behavior" or other considerations, have won favorable attention from guards and jail administrators. In some prisons and jails, the selection of trusties is formalized and regulated, but many institutions operate the system on informal understandings. In return for cigarettes, extra phone calls, money in the commissary fund, or other privileges, trusties help the guards with any number of tasks. At the most benign level, trusties help to process new prisoners, deliver meals to cells, organize supplies, and supervise other prisoners in cooking and cleaning and daily chores. In some jails and prisons, the system is far less benign. Many prisoners have reason to believe that some trusties serve as spies for guards, and there are instances in which trusties have been known to administer beatings at the behest of guards. Prison officials are conveniently insulated from the consequences of any illegal disciplinary measures that might be employed by trusties. No matter what privileges may accrue to them, trusties are victimized by the whole system. They are often regarded by both prisoners and guards as no more than tools in the service of the psychology of power: divide and conquer.

Handcuffs and chains and shackles were removed in the reception area, and we were ordered to strip. Nothing in prison life is designed to respect privacy or modesty, but the strip search seems to have been specifically concocted to peel away more than clothing. Dignity is stripped off as a means of introduction to a prison that is also meant to strip away your criminal character and replace it with . . . what? "Open your mouth. Lift your tongue," says a guard armed with flashlight and tongue depressor. And then another guard, "Lift 'em. Bend over and spread 'em." Every conceivable orifice is checked, ostensibly for the presence of weapons or contraband. I cannot imagine any weapons that would fit into the places that they checked and "contraband" seemed to matter little anyhow. I would later discover that jailhouse evenings were pervaded with the smell of marijuana smoke. Whether those smoking dope were trusties or guards or other prisoners or a combination I do not know, but it was clear that the guards knew about it. In a prison environment, altering the mind seems like a reasonable approach to maintaining sanity. I made no particular judgments on the drug users, but the blatant presence of marijuana made it all the more clear that the strip-search ritual was designed for purposes other than discovering contraband.[106]

Still nude, we were led from table to table for a series of questionnaires and fingerprinting, after which we were led in small groups to a shower room. A guard at the doorway handed each of us a plastic bottle filled with gold-colored goo that we were told to use for washing: "Make sure you use it in your hair." The stuff had the odor of perfumed pesticide. We were being deloused.

As we exited the shower room, trusties handed out jail garb that they reckoned might fit and small bags containing a toothbrush,

---

106. Introduction to jail or prison life corresponds precisely to the sociological observations Harold Garfinkel makes in his essay "Conditions of Successful Degradation Ceremonies," in *Deviance: The Interactionist Perspective*, pp. 89-94. Erving Goffman also notes the importance of "mortification processes" in his essay "Characteristics of Total Institutions," in *Deviance: Studies in the Process of Stigmatization and Societal Reaction*, ed. Simon Dinitz, Russell R. Dynes, and Alfred C. Clarke (New York: Oxford University Press, 1969), pp. 472-85.

toothpaste, and whatever permissible books and other items we had brought with us. After dressing, we were led individually into a room to see "the Doc." I expected that some sort of physical examination was forthcoming, but the room was occupied by just one technician and an ancient-looking X-ray machine. I was told to have a seat, but I remained standing and showed some resolve that is not well-liked by jail officials when it is seen in any prisoner. The proper attitude for prisoners is to "go with the program." But after being chemically deloused, I was unwilling also to be irradiated. I asked to see the technician's license and certification on when the machine was last inspected. "We do this for your own safety. We don't want people with tuberculosis running around the jail." My questions about how he knew that he and all of the prisoners were not being exposed to excessive doses of radiation and his responses about the equivalence of a few minutes in the sun were getting nowhere fast. Noncooperation is not countenanced for long. Either I submitted to the X-ray or I would be put in twenty-four-hour lockup. A guard was called to lead me to a cell.

Two heavy metal plates protruded horizontally out of the steel wall, one suspended over the other, with a stained mat an inch or two thick lying on each. One corner of the back wall of the cell was occupied by a small metal sink, and there was a toilet bowl tucked between the sink and the metal plate beds. The toilet tank and its contents were located on the other side of the back wall of the cell. (Supposedly, this was to prevent prisoners from fashioning weapons out of removed toilet parts, but it also prevented my cellmate and me from attempting repairs on the day that our toilet stopped flushing. It was three days before a guard decided that the toilet problem was genuine and merited fixing.) Such were the furnishings of the six-by-nine-foot cell in which my cellmate and I "did" our time. We got out of the cell only once a week for fifteen minutes to walk down the corridor to take a shower. After my release, I was told that city jail administrators were under court order to let all prisoners out of their cells for daily recreation. Apparently the prisoners were not the only lawbreakers at city jail.

The jail was in a sorry state of disrepair. Cells were tiered from floor to roof, six or seven stories high in the cell block where I was kept. Looking out the front of the cell, one first sees the walkway that runs along each tier and then an open space extending from floor to roof and then a wall streaked from the rainwater that leaked through the roof during storms. The cells on the lowest tier were sometimes flooded. Guards were able to prevent prisoners from getting out, but they were far less successful at preventing rats from getting in. After dark, rats moved from cell to cell in search of whatever food might have been dropped or stored away for later consumption. When I first saw a rat in the cell, my cellmate was amused by the way in which I treated the rat's presence as an extraordinary event. He just warned me to leave the rat alone (I had no intention of doing otherwise), because "the only time they bite you is if you try to kill 'em or if you scare one of 'em when you get up at night to take a leak." Watching the reactions of newly jailed people can be entertaining for prisoners who have been in a joint for a while. My cellmate was also amused by my reaction the first time a cockroach dropped from the ceiling onto my dinner tray.

After a certain hour, the nights were quiet except for the occasional sound of a flushed toilet and the periodic rounds by guards shining flashlights through the cells. During the first few nights inside a jail, you can wake up and forget where you are; for some, the nightmare is in the waking. On my third or fourth night at city jail, I was jolted awake by the sound of screaming. After orienting myself to the fact that I was in jail, I listened intently to try to decipher what was being screamed. It was just a jumble of yelled words and names that made no sense.

"You awake?" I asked in a low voice.

"Can't help but be awake with that carrying on," my cellmate answered. "It's just that crazy guy a few cells down. Every few weeks he just starts screaming in the middle of the night. I think the guy's nuts. Don't worry, they'll take care of him in a few minutes."

Call me naive, but I imagined that medical help was on the way. Some prisoners in adjacent cells were becoming impatient with the screaming.

"Oh man, not this again. Hey buddy, why don't you just shut the hell up."

Another minute or two and I heard a cell door being opened. The screaming stopped with the first sickening thud. There were two or three more thumps that sounded like nothing so much as someone's head being bashed into a cell wall. The cell door slammed, then all was quiet. I asked nothing more of my cellmate, and he offered no more information. I listened, half wishing that I would hear more screams to know that the "crazy man" was all right, half fearing that I would hear more screams and the whole scenario would be repeated. But the rest of the night was quiet and very long.

Next morning's breakfast was delivered by one of the trusties who I knew to be a bit more friendly and talkative than some of the others. I asked about the night before.

"Yeah, that guy's crazy."

I wondered what they did to him.

"Well, I wasn't there myself, but sometimes you have to handle these guys a little bit to get 'em to understand."

I wondered if he had ever "handled" any prisoners.

"Naw. What I usually use is that." He pointed past the walkway and down the water-streaked wall to a fire hose. "That baby packs a lot of pressure. You don't even have to go inside the cell. Just point it in and blast away. Of course, I've only had to actually use it a few times. Most guys'll start to cooperate if they think you're going for the hose." He explained that most prisoners were less afraid of being slammed against a wall by the high-pressure stream than they were cowed by the prospect of spending hours or days in wet clothing and sleeping on wet mats.

After my release from city jail, while consistently refraining from divulging any names of trusties or other prisoners, I spoke with some officials who would presumably be in a position to do something about conditions in the jail. The twenty-four-hour lockup, which contravened a court order of which I had been ignorant, seemed to hold the most interest for them. Regarding the rats and roaches, they simply asked, "Isn't everyone in the city plagued with them?" Regarding the "alleged" brutality, they wanted to know, "Did you personally see anyone being beaten?" I couldn't see anything outside my cell but a walkway and a water-streaked wall. "Did you personally see anyone being attacked with a fire hose?" I told you, I couldn't see anything outside my. . . . When it comes to making sure that there are no witnesses to your crimes, offenders can learn a thing or two from the prison system.

The one merciful aspect of the section of city jail in which I was kept was the absence of televisions. Nine months later and unrehabilitated, I was jailed in another city, and, while the physical conditions were not as bleak, my nerves were constantly assaulted by a battle of volumes from assorted TVs and radios. I developed a schedule of getting up at four in the morning and reading or writing letters by dim light before the daily volume wars began. But I can understand the jailhouse appeal of television. For some prisoners, it is the only release from boredom or the only contact with life on the outside. And so, prisoners sit for hours on end watching cops and robbers getting "blown away."

In 1976, I watched one of the Carter/Ford presidential debates from inside jail. I was surrounded by mostly black men, and we looked out between the bars and watched two white men talking about freedom and justice and equality. Presidential debates look different when viewed from behind bars. Next election, over a million Americans will see what I mean.

Scapegoats

Americans are at odds with some other societies in the degree to which they respect and pay deference to the wealthy and powerful. In some cultures, the motivations and actions of the rich and powerful are regarded as suspect, and their lives are hidden away from public view for fear of derision or worse. In contrast, the well-heeled in America are paraded before cameras and interviewed for glossy "human interest" stories in profitable magazines that have as their sole *raison d'être* coverage of the life-styles of the moneyed. The hero may be a Rockefeller or a Hunt or a Forbes or a Trump. Of course, even after all the glossy attention, we may know precious little about who these people are. No matter. Some in America are idolized not for who they are but for what they have.

It is the poor who are suspect in America. Politicos vie with each other to tell stories of "welfare queens" and food stamp recipients who drive their Cadillacs to and from the social service offices. For those homeless who seem genuinely down and out, there are no banks of cameras and glossy interviews. Indeed, many Americans hold the view that these homeless are already too visible and that their cardboard dwellings should be cleared from public parks and thoroughfares. A well-heeled celebrity caught short of change to make a phone call can expect a different reception than the panhandling homeless who are always suspected of wanting money for booze or drugs. Some in America are despised not for who they are but for what they do not have.

It is the poor who are suspect in America, and it would be sheer gullibility to believe that this prejudice does not assert itself in American jurisprudence. The poor are arrested, prosecuted, convicted, jailed, and hanged or electrocuted or otherwise dispatched at a rate far exceeding that of the middle class, let alone the rich. Whether the poor also commit an amount of crime commensurate with their rate of imprisonment is far less certain, even though one of the American prejudices against the poor is that they are more "prone to criminality."[107] Rather than being prone to criminality, the poor may simply be vulnerable to the judicial system for two closely related reasons: first, the poor lack the sort of political and economic clout that can influence which laws will be passed and how those laws will be enforced, and second, once they are caught in the wheels of the judicial process, the poor lack the resources that wealthier people use to extricate themselves. Regarding the first of these reasons, Joseph Lohman, former sheriff of Cook County, Illinois, has candidly acknowledged that "the police function is to support and enforce the interests of the dominant political, social and economic interests of the town, and only incidentally to enforce the law."[108] Regarding the second reason, what Alain René Lesage said in the eighteenth century is still true today: "Justice is such a fine thing that we cannot pay too dearly for it."[109]

Since one out of sixty-seven serious offenses results in imprisonment, it is revealing to examine who this one imprisoned person is likely to be. The prisoner is most often a low-income male and a person of color — usually black or brown. A recent survey of New York prisons found that about 80 percent of all prisoners in the State are black or Latino.[110] Moreover, in the nation as a whole, almost one-quarter of all black men between the ages of twenty and twenty-nine are either in jail or prison or on probation or parole.[111] Nor is the judicial system color

107. In their cross-national study, Dane Archer and Rosemary Gartner found that economic downturns and increases in the rate of unemployment do not have an inevitable impact on crime rates, although increased unemployment is more likely to be correlated to increased crime rates in nations that have greater economic inequality (*Cross-National Perspective*, pp. 157-62).

108. Lohman, cited in *Struggle for Justice*, p. 130.

109. Lesage, quoted by Gray and Stanley in *A Punishment in Search of a Crime*, p. 283.

110. The same survey found that over 80 percent of prison guards in the State are white. Of 165 chaplains in the State prison system, only six are Latino ("Problems of Latino Prisoners Studied," *Justicia*, January 1989, p. 6).

111. Twenty-three percent according to a report by Harry Smith on the *CBS This Morning* broadcast of 2 March 1990.

blind in capital cases. Blacks constitute slightly over 10 percent of the American population, but about half of all people executed in the U.S. are black. A black defendant convicted of killing a white person is several times more likely to be sentenced to death than either a white or black defendant convicted of killing a black person.[112]

Apart from bigoted presuppositions that black people are somehow genetically predisposed to break laws, the traditional explanation for why blacks are more frequently subjected to the workings of the American penal system maintains that crime rates are naturally higher in communities that suffer the frustrations of high unemployment, low per capita income, limited health care facilities, high rates of infant and overall mortality, and scarce or poor-quality community services. The legacy of institutionalized racism in America means that black people are disproportionately victimized by such circumstances. Indeed, over the past decade, the gap between whites and blacks in terms of both income and average life expectancy has been expanding.

One of the problems with this traditional explanation for the high number of imprisoned black people is that it entails a prima facie acceptance of the notion that the penal system offers a reliable measurement of who is committing crimes. It is straightforwardly assumed that because there are more poor people or black people in prison, therefore these people commit more crimes. The impact of white racism cannot be denied, but perhaps the traditional explanation for the high proportion of blacks in prison is posing the wrong questions. Instead of asking "How does the legacy of racism turn so many black people into criminals?" it might strike closer to the heart of the matter to inquire into the ways in which American law enforcement, judicial, and penal systems are pervaded by a racism that makes it more probable that black people will be labeled as criminal. In fact, a ten-year study by University of Colorado sociologist Delbert Elliott found only minor variations in crime rates between poor black and affluent white youth.[113] The major variation comes in the vehemence with which black suspects are pursued, arrested, convicted, and jailed. The higher rate of imprisonment for black people sets up the self-perpetuating justification for

112. Hugo Adam Bedau, *The Case against the Death Penalty* (New York: Capital Punishment Project, American Civil Liberties Union, 1984), pp. 10-15.

113. Elliott's study is cited by Colson and Van Ness in *Convicted*, p. 57.

dealing more harshly with the "black criminal type."[114] From this perspective, it is understandable that an imprisoned Eldridge Cleaver might suggest that the police and the penal system are meant solely to "protect the way of life of those in power":

> The whites are on top in America and they want to stay there, up there. . . . Everywhere the whites are fighting to prolong their status, to retard the erosion of their position. In America, when everything else fails, they call out the police. . . . Behind police brutality there is social brutality, economic brutality, and political brutality.[115]

Just as we cannot expect that American jurisprudence has been magically insulated from racism, there can be no pretense that the system has been unaffected by patriarchal sexist assumptions. Young women have historically been taught that some of their deviations from societal standards are less tolerable than those of their male counterparts, and the penal system has served to reinforce that message. The history of the family court and juvenile court systems in America shows that young women have most frequently been brought into these courts on charges of "waywardness" or "immorality" and that they have more often been sent to training schools or reformatories than have young men.[116] The sexual activity (whether real or suspected) of women has been criminalized in ways that have not applied to the male "sowing of wild oats," an indication that women have not been and still are not believed to have full

---

114. There can be no doubt that expectations of criminality and guesses about who is a "poor risk" play a powerful role in the penal treatment of black people. In an article in *Federal Probation,* William Breer first freely confesses that probation officers are "involved in the business of social control. This inherently means coercing subcultural groups into at least nominal acceptance of the laws of the dominant white society." Breer then explains the need to understand the various "types" of blacks, including "the transplanted rural southern type, the black bourgeoisie type, and the poor ghetto type. The poor ghetto variant is of most concern to the probation officer because it is the most criminally inclined" ("Probation Supervision of the Black Offender," in *Corrections in the Community: Alternatives to Imprisonment — Selected Readings,* 2d ed., ed. George G. Killinger and Paul F. Cromwell, Jr. [St. Paul: West Publishing, 1978], pp. 168, 171).

115. Cleaver, *Soul on Ice* (New York: McGraw-Hill, 1968), pp. 131-33.

116. For an exploration of this history and its implications, see Meda Chesney-Lind, "Girls' Crime and Woman's Place: Toward a Feminist Model of Female Delinquency," *Crime and Delinquency* 35 (January 1989): 5-29; and Kathryn Burkhart, "Women in Prison," in *In Prison,* pp. 73-88.

ownership of their own bodies. The assumption seems to have been that men's sexual activity violates no one's rights, but women's sexual activity might infringe on the property rights of fathers or husbands.

Statistically, men are more likely than women to be imprisoned for most categories of criminal offenses, although the numbers are changing. During the 1980s, the number of women in local jails in the United States increased at nearly twice the rate of men.[117] It seems likely to me that this increased jailing of women is part of the backlash against the gains that have been won by feminists in America, but a popular argument claims that feminism itself is the culprit. A California sheriff recently claimed that "women are enjoying a lot more freedom now, and as a result, they are committing more crimes."[118] The positing of a causal relationship between freedom and crime is an ominous prescription for totalitarianism.

On matters of violence within relationships, judicial practice betrays a prejudice that the violence of men is somehow more understandable. As Mary Nerney observes, "Women know that they are more likely to be killed than to kill. Yet when we look at women in prison, we see those who kill after an abusive relationship receive longer sentences than men who kill women in their relationships."[119] The attitude that the violence of men is somehow understandable is also prevalent when women appear in court as victims of rape. Once again, the judicial process ignores the needs of the victims of crime as attorneys rush to portray women who have been raped as seductresses.

Independent of the societal bigotries that have left women, poor people, and people of color especially vulnerable in the judicial system, there is another sense in which all offenders and prisoners serve as scapegoats for social ills. The president and other governmental officials have significant power to announce that a certain variety of criminal behavior has become so widespread that a crisis exists and a "war on crime" is necessary to confront the emergency, and then an obliging

117. See Russ Immarigeon, "Beyond the Fear of Crime: Reconciliation as the Basis for Criminal Justice Policy," in *Criminology as Peacemaking,* ed. Harold E. Pepinsky and Richard Quinney (Bloomington, Ind.: Indiana University Press, 1991), p. 70.

118. Cited by Susan Faludi in *Backlash: The Undeclared War against American Women* (New York: Crown Publishers, 1991), p. xii.

119. Nerney, "Women Fighting Back: Commitment and Cost," *Justicia,* November 1988, p. 9.

media will cover the war in detail.[120] Often, what the media and the public are responding to is not a new set of facts or experiences of crime but a new definition of the situation and a new perception created by official pronouncements.[121] Whether by design or not, the declaration of a war on this or that crime can serve the symbolic function of reinforcing certain cultural norms or the diverting function of removing public attention from social problems that are not being addressed.[122] The proclamation of a crisis and the mobilization of resources might be on a scale that is independent of the actual harm being done. While harm cannot be measured by mere body counts, and a single avoidable death is one too many, more American lives are lost to suicide than to murder. Yet no American president has declared a war on suicide. As Kevin Wright observes,

> Your chances of being murdered are less than your chances of dying in an accident in or around your home. And . . . you are much more likely to be killed in an automobile accident than to be murdered. But when was the last time a local politician ran on a platform to get tough on home accidents, or citizens formed a group to see that their neighbors wore seat belts?[123]

The anti-drug frenzy of the Reagan and Bush administrations is a case in point. By any measure, more lives are lost and greater economic loss is suffered from the use of legal drugs (e.g., tobacco, alcohol) than from illegal drug use. Even those of us who do not advocate the use of drugs have cause to wonder what mixed conscious and subconscious motivations may lie behind the frenzied "war on drugs." In an article in the *New Orleans Tribune*, Kalamu ya Salaam offered a reminder that earlier American anti-drug campaigns targeted "opium smoking

120. On media depictions of crime, see Steven M. Gorelick, " 'Join Our War': The Construction of Ideology in a Newspaper Crime-fighting Campaign," *Crime and Delinquency* 35 (July 1989): 421-36.

121. This point was also made by researchers who studied the basis of a government campaign against mugging in Britain in the 1970s. See Stuart Hall et al., *Policing the Crisis: Mugging, the State, and Law and Order*, Critical Social Studies Series (London: Macmillan, 1978), p. 29.

122. The symbolic and diverting functions are two of the functions of prisons cited by Thomas Mathiesen in *The Politics of Abolition*, Scandinavian Studies in Criminology, Law in Society Series (New York: John Wiley, 1974), pp. 77-78.

123. Wright, *The Great American Crime Myth*, p. 48.

Chinese" immigrants and "cocaine-crazed Negroes."[124] In the more recent version, it is the foreigners from Latin America who are portrayed as serving up the drug threat to the United States. The frenzy whipped up by the war on drugs provided some of the foundation for a very real war in December 1989: part of the pretext for the U.S. invasion of Panama was provided by claims that Panamanian leaders were channeling drugs into the veins of Americans.[125] At the same time, the war on drugs has provided additional justification for the U.S. export of police assistance to allied regimes in Latin America, even though many of these regimes have shown a proclivity to utilize such assistance for the repression of political opposition among their own people.[126]

The proclamation of crime emergencies and the institution of programs in a quest for "law and order" have also been utilized to combat dissent in America. One cause for alarm over the contemporary burgeoning of the prison system is the fact that many movements of conscience or of political opposition in this nation's history have been met by mass arrests and jailings. Quakers and members of the peace churches were persecuted during the American War of Independence for their refusal to take up arms against the British. So paranoid were the new American governments about possible Tory sympathies that states adopted loyalty oaths, and Virginia declared it illegal to wish health to the British monarch.[127] The movement against slavery was marked by judicial per-

---

124. Salaam, "Drug Frenzy Is Nothing New in the U.S.," *Utne Reader,* March/April 1989, p. 78.

125. A 1992 Supreme Court ruling upholds the practice of federal law enforcement officials kidnapping suspects in other countries and transporting them to the United States for trial. At times, this involves cases in which the alleged violations of U.S. law did not occur inside U.S. territory. If the force of U.S. law is held to be applicable to citizens of other countries residing outside the United States, the specter of America "policing" the world takes on new meaning. In addition to raising some frightening prospects, the ruling raises questions about the constitutionality of some potential actions that would clearly be absurd. For example, what would prohibit U.S. officials from kidnapping the British Prime Minister because she or he drives on the "wrong" side of the street? While the activity is not illegal inside England, it is a clear violation of U.S. law.

126. The export of U.S. penology and police assistance is discussed by Argenis Riera in "Latin American Radical Criminology," *Crime and Social Justice: Issues in Criminology,* Spring-Summer 1979, pp. 71-76.

127. See Charles Goodell, *Political Prisoners in America* (New York: Random House, 1973), p. 18.

secution of abolitionists and blacks who organized slave resistance. With Civil War pending, Lincoln suspended the writ of habeas corpus, and thousands of dissidents were imprisoned without charge until the Supreme Court revoked Lincoln's action. Suffragettes were among the first of thousands to be arrested in the movement for equal rights for women.[128] With the American entrance into World War I, those who were imprisoned included not only pacifists but also people prosecuted under the Espionage Act of 1917, a wide-ranging piece of legislation that enabled the imprisonment of genuine dissidents as well as people guilty of nothing but a slip of the tongue. One of the most famous victims of the Espionage Act was socialist Eugene Debs, but the many others who were imprisoned included a man who declined to kiss the U.S. flag and another who voiced the opinion at a family gathering that America was engaged in "a rich man's war."[129] With some frequency, federal and state governments have filled prisons while combating labor movements, the most infamous example being the Palmer Raids, which helped to seal the fate of the International Workers of the World.[130] More recent examples of the political use of imprisonment include the construction of concentration camps for Japanese-Americans during World War II, the blacklisting and harassment of suspected communists during the McCarthy era, and the arrests of civil rights activists and Vietnam War resisters during the sixties and seventies.

But focusing on the political, racial, sexual, and economic scapegoats of the prison system entails a danger of creating the impression that what is wrong with prisons can be fixed with some judicial or political tinkering — that what is most needed is kinder and gentler politicians, judges, police, or prison guards. Perhaps this survey of the penal ideologies of rehabilitation, deterrence, and retribution has served to provide a hint that there is something more fundamentally wrong with the practice of caging people, something that cannot be fixed by merely shifting personnel or altering procedures. The fundamental

128. In 1917, women suffragists were the first people ever to picket the White House. See Gene Sharp, *The Methods of Nonviolent Action*, part 2 of *The Politics of Nonviolent Action* (Boston: Porter Sargent, 1973), p. 133.

129. Goodell, *Political Prisoners*, pp. 56-64.

130. On the suppression of the Wobblies and related movements, see William Preston, Jr., *Aliens and Dissenters: Federal Suppression of Radicals, 1903-1933* (New York: Harper & Row, 1963).

problem with prisons is not bad police or bad guards. These people act at our behest and, more often than not, they are victimized and brutalized by the same system that victimizes and brutalizes prisoners.

And is there not an additional danger that focusing on the system's scapegoats will paint images of only "nice prisoners"? If one were to advocate prison abolition, would that not also be advocating freedom for the "bad prisoners"?[131] Not only blacks oppressed by the prison system, but also Ku Klux Klan members guilty of violence against blacks? Not only prostitutes, but also men guilty of rape? Not only war resisters, but also people guilty of murder?

Precisely. To talk of freedom for the "nice prisoners" leads us to a consideration of a liberal ideology. To talk of freedom for all prisoners leads us to a consideration of a biblical proclamation.

---

131. For an insightful and moving account of "good" and "bad" victims of the prison system, see Will D. Campbell, *Brother to a Dragonfly* (New York: Seabury Press, 1977), pp. 217-28.

Chapter III

Prisons and the Bible

He has sent me to proclaim release to the captives.
Luke 4:18

The first crime was Cain's killing of Abel. I mean "first" in an ethical rather than a chronological sense. In Genesis 4:1-16, the true nature of killing is revealed. Every act of killing calls into question the continuation of all of creation. It is more than wordplay to say that the ground *(adamah)* itself, the very ground of our being, cries out as blood *(dam)* is shed. Every act of killing is fratricide, is sororicide. Without exception, every killing takes the life of our sister or brother.

And as the Genesis account reveals, every act of killing is without excuse or justification. Exegetes and biblical scholars have gone on at some length concerning possible meanings in Cain's murderous behavior. Perhaps here we have the etiological explanation for the rejection of Canaanite religion and culture. Perhaps here we sense Israel's early struggles between nomadic and agrarian life. But no matter what historical or cultural meanings might be projected into the story, Cain's act is devoid of any sense. To all of God's questions ("Where is your brother? Why are you angry?") Cain can only answer, "I do not know." Every act of killing is empty of justification, and there is an ex post facto rush to fill the emptiness with excuses ranging from self-defense to patriotism to madness. All of these excuses are the same. All have the same meaning: "I do not know." Again and again in human history the story repeats itself. Cain kills Abel. There are no surprises here.

It is God who brings the surprise to the story. Cain is guilty as sin, and yet in violation of all human "justice," God protects him. Even before we are told of God's establishment of the law, we are told of God's mercy in the face of lawlessness.[1] In this sense, Karl Barth is right: the gospel does not come after the law; it precedes the law. Here already in Genesis 4, the history of God's relationship with humankind is summarized. As we persist in choosing death, God chooses life on our behalf. As we deny responsibility to care for sisters and brothers ("Am I my brother's keeper?"), God intervenes to show us how. God intervenes with a mark of protection and a place of refuge.[2] What would the alternative be? Blood vengeance would demand that a member of Abel's family exact retribution by killing the killer. But when the killer is a member of the family (as all killers are), there can be no end to the suicidal cycles of retribution and bloodshed. God calls an end to it by intervening with a mark of protection. God's freedom from the law is freedom for humanity and freedom for forgiveness. God acts in a way that shows that killing is far too serious a crime to be met with mere executions or tortures or imprisonments. It is a crime that must be met with the burning coals of love (Rom. 12:20-21). The killer has already shown himself capable of coping with punishing brutality. He is now made to face a much harder reality — forgiveness. Cain is a marked man. We would mark him for death. God marks him for life. That is the surprise in the story of Cain and Abel. It is the only surprise.

---

1. Ralph Scott's book *A New Look at Biblical Crime* (New York: Dorset Press, 1987) is an entertaining "attorney meets the villains of Scripture" fantasy, but the biblical commentary is outlandishly literalistic, including, e.g., the claim that Abel was killed 1,500 years before murder was legally prohibited (pp. 3-6). The J redactor of Genesis 4 was fully aware of the crime of murder, and the writer was not pretending to offer a literal history. Without displaying any concern to explain how spouses are found and cities are built in an unpopulated world, J tells of Cain going out to find a spouse and build a city. The need to explain this is not a biblical problem but rather a problem of modern literalism.

2. On allusions in Genesis 4 to the cities of refuge, see the chapter entitled "The Blood of the Innocent" in Giovanni Garbini's *History and Ideology in Ancient Israel,* trans. John Bowden (New York: Crossroad, 1988), pp. 111-20.

Prisons and the Old Testament

The power of the sword and the power of the cage have been perennial tools of human governance. It is a popular misperception that substantial reliance on prisons evolved only in the eighteenth century.[3] In fact, references to prisons appear in some of the earliest records of humankind. Another popular but misleading claim is that these earliest prisons were used only to detain defendants until trials could be held and sentences passed. Contrary to this picture of early imprisonment as a short-term affair, King Jehoiachin spent thirty-seven years in a Babylonian prison (2 Kings 25:27; Jer. 52:31), King Jehoahaz died in Egyptian imprisonment, and there is no trace of King Zedekiah after he was jailed in Babylon.[4] Apart from these examples of prisoners of war, the Persian King Artaxerxes empowered Ezra to appoint magistrates who could utilize imprisonment not only as a pretrial detention but also as a punishment (Ezra 7:26). When ancient Near Eastern kings did utilize prisons for pretrial detention, it was less than certain that the accused would be the only one detained. An early letter from the King of Carchemish mentions two men who had been arrested for a crime: "their accuser is being guarded here in prison. . . . If these men are saved, I will burn their accuser in fire; if the men die, here I will give their houses (and) their people to their accuser."[5] Whether for the detention of accusers or accused until trial or until death, prisons were a common feature of juridical systems long before the eighteenth century. History is full of cages.

Given the enduring prominence of prison and sword as tools of human governance, it is hardly surprising that jailings and executions were components of the juridical system in ancient Israel. Among the crimes that could bring the penalty of death in ancient Israel were murder, adultery, and the practice of magic, all of which were seen as particularly evil because of the way in which they broke the net of

3. See, e.g., the comments by Daniel W. Van Ness, *Crime and Its Victims* (Downers Grove, Ill.: InterVarsity Press, 1986), pp. 74-75.

4. Richard Elliott Friedman, *Who Wrote the Bible?* (New York: Summit Books, 1987), p. 155.

5. In *The Ancient Near East*, vol. 2: *A New Anthology of Texts and Pictures*, ed. James B. Pritchard (Princeton: Princeton University Press, 1975), p. 189. The first section of the Code of Hammurabi also prescribes the death sentence for false accusation.

relationships within the covenantal community or the relationship of the community with Yahweh. In the Old Testament, however, capital punishment was not related to any abstract demand for justice or to any calculations regarding the potential social benefits of deterrence; rather, it was rooted in the religious demand for expiation.[6] "Blood pollutes the land and no expiation can be made for the land for the blood that is shed on it, except by the blood of him who shed it" (Num. 35:33). If the murderer was not identified, then the city nearest the site of the murder was to offer up a sacrificial heifer to serve as a substitute in the ritual act of expiation (Deut. 21:1-9).

While executions were permitted by the juridical system in ancient Israel, there is early evidence of ambivalent attitudes toward capital punishment. Unlike many of its neighbors, Israel did not allow for the death penalty in cases of property crimes. Indeed, Israel's law was unique for its time in showing concern for the lives of thieves and intruders.[7] A householder was not permitted to kill a thief who was caught breaking and entering in daylight, for example. The irreconcilable conflict between the death penalty and the high value placed on human life can be discerned in the words of the Mishnah, words that likely reflect the debate of an earlier age. From Makkot in the fourth division:

> A sanhedrin which imposes the death penalty once in seven years is called murderous.
>
> Rabbi Eleazar ben Azariah says, "Once in seventy years."
>
> Rabbi Tarfon and Rabbi Aqiba say, "If we were on a sanhedrin, no one would ever be put to death."[8]

Jails were introduced into ancient Israel under foreign influence.[9]

---

6. See *The Church, the State, and the Offender*, Church and Society Series, no. 3 (Newton, Kans.: Faith & Life Press, 1963), pp. 9-11. This Mennonite report concludes that, since the expiation made by Jesus is all-sufficient, Christians no longer have recourse to expiation in the Old Testament as justification for capital punishment. In modified form, this is also the position of Jean Lasserre in *War and the Gospel*, trans. Oliver Coburn (Scottdale, Pa.: Herald Press, 1962), pp. 180-92.

7. See Brevard S. Childs, *The Book of Exodus: A Critical, Theological Commentary*, Old Testament Library (Philadelphia: Westminster Press, 1974), p. 474.

8. Jacob Neusner, *The Mishnah: A New Translation* (New Haven: Yale University Press, 1988), p. 612.

9. See Roland de Vaux, *Ancient Israel*, vol. 1: *Social Institutions* (New York: McGraw-Hill, 1965), p. 160. On the various Hebrew words used to refer to jails and

In this regard, it is of interest that the first prison experience mentioned in Scripture is that of Joseph in Egypt (Gen. 39). While jailings in Israel were often for the purpose of holding people until judgment could be reached on criminal charges, imprisonment was sometimes utilized for punishment (e.g., under Ezra) or for political purposes, as when Jeremiah and numerous others were jailed on charges of desertion and war resistance. But references to imprisonment in the Old Testament should not be viewed as an indication that jails were a common feature of life in Israel. Indeed, when Jeremiah was arrested, he had to be thrown into a makeshift prison in the house of Jonathan the secretary (Jer. 37:15). The descriptions of Jeremiah's prison experiences are noteworthy for what Gerhard von Rad called their "grim realism."[10] In later, apocalyptic writings (2 and 4 Maccabees, for example), we encounter depictions of prisoners who were emotionally and spiritually triumphant in the face of martyrdom that might serve as vicarious atonement for the oppressed people of Israel.[11] Jeremiah was not consoled by any notion of heroism in his suffering. For him, imprisonment was hell.

At least three separate factors combined to retard the development of a prison system in Israel:

1. Historically, prison systems have grown with the development of standing armies and a military establishment. Military garrisons often served as prisons, and soldiers worked as guards. Since a formalized military establishment was a comparatively late development in Israel's history, there were likewise few jails or officials with policing duties.

2. The Old Testament legal ethic was influenced by the principle of restitution, and imprisonment would have done nothing to facilitate restitution to the victims of crime. While texts such as Exodus 21:24 ("Eye for eye . . .") are often cited as evidence of the role of vengeance in the Hebrew legal system, these texts were actually regulations regarding limits to retaliation. Rather than revenge or retaliation, restitution was always the more central concern. If property was stolen, the prop-

---

prisons, see Daniel L. Smith, *The Religion of the Landless: The Social Context of the Babylonian Exile* (Bloomington, Ind.: Meyer-Stone Books, 1989), pp. 171-73.

10. Von Rad, *The Message of the Prophets* (New York: Harper & Row, 1962), pp. 176-77.

11. This later literature of the "martyrs" (literally, "witnesses") was also accompanied by a growing belief in the resurrection. See Otto Eissfeldt, *The Old Testament: An Introduction*, trans. Peter R. Ackroyd (New York: Harper & Row, 1965), pp. 46-47.

erty should be returned. If damage was done to someone's house or fields, the person responsible for the damage should repair it. Even in the case of physical injury, restitution should be made in the form of payment for care and loss of time (Exod. 21:18-19). Restitution was seen as a way of setting things right with one's neighbor and as a movement toward repentance before God. Reconciliation was the ulterior intent of restitution. It was in the spirit of this Hebrew concern for reconciliation that Jesus renounced those who would be guided by a simple "eye for eye" legal ethic (Matt. 5:38-42). For Jesus, the important element in the Jewish law was not the exchange or return of property but the restoration of proper relationships among people and between humanity and God. In the belief that reconciliation is better served by a willingness to suffer wrongs inflicted than by material restitution, Jesus admonished the disciples not to ask for the return of property stolen from them (Luke 6:30).[12]

3. An additional factor which likely contributed to the sparsity of jails in Israel was the Old Testament renunciation of the sort of scapegoating that made crime the responsibility of only a few evil individuals within the society. The prophets seemed especially aware of how an individualized view of crime inevitably favored the rich who were able to purchase the enactment of the statutes they desired (Isa. 10:1-2) and bribe their way to acquittal (Mic. 7:3; Amos 5:12).[13] While the Code of Hammurabi is blatant in its favoritism for the aristocracy, the law in Israel was to be viewed as a gift in which all people shared equal protection and equal responsibility.

Indeed, the prominence of the idea of corporate personality in Hebrew thought pointed to a level of corporate responsibility whenever the law was broken. H. Wheeler Robinson has noted that biblical covenants were always formed with the whole of the chosen people and

---

12. The movement from restitution to reconciliation is evident in biblical vocabulary. Thomas Sheehan notes, "Whereas the word 'repentance' has its root in the Latin *poena* (indemnification, satisfaction; cf. the Greek *poine*, blood money paid by the killer to the kinsmen of the slain), the Greek *metanoia*, used in the Gospels, stresses change of heart or mind (*noos/nous*, mind, perception, heart; *meta*, prepositional prefix, here with the sense of 'change')" (*The First Coming: How the Kingdom of God Became Christianity* [New York: Random House, 1986], p. 245n.34).

13. See the section on the poor in Israel in Richard Batey's *Jesus and the Poor* (New York: Harper & Row, 1972), pp. 83-97.

only with an individual insofar as that one was a "corporate personality" standing as a representative member of the covenanted community.[14] Likewise, when covenantal commitments were broken, the actions of one individual stood as indicative of a corporate malady. Violence and breach of law pointed to a crisis in the very fabric of the society. It is from this understanding that the prophets were able to warn that the entire nation was doomed because some widows had been mistreated or because the hungry had not been allowed to glean the fields. Not only all the people but the land itself was caught up in lawlessness and its consequences, for the meadows lay barren and the mountains quaked and the trees bore no fruit. For Israel, the fullest response to crime was not the isolated punishment of an individual lawbreaker but the repentance of the entire nation.

And what happened when the nation inevitably failed to repent? Once again, corporate personality came to the fore. Even if there was no denying the guilt of the people, perhaps God's mercy would be extended to all of the people if a handful of righteous ones could be found. Thus there arose the tradition of advocates such as Abraham (Gen. 18:16-33) standing before God and arguing on behalf of the people. Sometimes these arguments approximated scenes in a court of law in which advocates would approach God, who played the role of

14. H. Wheeler Robinson, *Corporate Personality in Ancient Israel*, Facet Books Biblical Series, no. 11 (Philadelphia: Fortress Press, 1964). This corporate "belongingness" also unites people with the earth, as Dorothee Sölle notes in her essay "Between Matter and Spirit: Why and in What Sense Must Theology Be Materialist?" in *God of the Lowly: Socio-Historical Interpretations of the Bible*, ed. Willy Schottroff and Wolfgang Stegemann, trans. Matthew J. O'Connell (Maryknoll, N.Y.: Orbis Books, 1984), pp. 86-102. For a discussion of "social personality" in Hebrew thought in the context of an exploration of the roots of the Pauline concept of the church as body, see John A. T. Robinson, *The Body: A Study in Pauline Theology*, Studies in Biblical Theology, no. 5 (Chicago: Alec R. Allenson, 1952), pp. 15-16. In another consideration of the Pauline concept of body, Eduard Schweizer notes, "the fact that the Hebrew did not need any word for 'body' shows that the distinction of his individual body from other human bodies was not of first importance for him. . . . Thus, the Hebrew is used to seeing first the nation, the people, mankind, and only afterward the individual member of that nation, people, or mankind. It was Martin Buber who once observed that the Hebrew first sees the woods and only then single trees; whereas we in the Western world would see first the single tree, and only after a process of reflection do we call a thousand trees a wood. We Western people really miss the woods for the trees" (*The Church as the Body of Christ* [Richmond: John Knox Press, 1964], p. 21).

both judge and defendant.[15] But in such a courtroom scene, was there anyone who could be called the accuser or (in modern parlance) the prosecuting attorney? There were no "district attorneys" in Israel; each plaintiff brought his or her own case before the judges. When Abraham and other advocates argued with God, however, it was not so much as accusers of God. After all, the guilt of the people was there for all to see, and, if God was a defendant against the arguments of the advocates, the advocates themselves were defendants of another sort. Their task was to coax God into setting aside a richly merited verdict of guilt.

But, standing in the shadows, an accuser was present. The understanding of Satan as "the accuser" (Zech. 3:1; 1 Pet. 5:8; Rev. 12:10) first developed in connection with the heavenly court-of-law scenario.[16] The earliest Hebrew depictions of Satan portray a fairly benign angel who was a servant of God. Gradually, this servant in the court becomes the law court opponent of humanity. The Apocalypse of Zephaniah (probably written before 70 C.E.) avoids dualism by still according Satan the status of a servant angel, though he is called "the ugliest angel." Under additional influence from apocalypticism, however, Satan is eventually depicted not only as the accuser and opponent of humanity but as the accuser and opponent of God as well. Nor is his mischief confined to accusation. Satan becomes the one who inflicts punishment. In 1 Enoch 53:3 we read of "the chains of Satan." The New Testament writings further establish a relationship between imprisonment and the demonic.

In order to move toward a biblical understanding of prisoners and prisons, we will have to examine the distinctions between the notion of justice as it has been inherited through a long Greco-Roman-Teutonic tradition and the biblical concept of justice. In the modern courtroom, despite the presence of well-intentioned judges and jurors, justice is largely a technical event — technical in that the concern is rather exclusively with the presentation of brute, empirical facts and the application of predetermined laws to those facts. Truth equals fact.

15. On the development and persistence of this theme even into modern times, see Anson Laytner, *Arguing with God: A Jewish Tradition* (Northvale, N.J.: Jason Aronson, 1990). In profound and insightful fashion, Laytner traces the tradition through the experience of the holocaust and the writings of Elie Wiesel.

16. On the history of the development, see Jeffrey Burton Russell, *The Devil: Perceptions of Evil from Antiquity to Primitive Christianity* (New York: New American Library, 1979), pp. 174-220.

In the Old Testament, justice has to do with something other than the application of the right law in the right circumstances. It is not meted out according to brute fact, nor is it determined by "the greatest good for the greatest number." To speak of biblical justice is to speak of the Hebrew concept of *tsedeka,* a word that has connotations of both "justice" and "righteousness."[17] Originally, this *tsedeka* is established between God and the Hebrew people, and it implies covenanted commitment. When the covenant is broken, justice demands that the wrong be righted, that the covenant be restored. With the restoration and maintenance of the covenant, the true fruit of justice *(tsedeka)* is revealed as peace *(shalom).* This peace, however, is the specific peace that is born of reconciliation between those who had previously seemed most at odds and most unreconcilable; it is, in short, a peace that is quite distinct from what often passes as "peace" but is in fact only the deadly silence that follows our having locked up or eliminated all potential "disturbers of the peace."

Once the covenant is broken, how does *tsedeka* influence its restoration and maintenance? In the biblical context, since God has always been faithful but the people have not been, the covenant was maintained only because of God's commitment to the accused, a commitment that entailed God's taking responsibility for the accused, nurturing them and protecting them, and ultimately acquitting them — not because the facts demanded acquittal (on the contrary, the facts demanded a finding of guilty) but because of God's own loving will to set the accused free to enter into covenant again. This understanding of *tsedeka* was not lost on the later rabbinical school of jurisprudence. Moses Maimonides summarized the spirit of *tsedeka* when he said that to accuse someone of a crime was to enter into a commitment with that person, to take responsibility for that person, to become that person's sister or brother. This understanding of justice harks back to the first crime, when God judged Cain and marked him and became his keeper (Gen. 4:9-15).

In contemporary understandings, when justice is present, when justice is "done," someone is prosecuted and jailed. But in the Judeo understanding, when the Just — the Zadik — are present, people are spared. Here again we note Abraham's intervention on behalf of the

17. For an excellent treatment of the concept of *tsedeka,* see Herman Bianchi, "Tsedeka-Justice," *Review for Philosophy and Theology,* September 1973, pp. 306-18.

accused, his pleading and coaxing with God that the city should be
spared if fifty of the Just are present, or forty, or ten (Gen. 18). Note
also the Hasidic legend: because there are a small number of the Just
among us, the world is given another day's grace. The identities of these
people are unknown to us, so when a stranger comes to your door, offer
overflowing hospitality, for it may be an angel or one of the Just. When
the Just are present, people are spared.

In modern understandings, those responsible as guardians of justice
are the judges and courts and, in some sense, national leaders as chief
executors of legislation. In Old Testament Israel, it was not the so-called
"judges" who were the representatives of justice and covenantal law.
Gideon, Deborah, and other charismatic leaders were given the title
"judge" as the term was derived from the Hebrew *shaphat*, meaning
"giving what is due" and indicating not that these leaders served in any
judicial capacity but that they rendered the service that was due to Israel.
Neither were the kings the guardians of the law; more often than not, they
stood accused of *violating* legal justice. While the Levitical priesthood had
a role in the enforcement of cultic laws, those who were chosen by Yahweh
as representatives of covenantal justice were the prophets. Amos and
Hosea, the first of the classical prophets, arose at a time when the people
were in danger of interpreting the fulfillment of cultic requirements as
meeting the totality of covenantal obligations.[18] In response, the prophets
protested that the law had to do with more than feasts, fasts, and sacrifices.
The weightier matters of the law had to do with the plight of the poor and
the widows and the victims of violence. The prophets provide no basis for
our later, postbiblical distinctions between distributive and legal justice;
tsedeka stood as a unified view of the various manifestations of righteousness and justice, and to pretend that legal obligation could be separated
from compassion for the oppressed would be to fall into the errors of the
cultic priesthood. The prophet represented justice by means of interference, by stepping in where he had no business, by intervening on behalf
of those who had no voice, and by boldly claiming that the interference
was in the name of God.[19]

18. See John Bright, *A History of Israel*, 2d ed. (Philadelphia: Westminster Press,
1972), pp. 256-63.
19. For a discussion of the prophets as representatives of justice, see Abraham J.
Heschel, *The Prophets*, vol. 1 (New York: Harper & Row, 1962), pp. 195-220.

The role of the prophet as the representative of justice was later given highly developed expression in the writings of Deutero-Isaiah. Here, God's justice is depicted as aggressive toward the so-called "justice" of the nations. The means by which God's justice will overcome the legalisms of others is the Suffering Servant (Isa. 42).[20] Hammurabi, Nebuchadnezzar, and other great lawmakers in the Near East spread their version of justice by means of conquest, but the Servant did not understand justice to be dependent on swords and cages. Justice is established through suffering persuasion. The Suffering Servant is a nonviolent transformation of the Near Eastern warrior king.[21]

It is in the context of the Servant Song in Isaiah 42 that an amazing proclamation is issued:

I am the LORD, I have called you in righteousness *(tsedeka)*,
I will also hold you by the hand and watch over you,
And I will appoint you as a covenant to the people,
As a light to the nations,
To open blind eyes,
To bring out prisoners from the dungeon,
And those who dwell in darkness from the prison. (Vv. 6-7)

Corporate responsibility, restitution, reconciliation — these are all important considerations. But we must not be misled into assuming that the biblical understanding of prisoners has to do with legal ethics and calculations about what should be done by and to criminals. Rather, the Servant Song in Isaiah 42 is one of the earliest indications that the biblical word regarding prisoners is at once both simple and scandalous: liberty for the captives.

The theme of freedom for prisoners has its roots in the Jubilee and Sabbath Year proclamations (Lev. 25:1-10; Deut. 15), which provided that land should be redistributed and slaves should be set free.

---

20. It is not necessary here to delve into the complex question of whether the Servant Songs should be attributed to Deutero-Isaiah or to one of his disciples. For a discussion of the various options on the identity of the Servant, see John L. McKenzie, *Second Isaiah*, Anchor Bible, vol. 20, ed. William F. Albright and David N. Freedman (Garden City, N.Y.: Doubleday, 1968), pp. xxxviii-lv.

21. For these insights, I am indebted to Millard C. Lind, *Transformation of Justice: From Moses to Jesus*, New Perspectives on Crime and Justice: Occasional Papers, no. 5 (Akron, Pa.: Mennonite Central Committee, 1986).

Every seven years (every fifty in the case of Jubilee), accumulated indebtedness was to be forgiven, land lost through indebtedness was to be returned to the prior owner, and those who had been forced into servitude through poverty were to be released. How faithfully did Israel adhere to the observance of the Sabbath and Jubilee Years? Many scholars contend that there is little historical evidence to indicate strict adherence. Indeed, one biblical mention of Sabbath Year (Jer. 34:8-16) portrays king and people abiding by the letter of the covenant by setting slaves free and then circumventing the spirit of the Sabbath Year by taking the freed slaves back into captivity. Similarly, there are indications (e.g., Deut. 15:7-11) that the forgiveness of debts was circumvented by some who refused to extend assistance to the needy when a Sabbath Year was approaching. But as with much of biblical history, the important point has to do with God's proclamation, not with the human efforts to circumvent it. Even if debts were rarely forgiven and slaves were rarely freed, the proclamation reemerged throughout biblical history.[22] The proclamation was God's encouragement for people to say to one another: Let us start anew, because all of our deciding about who should have ownership and who should not — who should have freedom and who should not — is sinful and divisive. Let us return to the equality we share in standing before God, who owns all and frees us all. As described by Martin Buber, the Sabbath and Jubilee Years told the people that "they ought not to thrust one another aside, they ought not to impoverish one another permanently or enslave one another; they must again and ever again become equal to one another in their freedom of person and free relation to the soil; they must rest together and enjoy the usufruct together; the times dedicated to God make them free and equal again and again, as they were at the beginning."[23]

What was this beginning? The Sabbath and Jubilee Years harked back to the very formation of Israel as a people, to God's liberating activity in the exodus of the Hebrew people from Egypt. It was on the basis of God's liberation of the slaves that a covenant was established

22. The Sabbath and Jubilee remained important themes in Judaism, as evidenced by extensive commentary in the Talmud. See Judah Goldin, *The Living Talmud: The Wisdom of the Fathers* (New York: New American Library, 1957), pp. 36-37.

23. Buber, *Moses: The Revelation and the Covenant* (New York: Harper & Row, 1958), p. 181.

with Israel,[24] and it was also on the basis of that history of liberation that Israel was to observe the Sabbath and Jubilee. In this context, the freeing of captives was not to be seen as an act of charity, nor was it based on any illusions that all of the poor and all of the captives were basically "good" people; rather, the proclamations of liberty to the captives were concrete social responses to God's liberating activity in the exodus of Israel from Egypt. Thus, the Jubilee and Sabbath Years were a type of social counterpart to Jewish Passover or Christian communion — do this in remembrance of me. The Jubilee and Sabbath Years were times of remembering, times to celebrate faith in the God who had been and is faithful. They were *social* programs, but they were at the same time proclamations central to the *faith* and worship of Israel. As James Muilenburg summarizes the relationship between faith and action, God and people, "the justice of God is to evoke Israel's justice."[25]

In the social/legal terminology of Israel, the Sabbatical and Jubilee liberations were based on God's standing as the *Go'el* for Israel's slaves. The *go'el* was the kinsperson who offered ransom to purchase the freedom of a relative who had been driven into slavery through indebtedness.[26] If some slaves were so totally abandoned that no one arose to offer ransom for them, then in the seventh year, God was *Go'el* for these forgotten slaves. In effect, God became the next of kin for the most hopeless of the captives. Refusing to grant liberation to these captives was a serious affront to God (Jer. 34:17-22), because it was cheating the *Go'el* out of the price of freedom. The ransom had already been paid

24. While some treaties and covenants in the ancient Near East were imposed by sheer force, Delbert Hillers notes that the covenant between Yahweh and Israel was based on history, a history that is repeatedly invoked throughout Scripture (*Covenant: The History of a Biblical Idea* [Baltimore: The Johns Hopkins University Press, 1969], p. 31).

25. Muilenburg, *The Way of Israel: Biblical Faith and Ethics* (New York: Harper Torchbooks, 1965), p. 70.

26. See Robert B. Sloan, Jr., *The Favorable Year of the Lord: A Study of Jubilary Theology in the Gospel of Luke* (Austin: Schola Press, 1977), pp. 6-7. André Trocmé noted that there was an early association of vengeance and redemption in that the *go'el* was also the one responsible for exacting blood vengeance when a relative was killed. God's role as *Go'el* was in part a plea to halt human retaliation ("Vengeance is Mine," Deut. 32:35; Rom. 12:19), and it eventually emerged in the Suffering Servant theme in which God serves as both *Go'el* and, through the Servant, as the one who suffers the impact of vengeance. See Trocmé, *Jesus and the Nonviolent Revolution*, trans. Michael H. Shank and Marlin E. Miller (Scottdale, Pa.: Herald Press, 1973), pp. 25-26.

for all future captives when God served as *Go'el* for all of the covenant people in the liberation from Egypt.

The Old Testament consciousness of liberation meant that Israel was never much at ease with slavery. While the Code of Hammurabi demanded the death penalty for those who helped slaves to escape,[27] there is no evidence that helping escaped slaves was a capital crime in Israel. But Old Testament statutes (e.g., Exod. 21:16; Deut. 24:7) did agree with the Code of Hammurabi in outlawing the practice of kidnaping people for the purpose of selling them into slavery.[28] In Babylon, an ear was cut off the slave who renounced his or her owner with the words "You are not my lord," but in Israel slaves were to be marked with degrading signs only if they renounced opportunities for freedom; slaves who declined liberation in the Sabbath or Jubilee Years were to have their ears pierced as a sign of perpetual servitude. Renouncing the master was shameful in Babylon, but it was forsaking freedom that was shameful in Israel.[29] Other cultures might mock the contrasts between slavery and freedom. "The Roman Saturnalia festival," writes Northrop Frye, "in which masters waited on their slaves in memory of the golden age of Saturn, was a dumb, helpless gesture which said symbolically that the slave structure of Roman society was all wrong, but that nothing could or would be done about it."[30] The Sabbath and Jubilee Years were constant reminders that God expected Israel to do something about slavery.

How was it that prisoners came to be included in the calls for liberation? There are echoes of the Sabbath and Jubilee Years in the "favorable year of the Lord" proclaimed by the prophet:

27. See sections 15 and 16 of the laws, in *The Ancient Near East*, vol. 1: *An Anthology of Texts and Pictures*, ed. James B. Pritchard (Princeton: Princeton University Press, 1958), p. 141.

28. Albrecht Alt is among the biblical scholars who maintain that the eighth commandment ("you shall not steal") was originally a commandment against the "stealing of persons" — i.e., kidnaping people in order to sell them into slavery. See S. Scott Bartchy, *First-Century Slavery and I Corinthians 7:21*, SBL Dissertation Series, no. 11 (Atlanta: Scholars Press, 1985), p. 46n.124. Bartchy's dissertation provides a helpful overview of the attitude toward slavery in the early church. Mistranslations of texts such as 1 Corinthians 7:21 have contributed to the mistaken view that Paul busily exhorted slaves to remain enslaved.

29. The contrast is noted by Buber in *Moses*, p. 145.

30. Frye, *The Great Code: The Bible and Literature* (New York: Harcourt Brace Jovanovich, 1982), p. 134.

The Spirit of the Lord GOD is upon me,
Because the LORD has anointed me
To bring good news to the afflicted;
He has sent me to bind up the brokenhearted,
To proclaim liberty to captives,
And freedom to prisoners;
To proclaim the favorable year of the Lord. (Isa. 61:1-2)

Lamentations 3:34-36 tells us that the crushing of "all the prisoners of the land" is one of the things of which "the Lord does not approve." And Psalm 146 is a hymn of praise to the Lord who cares for all of the oppressed, prisoners among them:

Praise the LORD!
Praise the LORD, O my soul!
I will praise the LORD while I live;
I will sing praises to my God while I have my being.
Do not trust in princes,
In mortal man, in whom there is no salvation.
His spirit departs, he returns to the earth;
In that very day his thoughts perish.

How blessed is he whose help is the God of Jacob,
Whose hope is in the LORD his God;
Who made heaven and earth,
The sea and all that is in them;
Who keeps faith forever;
Who executes justice for the oppressed;
Who gives food to the hungry.
The LORD sets the prisoners free. (Vv. 1-7)

How was it that prisoners were included among those to be set free?

In the palace of Sennacherib in Nineveh, a bas-relief portrays three singers, quite possibly Jews, playing musical instruments as they sat by a river. The singers are apparently captives, for standing to one side is an Assyrian guard armed with bow and club.[31] The scene calls to mind the lament of the psalmist: "How can we sing the LORD's song in a

---

31. The bas-relief is described by Gonzalo Báez-Camargo in *Archaeological Commentary on the Bible* (Garden City, N.Y.: Doubleday, 1984), p. 144.

foreign land?" (Ps. 137:4). But the scene also calls to mind the fact that captivity in exile was a brutal experience. The historians of Scripture mention the imprisonment of exiled kings (2 Kings 17:4; 25:27), but the kings were not the only exiles to be imprisoned. As the Nineveh bas-relief indicates, those taken into exile could not expect to roam about at will. As captives, many were likely subjected to forced labor under the watchful eyes of armed guards.[32] While some in Israel had displayed a penchant for imprisoning the prophets (2 Kings 22:26-27; Jer. 37:15-16), prisons and chains and fetters awaited many more in exile (Jer. 40:1).

It was from the period of exile that "prisons" and "prisoners" became important symbols for Israel.[33] And it was from the experience of exile that Israel learned of the fundamental kinship between enslavement and imprisonment. The experience of the exile prepared the covenantal community to understand the truth of the prophets' words: the same God who frees the slaves frees the prisoners too. In the calm reflections of the wisdom literature, the community even proclaimed the possibility that a freed prisoner would lead the people: "For he has come out of prison to become king, even though he was born poor in his kingdom" (Eccles. 4:14). And in moments of anguished hope, the community even proclaimed the messianic expectation that one would appear to say, "I have set your prisoners free" (Zech. 9:9-12).

Prisons and the New Testament

Walter Wink offers the observation that we are able to gain insight into a culture by examining what are *not* acceptable topics for conversation in polite circles. Those of Freudian bent could have a heyday analyzing

32. There is an ongoing debate regarding the history of the exiles. How many people of what socioeconomic classes from Judah and Israel were taken into exile in Assyria and Babylonia? What was their status under captivity? For a review of the various arguments, see Smith, *The Religion of the Landless*, pp. 26-41. There are few extrabiblical sources to assist in any effort to reconstruct a picture of the life of the exiles. While it is doubtless true that some of the exiles were accorded better treatment than others, I find no reason to dismiss the Old Testament portrayal of the fate met by some — slavery, fetters, prison.

33. See Smith, *The Religion of the Landless*, p. 31.

all of the sublimations involved in the repression of discourse on sexuality in America's past. But for the most part today, Americans take a certain pride in "open-mindedness." Though political life may have a twinge of the reactionary, conversations at social gatherings sparkle with liberality. "But if you want to bring all talk to a halt in shocked embarrassment, every eye riveted on you, try mentioning angels, or demons, or the devil. You will be quickly appraised for signs of pathological violence and then quietly shunned."[34] In an age that idolizes material, there is meager tolerance for any assertion that immaterial forces or spirits might have an affect on human life.

And yet there is no denying that certain historical events and moments are surrounded by something that can only be described as a "spirit." When a certain degree of political freedom spread quite rapidly through the Soviet Union and the nations of Eastern Europe, people referred to "the spirit of Glasnost." As one-party rule was eliminated in nation after nation, events took on a life of their own. The "spirit" that was loose could not be stopped. Events were "out of control," and many people viewed the results as positive. But there are some other spirits that few people would applaud. The spirit of evil that pervaded Nazi Germany also had a life of its own.

To speak of events that were out of control also calls to mind the American war in Southeast Asia. As bombs and napalm rained down, politicians and military commanders laid claim to schemes to end the war, but the light at the end of the tunnel kept receding until a million people had died. We were a nation "possessed," fighting for purposes that no one remembered, pretending that another few corpses would end the madness, covering the death with platitudes about freedom.

To speak of a nation possessed is not to erase human responsibility but is rather to point to the contagious quality of evil. There is no magical vaccine to guarantee immunity to this contagion. There is a hidden truth, however, in the use of the cross in ancient rites of exorcism. Insofar as the cross stands as a sign of Jesus' suffering and his forgiveness of those who crucified him, it also beckons us into the presence of God's kingdom, in which enemies are loved and wrongs are

---

34. Wink, *The Powers,* vol. 2: *Unmasking the Powers: The Invisible Forces That Determine Human Existence* (Philadelphia: Fortress Press, 1986), p. 1.

suffered rather than inflicted. The presence of demonic spirits in *every* call to arms and *every* appeal to death is revealed in the light of the contrasting call of Jesus: deny yourself; take up your cross and follow me (Matt. 16:24; Mark 8:34; Luke 9:23). While it may be possible to speak in a meaningful way of individuals who are "possessed," popular treatments such as *The Exorcist* trivialize the reality of the demonic. Exorcism is not effectuated by resorting to trinkets shaped like crosses. When whole communities and nations are possessed by the spirit of death, the path to exorcism is the *way* of the cross.

Even though talk of spirits and the demonic may seem awkward for modern people preoccupied with the material world, the willingness of biblical writers to address the spiritual realms should not automatically be dismissed as the residue of a primitive worldview. Indeed, the far more primitive view is that which often emerges from modern efforts to keep ethical analysis on a purely material plane; on a popular level, such analysis dissolves into a simplistic dualism that suggests the world is populated by good and bad people and the bad ones cause our problems. Paul was among the biblical writers who noted the mistake in assuming that we are merely assaulted by "bad people." Far more serious, we are assaulted by a deadly spirit in the air, a spirit that we breathe from birth,[35] a spirit which threatens to possess "good" and "bad" alike: "Put on the full armor of God, that you may be able to stand firm against the schemes of the devil. For our struggle is not against flesh and blood, but against the rulers, against the powers, against the world forces of this darkness, against the spiritual forces of wickedness in the heavenly places" (Eph. 6:11-12).[36]

Rather than representing a primitive view that is in need of demythologizing, this Pauline perspective points to inadequacies within our modern mythos. Eliminating "the bad people" does nothing to help us prevail in our struggle against "the spiritual forces of wickedness." Impris-

---

35. For an excellent summary of this aspect of Paul's thought, see Walter Wink, *The Powers*, vol. 1: *Naming the Powers: The Language of Power in the New Testament* (Philadelphia: Fortress Press, 1984), pp. 82-96.

36. Despite my unqualified reference to Ephesians as a Pauline epistle, I am aware of the considerable debate regarding the authorship of this epistle. If it was not written by Paul, it was certainly written by someone who shared many of Paul's perspectives. I believe that Markus Barth makes a convincing case for Paul's authorship in *Ephesians 1–3*, Anchor Bible, no. 34 (Garden City, N.Y.: Doubleday, 1974), pp. 36-50.

oning or assassinating a Stalin or a Hitler or a Pol Pot does not address the genocidal spirit to which they were merely pathetic servants.[37] In fact, such assassinations and imprisonments may give a freer reign to the spirit of violence by leading many people to assume that the "problem" has been eliminated or locked away. Indeed, violent struggle against flesh and blood merely serves to fuel the spirit or power that the violent struggle presumes to resist. It is a victory (both a spiritual and material victory) for the spirit of violence, because everywhere violence appears, no matter what the motivations and justifications, it is inevitably and tediously the same.[38] Paul shows the inadequacies of our modern mythos when he speaks of the "spirit" and the "power" that surround realities such as violence. Quite independent of human manipulations, the spirit of violence seduces people into its ranks with assurances that the violence is good or (in just this one instance) necessary or that it is just a little violence for the sake of averting major violence. It is all tediously the same.[39]

---

37. This brings the anguishing decision of Dietrich Bonhoeffer to mind. From our safe and comfortable distance, it would be far too easy and cheap to denounce his decision to join with those who were plotting to assassinate Hitler. No matter what judgments may be brought to bear on his decision, nothing can detract from the fact that Bonhoeffer was engaged in resistance while most German Christians were engaged in a far more deadly silence. The debate is explored in several helpful essays in *A Bonhoeffer Legacy: Essays in Understanding*, ed. A. J. Klassen (Grand Rapids: William B. Eerdmans, 1981). In "Dietrich Bonhoeffer's Way between Resistance and Submission" (pp. 170-77), Jørgen Glenthøj observes that Bonhoeffer's role with the resistance entailed laying plans for the German church after Hitler's demise rather than actually planning the attempt on Hitler's life. See also William Jay Peck's essay "The Role of the 'Enemy' in Bonhoeffer's Life and Thought," pp. 345-61.

38. This "sameness" is one of the laws of violence cited by Jacques Ellul in *Violence: Reflections from a Christian Perspective*, trans. Cecelia Gaul Kings (New York: Seabury Press, 1969), pp. 93-108.

39. While Paul certainly addresses the violence of the principalities and powers, he devotes even more attention to how, through legalism, the law has become one of the "powers" that govern and control humanity and separate us from God. Paul asserts that the victory of Jesus overcomes the power of the law along with all other principalities and powers. See Gustaf Aulén, *Christus Victor: An Historical Study of the Three Main Types of the Idea of the Atonement*, trans. A. G. Hebert (New York: Macmillan, 1969), pp. 67-68. By overcoming the power of the law, Jesus establishes a new relationship between humanity and God. As Paul Althaus puts it, "The law declares that the unclean cannot stand before God, only the clean. The gospel declares: God accepts the unclean!" (*The Divine Command: A New Perspective on Law and Gospel*, trans. Franklin Sherman, Facet Books Social Ethics Series, no. 9 [Philadelphia: Fortress Press, 1966], p. 23).

An understanding of the biblical perspective on spirits and powers has special relevance here, because in the Bible the prison is not viewed as a mere material entity. The Bible does not present the prison as simply one of many social institutions that may be more or less effective in pursuing the various goals assigned to them. The Bible identifies the prison with the spirit and power of death. As such, the problem with prisons has nothing to do with utilitarian criteria of deterrence. As such, the problem is not that prisons have failed to forestall violent criminality and murderous rampages; the problem is that prisons are *identical in spirit* to the violence and murder that they pretend to combat. The biblical discernment of the spirit of the prison demythologizes our pretenses. Whenever we cage people, we are in reality fueling and participating in the same spirit we claim to renounce. In the biblical understanding, the spirit of the prison is the spirit of death.

At numerous points in biblical literature, death is portrayed as a power that, though defeated, continues to manifest vain efforts to lay claim to humanity. One of these manifestations of death is imprisonment.[40] "There were those who dwelt in darkness and in the shadow of death, prisoners in misery and chains" (Ps. 107:10). In its origins, the identification of imprisonment with the power of death may be related to the ancient Near Eastern practice of imprisoning people in cisterns and pits and the association of these cells with the entrance to Sheol and the underworld.[41] Jeremiah 38:6 reports that guards imprisoned the prophet by lowering him with ropes into a cistern from which the water had been emptied, but "Jeremiah sank into the mud." Psalm 69 is the individual lament of one who was falsely accused and cast into a cistern; the rising waters that threaten death are compared to the primordial waters of chaos, but in the midst of them, "the Lord hears the needy, and does not despise His who are prisoners" (69:33). The identification of the prison pit with death is so close that the Hebrew

40. Christoph Barth cites imprisonment along with other manifestations of the power of death (e.g., injustice, opulence) in his *Introduction to the Psalms*, trans. R. A. Wilson (New York: Scribner's, 1966), p. 51.

41. See Othmar Keel, *The Symbolism of the Biblical World: Ancient Near Eastern Iconography and the Book of Psalms*, trans. Timothy J. Hallett (New York: Seabury Press, 1978), pp. 69-73.

bôr can alternately refer to the cistern pit, the grave (Isa. 14:19), or the entrance to Sheol.[42]

Through the influence of later apocalypticism, this underworld of pit and death, prison and Sheol is understood as the domain of Satan the Accuser. In Revelation 2:10 we read, "the devil is about to cast some of you into prison." The dialogue between Jesus and Peter recorded in Luke 22:31-33 may be read in the light of this identification:

> "Simon, Simon, behold, Satan has demanded permission to sift you like wheat; but I have prayed for you, that your faith may not fail; and you, when once you have turned again, strengthen your brothers."
>
> And he said to Him, "Lord, with You I am ready to go both to prison and to death!"[43]

Bearing in mind this identification of prison with the power of death, it is clear that Jesus' proclamation of liberty for the prisoners is not just an isolated saying within his ministry; it stands as a renunciation of the power of death, and it therefore points toward the resurrection itself.

It is Isaiah 61 that Jesus quotes in Luke 4 as he sets out the platform for his ministry.[44] The setting is the synagogue in Nazareth where, as

---

42. Without going far afield, I can only mention another interesting relationship — the biblical association of nets and snares with prisons. The association is linked to the practice of occasionally using nets to drag prisoners of war into captivity. Ensnared in nets, prisoners were treated in a fashion akin to hunted animals. Indeed, one ancient relief depicts an Assyrian king leading prisoners about with ropes attached to rings in their noses. See Báez-Camargo, *Archaeological Commentary on the Bible*, pp. 126, 188. For additional exploration on the symbolism of nets and snares, see Keel, *The Symbolism of the Biblical World*, pp. 89-95.

In the New Testament, 1 Timothy contains a reference to "the snare of the devil" (3:7) and warns that "those who want to get rich fall into temptation and a snare" (6:9). The biblical symbolism surrounding nets and snares points to fascinating potential for understanding the full range of meaning in Jesus' call, "I will make you fishers of men" (Matt. 4:19; Mark 1:17). While some traditional exegesis renders these verses as simple calls to proselytism, Ched Myers discerns a link between Jesus' call and the "fishing" depicted in Amos 4:1-2 and Ezekiel 29:1-4, where the fishers are called to renounce the snares of oppression and injustice (*Binding the Strong Man: A Political Reading of Mark's Story of Jesus* [Maryknoll, N.Y.: Orbis Books, 1988], p. 132).

43. Note that there is an echo of these words in Paul's declaration in Acts 21:13: "I am ready not only to be bound, but even to die at Jerusalem for the name of the Lord Jesus."

44. While Luke's is the only Gospel to portray this scene, the themes of Isaiah 61 also emerge as central for the writers of other Gospels. Robert Guelich notes, e.g., that

Luke reminds us, Jesus had lived most of his life up to that point. Liturgical practice likely dictated that the reading of the law was set by lectionary, but when Jesus rose to read from the prophets and he was handed the book of Isaiah, he was free to read a passage of his own choosing.[45] According to Luke, these are the words Jesus chose to read:

> The Spirit of the Lord is upon Me,
> Because He has anointed Me to preach the gospel to the poor.
> He has sent Me to proclaim release to the captives,[46]
> And recovery of sight to the blind,
> To set free those who are downtrodden,
> To proclaim the favorable year of the Lord. (4:18-19)

Here at the very outset of Jesus' ministry is the proclamation of liberty to the captives. And as he speaks, Jesus announces that the proclamation is fulfilled. As the Servant who is Lord, Jesus assumes a greater authority than that of the principalities and powers — authority to announce freedom to those who are imprisoned by the powers.[47]

It would be a mistake to assume that the words of Luke 4 can be

---

the presentation of the Beatitudes in Matthew is not intended to be "spiritualizing"; the language is an intentional alignment of the Beatitudes with Isaiah 61. Thus, "Matthew opens Jesus' teaching ministry with this deliberate allusion to Isaiah 61 in the Beatitudes (cf. Luke 4:16-21)" (*The Sermon on the Mount: A Foundation for Understanding* [Waco, Tex.: Word Books, 1982], p. 74).

45. Eduard Schweizer, *The Good News according to Luke*, trans. David E. Green (Atlanta: John Knox Press, 1984), p. 88.

46. Some may note a contrast between "prisoners" in Isaiah 61:1 and "captives" in Luke 4:18. If anything, the Greek term used here by Luke (*aichmalōtos*, literally "one taken by the spear") is even more *inclusive* than possible alternatives. It carries the sense of slaves and captives of war as well as prisoners. Certainly the term is not meant to connote only the Israelites of the Babylonian or Assyrian captivity, as some have argued. See Sloan, *The Favorable Year of the Lord*, pp. 38-39.

47. This statement and some of what follows presuppose that Jesus possessed a firm understanding of the direction of his own ministry and, in fact, a degree of awareness that he was the Messiah. Some in the Bultmann school would regard such a suggestion as anathema. More recently, however, some biblical scholars have convincingly argued that the complex layers of synoptic traditions do not permit the automatic assumption that all titular references to Jesus' self-understanding are necessarily constructions of a later community of faith. See, e.g., Leonhard Goppelt, *Theology of the New Testament*, vol. 1: *The Ministry of Jesus in Its Theological Significance*, trans. John Alsup (Grand Rapids: William B. Eerdmans, 1981), pp. 159-205.

limited to the pronouncement of a psychological or soteriological liberation for those who are "imprisoned by sin."[48] The direct reference to the concrete social programs of the Sabbath and Jubilee Years would have been obvious to those who heard Jesus as he spoke.[49] But there is an additional allusion to concrete social realities. It was not uncommon in the Near East for the enthronement of a king to be accompanied by the declaration of amnesty for prisoners. A ceremonial hymn such as that from the enthronement of Ramses IV in Egypt (ca. 1167 B.C.E.) is illustrative: "Oh happy day. . . . Those who had been hungry were fed. . . . Those who had been naked were clad. . . . Those who were in prison were set free."[50]

The proclamation in Luke 4 is issued by Jesus the Servant King, though his is a kingship with eschatological rather than merely political authority — and his is an amnesty with eschatological rather than merely momentary significance. The principalities and powers only have the ability to make a mockery of freedom. New rulers declare amnesty only to quickly pack the prisons fuller than before. Jesus has nothing to do with such mockery. He does not lead a violent assault on the prison walls, nor does he cut loose a few captives so that the governing authorities can send in more prisoners to take their places. Rather, Jesus unmasks the powers and renders them visible, much as Satan is rendered visible when he is "cast down from heaven" (Rev. 12).[51] The powers may pretend that captivity is based on justice, but Jesus declares that henceforth all prisoners have a right to liberty — the only possible right to liberty, based in the Word of God. Biblically understood, prisons are based on the spirit of death. Biblically understood, liberty is based on "the Spirit of the Lord" (Luke 4:18).

When Jesus' proclamation of liberty is viewed in the light of the resurrection, it can be said that Christ led captivity captive or that he

---

48. The material in Isaiah 61 from which Jesus was reading fails to lend support to such "spiritualizing" of the text. John L. McKenzie notes that the "material element of salvation" is prominent in both Deutero- and Trito-Isaiah (*Second Isaiah*, pp. lxiii, lxix).

49. For considerations of the scope of jubilary theology in the teachings of Jesus, see Trocmé, *Jesus and Nonviolent Revolution*, pp. 27-52; and John Howard Yoder, *The Politics of Jesus* (Grand Rapids: William B. Eerdmans, 1972), pp. 26-77.

50. This and additional examples are cited by Sloan in *The Favorable Year of the Lord*, pp. 54-57.

51. Wink, *Unmasking the Powers*, p. 65.

captured captivity (Eph. 4:8).[52] The word *gospel* carries the sense of "the good news of victory,"[53] but unlike the gospel of imperial Rome, the gospel of Jesus proclaims victory over principalities, over captivity, over the power of death itself. Generals and kings celebrated their military gospels with parades in which prisoners of war and statues of the gods of the conquered people were led through the streets of the victorious nation.[54] In Colossians 2:15, Paul writes of the victory parade of Christ: "When He had disarmed the rulers and authorities, He made a public display of them, having triumphed over them through Him." (A better translation might be "through *it*" — i.e., through "the cross," which is mentioned in the preceding verse. The cross is just one of the elements that radically distinguishes the gospel of Jesus from military gospels.)[55]

52. While several versions translate Ephesians 4:8 to say that Christ "led captive a host of captives," J. L. Houlden notes that this is an instance of an abstract noun being rendered concrete and that the literal translation is "captured captivity" (*Paul's Letters from Prison: Philippians, Colossians, Philemon, and Ephesians*, Westminster Pelican Commentaries [Philadelphia: Westminster Press, 1977], p. 311). Since Ephesians was composed in prison, this virtual personification of "captivity" is understandable. Ephesians 4:8 is a somewhat altered quotation of Psalm 68:18. In Psalm 68, there is an awareness of God as the one who "leads out the prisoners into prosperity" (v. 6). "God is to us a God of deliverances; and to GOD the Lord belong escapes from death" (v. 20).

Markus Barth rejects the "captivity is captive led" translation because he fears that such a rendering evokes Platonic or Gnostic images of combat against demons who have taken control of the "souls" of people (*Ephesians 4–6*, Anchor Bible, no. 34A [Garden City, N.Y.: Doubleday, 1974], pp. 431-32). Of course, Barth is right in warning against any implication that Ephesians is a Gnostic writing. But still, Barth agrees that the verse refers to a victory over the principalities and powers. Once these powers are identified specifically as the powers of slavery and imprisonment, it is possible to translate the verse in its literal sense of "captured captivity" without needing to posit any Gnostic belief in demons exercising power over human "souls."

53. See the comments by Myers in *Binding the Strong Man*, p. 123.

54. For an illustration of Assyrian soldiers parading with the statues of captured gods, see plate 145 in *The Ancient Near East*, 1:351.

55. In the context of the good news of victory, we should briefly take note of the much-discussed passage 1 Peter 3:18-22, which speaks of Christ dying and going (we are not told where) to preach to "the spirits in prison." The context and the vocabulary of the passage make it clear that Christ is not depicted as preaching to human prisoners but rather to spirits and powers that have been restrained. Bo Reicke suggests that the import of this passage is that Christ's preaching is to serve as a prototype for the preaching of the church community. The gospel is to be proclaimed without regard to threats and dangers. "By taking him as their example, they will be prepared to defend the gospel before the heathen magistrates" (*The Epistles of James, Peter and Jude*, Anchor Bible, no. 37 [Garden City, N.Y.: Doubleday, 1964], p. 111).

According to Luke, it was in the synagogue at Nazareth that Jesus read the words of "liberty for the captives." And then he sat down (the posture of a rabbi who is about to teach) and said, "Today this Scripture has been fulfilled in your hearing" (4:21). Eduard Schweizer comments:

> The first words from the mouth of the adult Jesus are not his own words but the words of the prophet. What he preaches is not something new. What is new is the "today" in which God seeks to become reality, to aid all those who are oppressed . . . the Gentiles (4:25-27), prostitutes (7:36-50), tax collectors (15:1-2), and criminals (23:40-43). This is where the interpretation of Jesus begins. . . . Happy assent to such preaching of grace must not deceive anyone; grace for the poor is always judgment for the rich. This programmatic narrative also censures a religious luxury so certain of the divine that it has ceased to realize that God could come "today," to judge and to transform.[56]

In short, writes Schweizer, "God really encounters only those who allow him to take them by surprise."[57]

The people in the synagogue at Nazareth were not taken by surprise over the words from Isaiah, which they had doubtless heard many times, nor even over Jesus' rather startling pronouncement that the words were being fulfilled in their hearing. Indeed, Luke portrayed the people as having a certain degree of pride in the fact that such words came from one of their own (4:22), from someone who shared their turf, someone who shared their God and country. Of course, the subtlest challenge to the holiness of religion, race, or homeland can cause a crowd's ire to be raised even against one of its own. Jesus was not subtle. According to Luke, Jesus not only omitted Isaiah's references to the judgments and vengeance against the Gentiles (Isa. 61:2bff.) but even spoke of how God's glory is revealed to the Gentiles (Luke 4:23-27). Suddenly it became clear that Jesus was proclaiming good news not only for the poor of Israel but also for the *undeserving* poor, not only for the good prisoners but also for the *bad* ones. When the crowd had thought that Jesus was proclaiming liberty to people like themselves, they praised him. When the crowd realized that Jesus was proclaiming liberty to all people, they tried to kill him.

56. Schweizer, *The Good News according to Luke*, pp. 91-92.
57. Schweizer, *The Good News according to Luke*, p. 94.

Luke's account of the proclamation of liberty for prisoners does not end with Jesus' teaching at the synagogue in Nazareth. The proclamation also resonates through the accounts of miraculous deliverance from prison in Acts 5 and 12. Structural analysis offers the helpful observation that all language and literary texts serve both an informational and symbolic function.[58] On both of these levels, the accounts of release from prison serve to echo the message of liberty and renounce the power of the prison:

> But about midnight, Paul and Silas were praying and singing hymns of praise to God, and the prisoners were listening to them; and suddenly there came a great earthquake, so that the foundations of the prison house were shaken; and immediately all the doors were opened, and everyone's chains were unfastened. (Acts 16:25-26)

The chains fell away not only from the apostles and the "good" prisoners but from everyone.

In fact, it may be untenable to draw a sharp differentiation between the apostles and other prisoners. Any notion that the apostles were consistently innocent of legal infractions is less a product of the biblical account than of more recent theologies that assert that obedience to God and obedience to the legally constituted authorities are mutually supportive. If the will of God is represented by the will of the courts, the idea of a criminal apostle becomes an impossibility. And yet at several points in Scripture and particularly in Acts, the apostles are represented as criminals, albeit "righteous criminals." In order to recognize the extent of the criminality of the apostles, we must remember that there was a Roman stamp of approval on the authority of the Sanhedrin to adjudicate a wide range of legal matters in Judea. While the Sanhedrin is often regarded as a "religious court," there was no clear demarcation between the "religious" and the "civil" in Jewish law. It was in open defiance of the legally constituted authority of the Sanhe-

---

58. For example, on a strictly informational level, the word *Vietnam* refers to a nation in Southeast Asia, but the word also has an additional symbolic-connotative dimension for many Americans. Raymond Collins offers this example in the context of a discussion of contributions to biblical studies made by Claude Lévi-Strauss and others from the school of structural analysis (*Introduction to the New Testament* [Garden City, N.Y.: Doubleday, 1983], p. 243).

drin that Peter and other apostles spoke of the need to obey God rather than people (Acts 5:26-29). But it was not only on religious grounds nor only by religious courts that apostles were arrested, tried, and convicted. Like John the Baptist (Luke 9:9), James the brother of John was executed by the sword (Acts 12:1-2), a form of capital punishment reserved for those convicted of political crimes and/or treasonous behavior.[59] Indeed, Paul himself was in a legal double bind that inherently meant he was guilty of something. If the church community was Jewish and therefore fully subject to the rulings of the Sanhedrin, Paul was guilty of disobeying court rulings: at best he was a heresiarch; at worst, a blasphemer. If, on the other hand, the Christians were not Jewish, then Paul was preaching a new religion that did not have official Roman recognition, and such evangelism could merit the death penalty under Roman law. If Paul was innocent of one of the two charges, it meant that he was automatically guilty of the other.[60]

Some biblical commentators have represented Luke's writings in the Gospel and Acts as a political apologetic, an effort to demonstrate to Roman authorities and loyal Roman citizens that the church community posed no threat to the empire. These commentators cite as evidence of the apologetic such features as what they take to be Luke's attempt to portray "the Jews" rather than the Romans as responsible for the execution of Jesus (a point to which I will return shortly) and the imprisoned Paul's appeal to his Roman citizenship (Acts 22:25-29; 25:11). But Paul's legal appeal to Caesar can hardly be understood as lending support to a political apologetic or as constituting an endorsement of the Roman legal system, for the right of Jews to hold citizenship was itself a point of controversy. Apion recommended the revocation of Jewish citizenship in Alexandria, and around 13 B.C.E. Ionian cities petitioned Marcus Agrippa to revoke the citizenship of all Jews who failed to give proper reverence to the patron gods of cities and empire.[61]

---

59. Richard J. Cassidy, *Society and Politics in the Acts of the Apostles* (Maryknoll, N.Y.: Orbis Books, 1987), pp. 47-48.

60. On this, see Johannes Munck, *The Acts of the Apostles*, rev. ed. by William F. Albright and C. S. Mann, Anchor Bible, no. 31 (Garden City, N.Y.: Doubleday, 1967), p. lxxvi.

61. See Martin Hengel, *Judaism and Hellenism: Studies in Their Encounter in Palestine during the Early Hellenistic Period,* vol. 1 (Philadelphia: Fortress Press, 1981), pp. 67-68.

Paul's appeal to Caesar is more likely to have been viewed as bothersome than as an affirmation of Roman jurisprudence. Contrary to his intent, Paul's appeal may actually have helped to secure his death sentence because of the manner in which Rome saw this new Jewish sect displaying evangelical tendencies that threatened the unifying power of emperor worship.[62] Rather than an affirmation of Roman jurisprudence or citizenship (Phil. 3:20: "our citizenship is in heaven"), Paul's appeal to Caesar may best be understood as Luke explains it — as an opportunity to bear witness in Rome (Acts 23:11). Indeed, rather than a political apologetic, Luke's writing in Acts may have served as instruction for the early church to remain steadfast under persecution.[63]

Occasional comments in the epistles provide additional insight into Paul's own view of his imprisonment. Paul's assertion that "we are ambassadors for Christ" (2 Cor. 5:20) takes on an ironic meaning in Ephesians 6:20: "I am an ambassador in chains." As Markus Barth notes, the latter statement is an oxymoron.[64] An old diplomatic tradition applicable both today and in Paul's time stipulates that, except in extraordinary circumstances, ambassadors are immune from arrest or legal prosecution in the host countries to which they are sent. Rather than a confirmation of the justice of the Roman juridical system, the phrase "ambassador in chains" points to the fundamental injustice of the imprisonment of those who have been set free by "the mystery of the gospel" (Eph. 6:19).

But rather than bemoaning the injustice of his imprisonment, Paul viewed his circumstance as providing an opportunity to bear witness in Rome. It was without any lament that he referred to himself as "a prisoner of Christ Jesus" (Philem. 1; Eph. 3:1) or "the prisoner of the Lord" (Eph. 4:1). It must be emphasized, however, that these titles did not imply that the governing authorities had Christ's blessing in impris-

---

62. See Munck, *The Acts of the Apostles*, pp. lxxxii-lxxxiii.

63. The theory that this was one of Luke's purposes is offered by Cassidy in *Society and Politics in the Acts of the Apostles*, pp. 158-60. Cassidy notes that the political-apology theory of Luke-Acts is untenable in view of Luke's inclusion in his story of many elements that would have been blatantly scandalous for loyal Roman subjects, such as the references to Jesus as "Lord," the identification of Simon as a zealot, the forthright account of the disruptions that seemed to follow Paul and other apostles wherever they went, and so on.

64. Barth, *Ephesians 4–6*, p. 782.

oning Paul or others. There is no doubt that Paul believed that suffering, imprisonment, and death could ultimately serve to further the proclamation of the gospel (Phil. 1:7, 29), but that should never imply divine endorsement of prisons or death. The title "prisoner of Christ Jesus" carries a connotation similar to the Pauline references to believers as "bondservants" or "bondslaves of Christ" (e.g., Phil. 1:1; Col. 4:12). The import of such titles is mentioned by Paul in 1 Corinthians 7:22-23: "For he who was called in the Lord while a slave, is the Lord's freedman; likewise he who was called while free, is Christ's slave. You were bought with a price; do not become slaves of men." According to an old inscription in a Delphic temple in Greece, slaves could be redeemed if they were purchased in the name of Apollo; henceforth, such freed slaves were known as "the slaves of Apollo."[65] For his Hellenistic audience, Paul depicted the freedom bought by Christ in similar terminology. Thus, the phrase "bondslave of Christ" points less to slavery than it does to the freedom that Christ won for former slaves (Gal. 5:1; note, too, the allusion to the Hebrew *go'el*). Similarly, the title "prisoner of Christ Jesus" speaks less of imprisonment than of the one who breaks the power of the prison. Rather than carrying any sense of Jesus endorsing prisons, the title suggests the exact opposite — namely, that Jesus is the one who sets the prisoners free. Noting that Paul was a disciple of the one who is victorious over the principalities and powers, Calvin offered an appropriate commentary on his imprisonment: "Paul's chains adorn him with an authority higher than that deployed by a king's pomp."[66]

The miraculous nature of the apostles' deliverance from prisons in Acts can be understood in light of the identification of prisons with the power of death and the identification of Jesus as the one who frees the prisoners.[67] It is not because of anything "magical" that these releases are miraculous. Rather, in New Testament accounts of miracles, at least one of two elements is inevitably present: (1) an assertion of divine authority, as in the defeat of demons or the assertion of nurturing authority over the natural creation, and (2) life-affirming activity, as in feeding or healing or resurrecting. Both of these elements are present

65. See Báez-Camargo, *Archaeological Commentary on the Bible*, p. 250.
66. Calvin, quoted by Barth in *Ephesians 4–6*, p. 426n.6.
67. It is symbolically significant that in Acts 4:1-3, Peter and John are said to have been arrested for the crime of "proclaiming in Jesus the resurrection from the dead."

in the deliverance accounts. The release is an assertion of divine authority over the state and over the fallen principalities and powers, and the deliverance is also life-affirming in that it is a renunciation of that death with which imprisonment is biblically identified.

The Bible makes an important distinction between the power and spirit of the prison on the one hand and the people who are jailers on the other. Rather than harboring any grievances against their jailers, the apostles are portrayed at several points as saving their jailers' lives. Roman penal procedures mandated that any guards who permitted the escape of prisoners would pay with their own lives.[68] Acts 16:27-28 indicates that the Philippian jailer believed that his prisoners had escaped and was about to kill himself when Paul called out to prevent the suicide. The jailer was subsequently converted. The incident is a concrete example of how "our struggle is not against flesh and blood" (Eph. 6:12).

In proclaiming Jesus victorious over the principalities and powers, it was natural that Paul should admonish believers not to rely on the court systems of the fallen principalities: "Does any one of you, when he has a case against his neighbor, dare to go to law before the unrighteous, and not before the saints?" (1 Cor. 6:1). In fact, the admonition is not only Pauline. While the impact of the verse is usually skewed by mistranslation, Matthew cites Jesus in the Sermon on the Mount as calling for avoidance of the courts even when faced with an evildoer. As Joachim Jeremias notes, after Jesus cites the *lex talionis*, the literal translation of Matthew 5:39 is as follows: "But I say to you, Do not go to law with one who is evil; but if anyone strikes you on the right cheek, turn to him the other also."[69]

Linked to both Jesus and Paul, this tradition of refraining from reliance on courts of law did not mean that the church community was to be unconcerned for those who were victimized by crime and wrongdoing. Someone who was wronged was to seek redress within the church community. It is possible that Paul's vision of the church as an alternative body for seeking the reconciliation that could not be fostered in the

68. See Munck, *The Acts of the Apostles*, p. 114. As Paul was taken to Rome by prison ship, the guards had a plan to kill prisoners in order to prevent escapes (Acts 27:41-44).

69. Jeremias, *The Sermon on the Mount*, trans. Norman Perrin, Facet Books Biblical Series (Philadelphia: Fortress Press, 1963), p. 28.

courts of the "unrighteous" was partially influenced by the Jewish diaspora communities, which had their own courts to deal with internal disputes.[70] But Paul still admonished against reliance on criminal and civil courts even if the victimization came from one who was outside the church community. Rather than relying on the judgments of courts, Paul gave the outsider over to God's judgment (1 Cor. 5:12-13). "God has forbidden his people to play judge with each other," says Markus Barth, "because they would only be convicting and damning each other as they took the administration of law and justice out of God's hands and into their own. But 'there is one lawgiver and judge: he who can *save* and destroy. Who are you to condemn your neighbor?'"[71] Although the reference is to eschatological signs, the imagery attributed to Jesus in Luke 12:57-59 makes the point clear that the courts can offer only prison, not reconciliation.

What, then, did the early church community set forth as our responsibility to prisoners? Matthew quotes Jesus as speaking of a responsibility to "visit" the prisoners (25:31-46). While this "visiting" can certainly be understood as establishing relationships and personal contacts with prisoners, the Greek term *episkeptomai* connotes more than spending time with people. The same term is used most often to refer to the divine activity of redeeming and freeing and caring for people. There are numerous biblical references to being visited by God or an angel of the Lord and being freed by that visitation. In Luke 1:68, for example, we read that God "has visited us and accomplished redemption."

70. See Wayne A. Meeks, *The First Urban Christians: The Social World of the Apostle Paul* (New Haven: Yale University Press, 1983), p. 229n.143. The "courts" were certainly not the only alternative structures in Judaism and the early church. Abraham Malherbe notes that the theological and social importance attached to hospitality in the Judeo-Christian tradition gave rise to networks of private homes that in effect served as alternative inns so that even the poor need not be restricted in their travels (*Social Aspects of Early Christianity*, 2d ed. [Philadelphia: Fortress Press, 1983], pp. 66-67).

71. Barth, *Justification: Pauline Texts Interpreted in the Light of the Old and New Testaments*, trans. A. M. Woodruff III (Grand Rapids: William B. Eerdmans, 1971), p. 52. The quotation cited by Barth is from James 4:12. See also Romans 2:1-2. The same juridical language is often used in the Bible to describe the judgments of God and the workings of human courts, but God's judgments have the effect of turning the human judgments upside down. For an examination of the theme, see Markus Barth, *Acquittal by Resurrection* (New York: Holt, Rinehart & Winston, 1964).

In Matthew 25:31-46, the meaning of the reference to prisoners is clarified if we bear in mind that the text depicts Jesus teaching about God's eschatological judgment of *the nations* (25:32). Walter Wink suggests that the changes in the gender of the pronouns within the text imply a judgment of both individuals as representatives of various nations and the nations themselves as corporate entities.[72] The idea of a nation "visiting" its prisoners suggests that *episkeptomai* here carries the additional sense of redeeming and freeing. In Matthew 25 we read that Jesus preaches to individuals and to nations: care for prisoners, visit them, set them free.

Finally, there is a biblical word that all believers need to hear again and again: you have kinship with the prisoners. In origins, your faith is a prison faith. Your roots are not to be found among the powerful and the wealthy and the religious. Your roots are not in palaces and holy places. Your roots are in cisterns and dungeons and prison ships and jailhouses. Your mothers and fathers were shackled there. And your sisters and brothers still are.

Who are the prisoners? As Karl Barth noted, the first true Christian community was composed entirely of prisoners — the three criminals on the crosses at Golgotha.[73]

Jesus the Prisoner

Empires past and present have displayed a considerable knack for mollifying masses of people with bread and circuses. The Romans were among the first to recognize that the execution of criminals and dissidents carried a certain morbid entertainment value that could be incorporated into the circus. The Romans apparently thought that, though the killing be clothed in the guise of justice or deterrence or law and order, there was no reason to deny the added benefit of spectator appeal. So at circuses in various corners of the empire and at the huge Circus Maximus in Rome itself, condemned prisoners were ushered into arenas where they were torn asunder by wild beasts or dispatched by sword-toting soldiers. But when viewed alongside the excitement of chariot races or the bloody duels of

---

72. Wink, *Unmasking the Powers,* pp. 96-97.
73. Barth, "The Criminals with Him," in *Deliverance to the Captives* (New York: Harper, 1961), pp. 77-78.

gladiators, there was a certain flatness to the public executions. It was not that the condemned prisoners evoked any particular sympathies from the spectators nor that the bloodshed seemed excessive. (The crowds were capable of protesting excesses: in 55 B.C.E., one crowd let it be known that Pompey's butchering of 600 elephants was a bit much.) It was just that the straightforward killing of an unarmed prisoner never carried the excitement of contests between two equally armed opponents. The schedule for a day at the circus was eventually adjusted so that executions did not intrude on the Roman version of prime time. Prisoners were killed over the lunch hour so that spectators could come and go without fear that they were missing much.[74]

Crucifixion was another matter. Although it became a fairly commonplace form of execution during various periods in Roman history, crucifixion never failed to evoke a sense of horror. Compared to the rapid snuffing of life by sword or beast, the cross entailed the torturous death of gradual suffocation as the weight of the crucified's body slowly restricted the movement of the diaphragm and rendered breathing difficult. For some victims, the tortured breathing may have contributed to heart failure in a matter of hours, but others hung from crosses for days before dying. As Juvenal noted, vultures flocked around at crucifixion time, and, provided human gawkers kept their distance, the birds would pick at the flesh of the dead or the near-dead. Bugs buzzed and crawled over the immobile bodies on the crosses. The pain from the driven nails and the stares from the gathered crowds added to the agony and humiliation. This degrading form of death was not deemed appropriate for those of higher station in life. With rare exceptions, crucifixion was reserved for the "common" criminals, the poor, and especially the slaves.[75] Any society that holds masses of people in subservience must keep a wary eye on the potential for revolt. The Romans hoped the cross was ugly enough to serve as warning for the slaves: don't even think of freedom.

Over the centuries, ecclesiastical authorities could not abide an ugly cross. With gold, with silver, with ornate carving here and there, the cross became a thing of beauty. It is clear that Jesus of Nazareth

74. See John E. Stambaugh and David L. Balch, *The New Testament in Its Social Environment*, Library of Early Christianity, no. 2 (Philadelphia: Westminster Press, 1986), pp. 120-21.

75. John Romer, *Testament: The Bible and History* (New York: Henry Holt, 1988), pp. 178-79.

never saw the cross as beautiful. The Gospels each portray him as having had a profound sense of his own impending arrest and torturous death on a cross that was anything but pretty. Nonetheless, Jesus set his face toward Jerusalem (Luke 9:51, 53). He moved resolutely toward the center of political power, toward the center of religious piety and holiness. He moved resolutely toward death.

An unresolved debate has raged for nigh onto two millennia regarding the reason for Jesus' crucifixion, the specific nature of the charges leveled against him, and the identity of those who were culpable in his death. Some have pointed to the religious nature of the proceedings against Jesus, while others have noted the political character of the trial and execution.[76] Some theologies of the atonement have gone so far in the direction of asserting a divine need of satisfaction and payment for the multifarious sins of humanity that they virtually portray God as the one who drove the nails. Some interpret Paul's words in 1 Corinthians 2:8 as assigning the blame for the crucifixion to "evil angels."[77] Some point to the guilt of Pontius Pilate, while others have absolved him so completely that the Coptic and Ethiopic churches have accorded Pilate and Procla (the woman he married) the status of sainthood.[78] Still others (and here the debate is far from academic) blame the Jews.

---

76. Regarding the political character of the proceedings, see S. G. F. Brandon's classic work *Jesus and the Zealots: A Study of the Political Factor in Primitive Christianity* (New York: Scribner's, 1967). There is no denying the profound political implications in the life, death, and resurrection of Jesus, but some portions of Brandon's thesis have been severely challenged in recent years. Specifically, there is considerable reason to doubt that Jesus was affiliated with any organized political party, let alone one that advocated violence. Richard Horsley notes that the organized movement known as "the Zealots" did not even come into existence until 67-68 C.E. Insofar as there was reference to "zealots" before that date, the term was a fairly generic reference to the popular prophetic movements and the social banditry that emerged as the primary expression of opposition to Roman rule. (Social banditry is implied with the use of *lestēs* in Mark 14:48; Jesus asked the soldiers if they were coming to arrest him "as though I were a robber.") See Richard A. Horsley with John S. Hanson, *Bandits, Prophets, and Messiahs: Popular Movements at the Time of Jesus*, New Voices in Biblical Studies, ed. Adela Yarbro Collins and John J. Collins (New York: Harper & Row, 1985).

77. Such an interpretation is offered by James L. Kugel and Rowan A. Greer, *Early Biblical Interpretation*, Library of Early Christianity, no. 3 (Philadelphia: Westminster Press, 1986), p. 159.

78. Raymond E. Brown, *The Gospel according to John XIII–XXI*, Anchor Bible, no. 29A (Garden City, N.Y.: Doubleday, 1970), p. 795.

Those who join with Pilate in washing his hands of any guilt usually depict him as genuinely convinced of Jesus' innocence but unable to withstand the crowd's demands for crucifixion. Such a portrayal contradicts the historical information we have about him. Pilate exhibited no respect for Judaism, and there is no reason to believe that he would have allowed himself to be browbeaten by a Jewish crowd. During his reign, he insulted the Jews by bringing military insignia bearing the emperor's image into Jerusalem and by confiscating Temple funds in order to build an aqueduct; when this latter action met with Jewish protest, Pilate called out the troops. The Romans finally thought it prudent to remove Pilate from office in 36 C.E. after he had ordered an unprovoked attack on unarmed Samaritans at Mount Gerizim.[79] Pilate never demonstrated an inclination to do the Jews any favors or to allow himself to be harangued into acting against his will.

The major political and ideological division in first-century Palestine might be characterized as a conflict between the Romans and the Jewish ruling groups on one side and the peasants who constituted the vast majority of Jews on the other.[80] The high priests were appointed by the Romans, and in specific instances such as the trial of Jesus, it would not have been unusual for some members of the Sanhedrin to share interests with the Romans. Indeed, at some points in the New Testament, the phrase "the Jews" seems to refer specifically to the ruling group that had allied itself with Rome, while "the people" refers to the vast majority of Jews who, like Jesus and the apostles, were excluded from this ruling elite.[81] Bearing in mind the divisions within Palestinian society, it is possible to understand some Gospel accounts of Pilate's banter with the crowd during the trial of Jesus as Pilate's attempt to precipitate the death penalty by manipulating the crowd rather than vice versa.[82] While the interpretations of the actions and motives of Pilate and the Sanhedrin and the crowd can become quite

79. Howard Clark Kee, *Understanding the New Testament*, 4th ed. (Englewood Cliffs, N.J.: Prentice-Hall, 1983), p. 41.

80. Horsley, *Bandits, Prophets, and Messiahs*, p. 245.

81. Cassidy, *Society and Politics in the Acts of the Apostles*, pp. 48-49.

82. Ched Myers points to the manner in which the Gospel of Mark depicts Pilate as engaged in such manipulation (*Binding the Strong Man*, p. 374). As Myers notes, "What is *least* plausible is that a Jewish crowd would have advocated that *any* Jew be crucified by the Romans."

speculative, the outcome is historically clear: Jesus was killed by "cruci-fixion on a Roman cross, supervised by a Roman centurion acting on orders from a Roman governor."[83]

On a deeper level, however, the specific religious or ethnic or national identity of those who executed Jesus is really quite irrelevant. In their prayers from Jerusalem, Peter and John were very inclusive when identifying those who plotted against Jesus: "For truly in this city there were gathered together against Thy holy servant Jesus, whom Thou didst anoint, both Herod and Pontius Pilate, along with the Gentiles and the peoples of Israel" (Acts 4:27). Two thousand years later, blaming the Jews is as absurd as blaming the Italians. Consistently, the biblical point was not that the high priest or the Sanhedrin or particular Pharisees were Jewish but that they constituted the epitome of good religious order and piety, just as Pilate was representative of the best government the civilized world had to offer. To seek to assign blame to a specific group is to deflect attention away from what actually happened. Jesus was killed in the name of good government. Jesus was killed in the name of good religion.[84]

The debate about the precise nature of the charges against Jesus can be as misleading as the debate over who bears the blame. No matter whether the charges against him were religious or political or both, Jesus' fundamental offenses had nothing to do with mere legal infractions. Much more serious than that, his whole life and ministry had challenged the very spirit and power of politics, religion, and society. Walter Wink explains that

> it is impossible to discover in the Gospels an "adequate" cause for Jesus' execution. Every such attempt has presupposed that he must have done something punishable by death. But he did not. That is the whole point. He was innocent and yet executed. But the Powers did not err. He had rejected their spirituality; he had shaken the

83. Cassidy, *Society and Politics in the Acts of the Apostles*, p. 20.
84. Besides being a founding member of the Koinonia Community and a person who took the cost of discipleship seriously, Clarence Jordan was also a scholar of biblical Greek. His "Cotton Patch Versions" of biblical writings often manage to capture the spirit of a text by putting it in a modern setting. When Jordan translated references to the chief priest as "archbishop," the Sanhedrin as "ministers and elders" and the Jews as "good church folks," he was well within the spirit of the biblical text. See, e.g., *The Cotton Patch Version of Matthew and John* (New York: Association Press, 1970), pp. 89-90.

invisible foundations by a series of provocative acts. He was therefore a living terror to the order of things. He *had* to be removed.[85]

And insofar as he continues to challenge our politics, religion, and carefully constructed sense of security and order, he still has to be removed. Northrop Frye observes that "society will always sooner or later line up with Pilate against the prophet."

> Christianity is founded on a prophet who was put to death as a blasphemer and a social menace, hence any persecuting Christian is assuming that Pilate and Caiaphas were right in principle, and should merely have selected a different victim. The significance of the life of Jesus is . . . that of being the one figure in history whom no organized human society could possibly put up with. The society that rejected him represented all societies: those responsible for his death were not the Romans or the Jews or whoever happened to be around at the time, but the whole of mankind down to ourselves and doubtless far beyond. "It is expedient that one man die for the people," said Caiaphas (John 18:14), and there has never been a human society that has not agreed with him.[86]

So while the Gospels are basically silent on the legal charges, almost as if they do not matter, they do cite in explicit detail the real factors motivating the crucifixion. The Gospel of John, for example, recounts the trial sequences in a series of dialogues leading to crucifixion. We read of the utilitarian sentiments of Caiaphas, who asserted that it was "expedient for one man to die on behalf of the people" (18:14). Once the means are understood as being justified by a noble end, crucifixion follows. We read of the cynicism of Pilate: "What is truth?" (18:38). This is not a question from one who yearns to be found by truth, but an assertion by one who believes that all things are relative, including the value of human life. We read of the law-abiding public: "We have a law, and by that law He ought to die" (19:7). Rather than being a precursor of decency and peace, the law is a precursor of death. And we read of those who pledge their patriotic allegiance: "We have no king but Caesar" (19:15). From that proclamation, the next verse flows quite

85. Wink, *Naming the Powers*, p. 109.
86. Frye, *The Great Code*, pp. 132-33.

naturally and automatically: "So he then delivered Him to them to be crucified" (19:16). Whenever the state is regarded as the final arbiter of right and truth, people are delivered up to be crucified.

So it was not God who demanded that Jesus be crucified. Theologies that maintain God received a magical, substitutionary "satisfaction" by seeing Jesus die ignore the Gospel accounts: the only reference to "satisfaction" concerns the manner in which Pilate satisfied the murderous calls for crucifixion (Mark 15:15). This was a senseless act of human "justice." God did not demand it. God transformed it into an event of significance. Through the crucifixion, the true nature of the principalities and powers is revealed. Through the resurrection, the triumph over the principalities and powers is proclaimed.[87] The blood of the crucified Lord is not a magical potion but a sacrifice that cries out before God and humanity.[88] As the Epistle to the Hebrews notes, it is along with the blood of Abel (11:4) and the prophets and the prisoners (11:36) and all of those among the "cloud of witnesses surrounding us" (12:1) that the blood of Jesus cries out against the power of death in all its manifestations. The suffering and crying out of Jesus is different from that of the martyrs (Heb. 12:24) in that his is the suffering of one who is truly faithful, of one who is truly the Son of God. Indeed, it is possible to join with Jürgen Moltmann in speaking of "the crucified God":

> The symbol of the cross in the church points to the God who was crucified not between two candles on an altar, but between two thieves in the place of the skull, where the outcasts belong, outside the gates of the city. . . . It is a symbol which therefore leads out of the church and out of religious longing into the fellowship of the oppressed and abandoned. On the other hand, it is a symbol which calls the oppressed and godless into the church and through the church into the fellowship of the crucified God. . . . To make the cross a present reality in our civilization means to put into practice the experience one has received of being liberated from fear for oneself; no longer to adapt oneself to this society, its idols and taboos, its imaginary enemies and fetishes; and in the name of him who was once the victim

87. See Hendrikus Berkhof, *Christ and the Powers*, trans. John H. Yoder (Scottdale, Pa.: Herald Press, 1977), pp. 36ff.

88. Markus Barth explores the biblical understanding of the sacrificial blood in *Justification*, pp. 42-45.

of religion, society and the state to enter into solidarity with the victims of religion, society and the state at the present day, in the same way as he who was crucified became their brother and their liberator.[89]

Clearly, the prisoners are among the victims of religion, society, and state.

For Christians, however, the effort to arrive at a biblical understanding of prisoners and prisons can never be based on an abstract theory about who is or is not a "victim," nor on calculations about who was first victimized by whom. To listen for the Word in the words of the Gospels genuinely, we must first silence all of our noisy, media-fed images of prisoners and prisons, be those images good, bad, or indifferent. And above all, we must silence all of our technological scheming for solutions that will "really work" or for alternatives that will be "more humane." It is only by silencing these noises that we can really hear the stubborn biblical truth: Jesus was a prisoner.

Abandoned by the apostles who claimed that they would go with him to prison and to death, the prisoner Jesus was left with just two other criminals by his side (Luke 23:32).[90] And yet, this prisoner was able to show love for both executioners and victims (Luke 23:34, 43). He went to his death as a prisoner, but the imprisonment of Jesus does not end even with death. In the Gospel of Mark, the wrapping of Jesus' body is described in the same terminology used for the fettering of prisoners (Mark 15:46).[91] A stone was rolled in front of the prison tomb, and Matthew says that guards were posted (27:62-66). The prisoner on the cross was a prisoner even in death. The power of the prison is broken by resurrection.

But the stubborn biblical truth has to do with far more than the historical fact that Jesus was a prisoner. Along with the fact that Jesus *was* a prisoner is the proclamation that Jesus *is the* prisoner. There can be no pretending that Jesus was only alongside the prisoners for a short

89. Moltmann, *The Crucified God: The Cross of Christ as the Foundation and Criticism of Christian Theology*, trans. R. A. Wilson and John Bowden (New York: Harper & Row, 1974), p. 40.

90. While some versions hedge on the translation, Luke 23:32 clearly says "two *other* criminals," thus identifying Jesus as a criminal himself. Eduard Schweizer calls it a "remarkable phrase" (*The Good News according to Luke*, p. 356).

91. Myers, *Binding the Strong Man*, p. 395.

time on the cross. Even before his arrest, in words that could be either joyful promise or harsh admonition, Jesus proclaimed that we do to him whatever we do to *any* and *every* prisoner, even to the very least of them (Matt. 25:31-46).

The profound scandal of Matthew 25:31-46 cannot be overlooked. Jesus' Jewish faith emphasized the transcendent holiness of God. Even God's name was so unutterably holy that it was not to be pronounced. One could never hope to see this holy and transcendent God face to face. One could only see the burning bush or hear the voice on Sinai. In the wilderness, the ragtag group of former slaves could not see God; they could see only the pillar in the sky leading the way toward the promised land (Exod. 13:21-22). One does not see God. How much more amazing, then, is Jesus' teaching that the "Lord" is to be met in the naked and the hungry, the homeless and the sick, the prisoners and the social rejects. What Jesus was telling his disciples is that, if you want to meet God face to face, the nearest you are going to come to it on this planet is to look into the faces of your sisters and brothers — and especially your sisters and brothers who have been declared unrighteous, unclean, unacceptable. It is not that we find God there; it is that God finds us there. That is where our faith is nurtured and bears fruit. There where we expect to meet monsters, we meet God instead. The opportunity to serve God lies there among the prisoners who have been reckoned to be least deserving of any service at all.

So, for Christians all talk of prisoners must begin and end with Christ Jesus. This is the position in which the Word places us. We are so placed that we cannot talk about prisoners without a recognition of Jesus the Prisoner. We are so placed that we cannot talk about prisoners without a clear recognition that it is precisely these men and these women who have a right to freedom, who have the *only possible* right to freedom — the right that is based in the Word and activity of God. By so placing us, the Word demythologizes all of our social realities. It is a scandal for all of us good, law-abiding citizens. We can no longer talk of people who are "paying their debt to society"; we must now talk of people who are robbed of their freedom. We can no longer talk of "monsters" who deserve to suffer; we must now talk of the call to serve Jesus by serving the least of the prisoners. Whether we hear them with joy or with fear and trembling, the Word so places us that we must hear the words of Jesus: the Good News is freedom for the prisoners.

Chapter IV

Prisons and the Churches

Behold, the men whom you put in prison are standing in the temple and teaching the people.

Acts 5:25

For some reason, round numbers on the calendar evoke expectations that time is about to end. The advent of a new century or (even more) a new millennium provokes speculations about whether God might be thinking it a propitious time to draw down the curtain on history. A certain arrogance is betrayed by the notion that God's deciding and acting on such matters is determined by the calendars that humans have concocted, but our calendars have been known to fuel assortments of millenarianism and apocalypticism nonetheless.

The year 1300 was an example. Though Joachim de Fiore had died in 1202, his apocalyptic theology remained a powerful force as the fourteenth century approached. The prophecies of Joachim even held sway among the Franciscans and other "orthodox" circles.[1] Among laypeople, a spirit of expectation prevailed. In 1300, something big was going to happen.

---

1. Orthodoxy is a tenuous designation. In 1318, Pope John XXII declared that some Franciscans (a group known as the "Spirituals") were entirely too serious about their vows of poverty. Absolute poverty was unorthodox, said John. Within five years, the whole Franciscan movement was pronounced heretical. While the order was later restored, Franciscan "orthodoxy" was repeatedly questioned.

127

And it did. Harking back to the teachings of Leviticus 25, Pope Boniface VIII proclaimed that 1300 would be a year of Jubilee. The Bible had declared that the Sabbath and Jubilee years were to be times of freedom; land was to be redistributed and slaves and prisoners were to be set at liberty. But the Jubilee of 1300 had precious little to do with the plight of the poor or slaves or prisoners. Instead, Boniface responded to the plight of the many people who feared eternal damnation. If Christ should appear in the clouds in 1300 (and the calendar itself suggested the possibility), preparations were in order. Rather than freedom from human captivity, the Jubilee of 1300 offered freedom from purgatory and hell.[2] From all over Europe, masses of people flocked to Rome in a mixed atmosphere of pilgrimage and carnival. No matter what his other motivations, Boniface recognized the Jubilee as an opportunity for the church to raise some badly needed funds. Indulgences were sought and acquired.[3] This was a Jubilee of freedom from the punishment of hellfire.

But the people of 1300 also had cause to beware of other punishments. The ecclesiastical hierarchy of the thirteenth century had shown itself to possess a certain zeal (if not paranoia) in searching out and extirpating heresy. Around 1220, Conrad Dorso, John the One-eyed, and several other self-appointed heretic hunters roamed the Rhine Valley and utilized blatant brutality in an effort to enforce their own understandings of the true faith. In part, it may have been a desire to forestall such independent efforts to combat heresy that led the papacy

2. The idea of purgatory as a "place" of virtual confinement and rehabilitation for those who lack qualifications for heaven is a comparatively late invention in the history of the church. Some attribute the idea to Dante (who was living in 1300), but while he may have contributed to systematizing the idea, purgatory antedates him by some years. For example, the German mystic Mechthild (ca. 1207-1282) alludes to purgatory in her visions of heaven and hell (Colleen McDannell and Bernhard Lang, *Heaven: A History* [New Haven: Yale University Press, 1988], p. 100). Jaroslav Pelikan notes that the germ of the idea might be traced all the way back to Origen's universalist hopes that the opportunities for purification and salvation might not end with earthly existence (*The Emergence of the Catholic Tradition, 100-600*, vol. 1 of *The Christian Tradition: A History of the Development of Doctrine* [Chicago: University of Chicago Press, 1971], p. 355).

3. For a description of the Jubilee of 1300, see Rosalind and Christopher Brooke, *Popular Religion in the Middle Ages: Western Europe, 1000-1300* (New York: Thames & Hudson, 1984), pp. 153-55.

gradually to develop a system that invested certain church officials with inquisitorial powers and regulated their procedures.[4]

The increasingly formalized procedures for rooting out alleged heresy were evident in the decades-long thirteenth-century battle against the Cathars in the region of Languedoc, France. As with many of the efforts to combat theological outlaws, a complex mixture of political and economic struggles contributed to ecclesiastical involvement in the attempt to rid Languedoc of Cathars, real and imagined. A crusade had been waged against the Cathars even before the inquisitors set about their work. Town after town fell to crusaders who sometimes cared little about the orthodoxy of their victims. As the walls of the town of Béziers were breached and the troops wondered how Cathars could be distinguished from other residents, a Cistercian abbot is said to have offered the memorable solution: "Kill them all! God will recognize his own."[5]

As the open warfare subsided, the Dominicans (founded in 1220) led the inquisitorial battle. Boys and girls as young as twelve were required along with the other citizens of Languedoc to swear allegiance to Rome and the hunt for Cathars, and they were required to renew the oath every two years. All were suspected of harboring Cathar sympathies who refused to take the oath, who possessed a Bible in the vernacular, who were absent from regular worship, or who displayed other abnormal behavior. Since the Cathars were known as ascetics, behavior suggestive of self-denial was prone to suspicion. When a suspect by the name of Jean Tesseire was summoned before the inquisitors, he pleaded his innocence: "I am not a heretic, for I have a wife and I sleep with her. I have sons. I eat meat, and I lie and swear and I am a faithful Christian."[6]

In fact, Tesseire had a valid point when he based his defense on his propensity for lying. Evidence suggests that when genuine Cathars

---

4. See Edward Peters, *Inquisition* (Berkeley and Los Angeles: University of California Press, 1989), p. 55. In the later sections of this book, Peters notes that "the Inquisition" never existed as a monolithic reality. It is more accurate to speak of inquisitorial powers accruing to certain offices within the church. If "inquisition" refers to ecclesiastical prosecution, there were many separate inquisitions throughout different periods of church history.

5. Cited by Otto Friedrich in *The End of the World: A History* (New York: Fromm International, 1986), p. 77.

6. Cited by Friedrich in *The End of the World*, p. 96.

(also known as "Albigenses") were hauled before tribunals, they were often quite forthright in professing their beliefs, even though such honesty carried heavy consequences. Inquisitors welcomed such professions of "guilt" but not claims of innocence. There seemed to be a presupposition that it was not for nothing that people were charged with heresy. The accusation itself indicated some form of guilt, and, for those who refused to confess it, other means were available for the extraction of truth. In the thirteenth century, torture was formally approved as a tool available to inquisitors. There were rules and regulations that ostensibly governed the use of torture. To be considered valid, a confession made under torture had to be freely repeated the following day without any torture being applied.[7] The regulations stipulated that inquisitors could have each defendant tortured only one time, but that restriction was effectively circumvented by inquisitors who counted successive days of torture as parts of a single episode. Since pregnant women were exempt from torture, many pregnant suspects were imprisoned so that torture could commence after they gave birth.[8]

Those who refused to recant their heresy after a finding of guilt and those who lapsed back into heresy after having recanted were handed over to secular authorities. Formally, inquisitors had no power to impose the death penalty, but handing alleged heretics over to civil authorities was the equivalent of sentencing them to death; it had been at the urging of the church that most secular laws required that unrepentant heretics be burned at the stake.[9] Those who recanted their heresy might be sentenced to penances of flogging, fine, or (increasingly during the thirteenth century) imprisonment. In regions where heresy was especially prominent,

7. Peters, *Inquisition*, p. 65.

8. Susan Jacoby, *Wild Justice: The Evolution of Revenge* (New York: Harper & Row, 1983), p. 133. The use of torture in trials antedates Christianity, but the introduction of torture into ecclesiastical trials may have been related to combat theories of trial. The Normans settled legal disputes through judicial duels with weapons in the belief that "the right" would win such battles. There was a presumption that torture set up analogous combat between the body and spirit of the accused. If the accused was actually innocent, no amount of bodily suffering would defeat the truth. On the impact of Norman trial by combat on our own jurisprudence, see Karl Menninger, *The Crime of Punishment* (New York: Viking Press, 1969), pp. 54-58.

9. The procedure of having heretics executed by secular authorities was endorsed by the thirteenth-century theologian Thomas Aquinas. See David Christie-Murray, *A History of Heresy* (New York: Oxford University Press, 1989), p. 108.

prisons were made available for the sole use of inquisitors. In other areas, inquisitors could rely on the prisons of bishops or monasteries. Offenders might be sentenced to *murus largus,* a form of imprisonment that resembled monastic existence, or *murus strictus,* confinement in a single cell.[10] The typical sentence was for "perpetual imprisonment," but the sincerity of the recantation could mitigate the actual time spent in prison. The recanting "heretics" of Languedoc knew that they could demonstrate their sincerity by naming others who shared in their heresy; in a decent show of concern for the living, they named mostly the dead. Acting on their information, Dominicans raided graveyards, disinterred corpses, and burned the departed.[11]

The inquisition at Languedoc was not the first time that the legal arm of the church reached beyond the grave. One of the more grotesque instances of prosecuting the dead occurred in 897, when Stephen VI exhumed the corpse of one of his predecessors, Pope Formosus. Clad in pontifical vestments, the decaying body of Formosus was present at the trial over which Stephen presided. Formosus was found guilty of a number of charges, including perjury. After a bit of ceremonial mutilation, the corpse was thrown into the Tiber River. Stephen's motivation in the whole grisly affair may have been a desire to have some of Formosus's ecclesiastical appointments declared null and void, but he misjudged his own stability in office. A popular rebellion deposed Stephen, and he was thrown into a prison where he was subsequently strangled. What was assumed to be the corpse of Formosus was retrieved from the Tiber and given proper burial.[12] This whole bizarre sequence of events took place during a period of decadence that was by no means typical of the papacy, but the exhumation and prosecution of the dead was a practice that recurred with some frequency.[13]

10. Peters, *Inquisition,* pp. 66-67.

11. Friedrich, *The End of the World,* p. 96.

12. The Lateran Basilica in which the corpse of Formosus was being tried happened to collapse during the trial proceedings, a piece of bad luck that further detracted from Stephen's public standing. At the time, most people understandably interpreted the collapse of the Basilica as a sign of divine disfavor. For accounts of these events, see J. N. D. Kelly, *The Oxford Dictionary of Popes* (New York: Oxford University Press, 1988), pp. 114-16; and Nicolas Cheetham, *Keepers of the Keys: A History of the Popes from St. Peter to John Paul II* (New York: Scribner's, 1983), pp. 75-76.

13. For a description of the seventeenth-century ecclesiastical trial of the exhumed corpse of Marco Antonio de Dominis, see Pietro Redondi, *Galileo: Heretic,* trans. Ray-

While there was general agreement and cooperation between medieval church and state on the punishments for heresy, there was often substantial disagreement on more basic jurisdictional questions. In a show of bravado, the same Pope Boniface who proclaimed the Jubilee of 1300 issued a bull entitled *Unam Sanctam* which very nearly claimed that papal power was absolute over all matters ecclesiastical *and* secular. While Boniface apparently took himself seriously, not many others did. The main accomplishment of Boniface's *Unam Sanctam* was to fuel the anger of medieval princes who had their own designs on absolutism.[14] The most for which Boniface and his successors could hope was that secular rulers would recognize the church's jurisdiction over clerics and monastic orders. Out of a fairly tenuous clerical immunity from capital punishment sprang a legal artifact known as "benefit of clergy." In theory, secular judges were barred from executing clergy, and so, prior to passing sentence, judges were expected to inquire into the profession of the defendant. In the fourteenth century, English monarchs recognized that clerical garb was too easily acquired and that more than a few defendants were falsely claiming benefit of clergy. A ruling was issued that the ability to read would be the sole criterion for determining the clerical status of the accused. Henceforth, anyone claiming benefit of clergy was required to read Psalm 51:1, a passage that became known as "the neck verse." Of course, a single verse was easily memorized, and many "clergy" saved their necks by "reading" the verse without even looking at the Bible in front of them. Benefit of clergy remained legally binding for some offenses as late as the nineteenth century in some regions of America. Still today, there is a judicial remnant of the medieval jurisdictional conflicts: in its historical origins, the opportunity for a defendant to

---

mond Rosenthal (Princeton: Princeton University Press, 1987), pp. 107-18. In many areas of Europe, punishment in the form of mutilation was inflicted on the corpses of those who committed suicide. As late as the nineteenth century in England, those who failed in suicide attempts were executed! See Jacoby, *Wild Justice*, pp. 133-34.

14. The jurisdictional disputes raged both before and after Boniface VIII. In the fifteenth century, a series of concordats between the papacy and various kingdoms sought (with limited success) to sort out questions of who should be tried and punished by whom. The history is traced by John A. F. Thomson in *Popes and Princes, 1417-1517: Politics and Polity in the Late Medieval Church*, Early Modern Europe Today Series (Boston: George Allen & Unwin, 1980), pp. 181-200.

speak before sentencing is provided so that benefit of clergy may be claimed.[15]

To get caught in the middle of jurisdictional battles between the medieval church and state could be deadly, as the members of the Order of Knights Templar discovered. Despite the bravado of Boniface's *Unam Sanctam,* one of his successors, Pope Clement V, found himself in a rather powerless position when King Philip IV of France decided to move against the Templars in 1307. The Knights Templar were originally organized as a military order to assist in the crusades of the church,[16] but King Philip's interest in them had more to do with the extensive Templar holdings of property and wealth in France. Philip sought to rally pressure for a papal inquisition against the Templars by trumping up charges that the Order was promulgating heresy and homosexuality.[17] On 13 October 1307, in an act that was both sudden and well-coordinated, Philip had all Templars in France arrested, and he called on other Christian rulers to do the same with the Templars in their own countries. Philip claimed that he took the action to defend the church against vile heresy, and he even managed to have some of the Templars confined in the prisons of French bishops. Pope Clement would have had legal grounds for protesting that Philip had no right to arrest the Templars or to make use of the prisons of the church, but in doing so he would have run the risk of showing just how powerless the papacy was in the face of disobedient secular rulers. Clement cloaked his anger in a show of courtesy. He communicated his appreciation for Philip's

15. George W. Dalzell, *Benefit of Clergy in America and Related Matters* (Winston-Salem: John F. Blair, 1955), p. 270.

16. On the origins of the Templars, see Richard A. Newhall, *The Crusades,* rev. ed., Berkshire Studies in European History (New York: Holt, Rinehart & Winston, 1963), pp. 54-56.

17. While most medieval inquisitors considered homosexuality to be the ultimate "unspeakable" crime, questions of jurisdiction intruded on the prosecution of homosexuals. Was homosexuality a "crime" against church or state or both? In 1509, the supreme inquisitor in Spain instructed church tribunals not to prosecute gay people unless heresy was also involved. In 1524, Pope Clement VII ruled that homosexuality sans heresy could indeed be prosecuted by the church. See Henry Kamen, *The Spanish Inquisition* (New York: New American Library, 1965), pp. 200-201. For additional information, see John Boswell's excellent study *Christianity, Social Tolerance, and Homosexuality: Gay People in Western Europe from the Beginning of the Christian Era to the Fourteenth Century* (Chicago: University of Chicago Press, 1980).

zeal in defending the church. His hand having been forced, Clement ordered an investigation of the Templars, but he showed his contempt by dragging out the investigation over a period of years. Philip badgered Clement with constant reminders that speed was of the essence if the church was to be defended, and he suggested that perhaps additional torture could be used to good effect against imprisoned Templars here or there. A considerable number of the Templars who languished in prisons were farm workers and cooks whose only involvement with the Order consisted of the manual labor they had provided for monasteries. On 12 May 1310, a bishop more loyal to king than pope had fifty-four Templars burned at the stake outside of Paris. The event made it clear that the remaining Templars could not depend on papal protection and that confession and recantation offered the best hope for survival. For the accused who confessed and recanted, inquisitors usually followed the procedure of first absolving them of their sins, then reconciling them to the church, then sentencing them to penitential punishment — often life in prison. In 1312, Pope Clement V grew tired of resisting Philip and issued a bull suppressing the Order of Knights Templar. By confiscating properties of the order, Philip became richer. Caught in the middle, many former Templars remained imprisoned.[18]

But Christians (heretical or otherwise) were not the only victims of the legal machinations of church and state. Greater horrors were inflicted on the Jews. Even by the medieval standards of ecclesiastical jurisprudence, there was no legal basis for church officials to claim jurisdiction over Jews. If legality mattered (and at times it did not), how was it that so many Jews were tried before ecclesiastical courts in medieval Europe? Part of the explanation is rooted in the crusades of the eleventh, twelfth, and thirteenth centuries. As crusaders traversed Europe on the avowed mission of retaking the Holy Lands from Muslims, their crusading zeal was often first expended on the Jewish communities they encountered along the way. The claim that the Jews were "Christ killers" served as a pretext for the attacks, but in many cases the crusaders were principally interested in nothing more than taking advantage of an opportunity to seize the property of Jews. Members of the Jewish communities were often summarily murdered, but

18. For a detailed record of these events, see Malcolm Barber, *The Trial of the Templars* (New York: Cambridge University Press, 1980).

at times they were forced to make a choice between death or "conversion" to Christianity. There were many Jewish martyrs who refused to renounce their faith, but some Jews chose conversion in the belief that they could thereby save themselves and their families and that they could revert to the Jewish faith once the crusaders had passed. Once they "converted" to Christianity, however, Jews were under the sway of ecclesiastical jurisdiction, and any indication of a return to Judaism was met with a charge of heresy. If any Jews sought to defend themselves by noting that their conversion had been forced by threats of death, such a defense was interpreted as an automatic sign of guilt, since the defendants were simultaneously admitting that they had become Christians and that they were lapsing from the faith; the death threats of the crusaders were considered irrelevant to the investigation of heresy. Many of the inquisitions in Spain focused their fury on the so-called "conversos" or "judaizers" — the unwilling converts who reverted to Jewish practice.[19]

For the Jews who remained beyond the pale of ecclesiastical jurisdiction, church councils (e.g., the Fourth Lateran Council at Rome in 1215, the Council of Arles in 1235) encouraged secular rulers to adopt and enforce anti-Jewish legislation, including a rule that all Jews should wear identifying yellow badges. In the mid-thirteenth century, the papal reigns of Gregory IX and Innocent IV were marked by additional efforts to claim church jurisdiction over the Jewish faith. It was brought to Pope Gregory's attention that some sections of the Talmud contained "blasphemies" against Christians and the Virgin Mary. There followed a series of inquisitional proceedings that historians have called "the trial of the Talmud." The books were found guilty. Pope Innocent IV declared that since Jewish leaders had not been responsible in maintaining their own doctrinal purity and adherence to the Old Testament, he would have to intervene for the sake of Jewish orthodoxy. Since the books were guilty of heresy, Innocent ordered that copies of the Talmud be burned — with the exception of a version edited by the church.[20] In theory, Jews possessing the heretical Talmud now came under ecclesiastical jurisdiction.

19. Kamen, *The Spanish Inquisition*, pp. 22ff.
20. James Muldoon, *Popes, Lawyers, and Infidels: The Church and the Non-Christian World, 1250-1550*, Middle Ages series (Philadelphia: University of Pennsylvania Press, 1979), pp. 30-31.

In times both modern and medieval, the persecutors of Jews have sought justifications in a variety of outlandish and pernicious rumors. Thousands of Jews were killed as the result of three tales that were especially prominent in medieval Europe. (1) When contagious plagues swept through a region, the illness was often claimed to be the result of Jews dumping poison into rivers and wells. When the "black plague" swept Europe in the mid-fourteenth century, Jews had to fear both the disease and the retribution of Christians. (2) There was a rumor that Jews used the blood of murdered children in Passover rituals. Whenever a Christian child was murdered or said to have been murdered, persecution followed. The dead Christian child was often elevated to a status of reverence, as with the death of St. Hugh of Lincoln in 1255 (after which eighteen Jews were executed in Lincoln, England) and the death of Good Werner near Oberwesel, Germany, in 1286 (after which forty Jews were executed and many more died at the hands of rioters). While they were spreading the rumor that Jews murdered children, those who professed to be Christians were themselves engaging in an ugly kind of child abuse: in some cases, the children of Jews that had been murdered in persecutions were baptized and raised as Christians, but in many cases they were sold into slavery. (3) In 1215, the doctrine of transubstantiation was declared dogma. Within only a few years, rumors started that Jews stole consecrated wafers and desecrated the host.[21] A surviving fifteenth-century German broadside uses drawings and captions to tell the story of the alleged desecration of the host in Passau, Germany, in 1478. It shows a Christian stealing eight wafers from a church and selling them to the Jews. The Jews take the wafers to their synagogue and stab them in a reenactment of the crucifixion. The wafers bleed, and the face of a child appears on one of them. The desecration is discovered, and the Jews are arrested and brought to trial. After all of the Jews are tortured and either beheaded or burned to death, their synagogue is converted into a church.[22]

---

21. As Lester Little notes, the doctrine of transubstantiation was met with incredulity in some quarters of Christendom. The rumors that the wafers bled when Jews drove nails into them may have been designed to combat Christian doubts that the wafers were literally the body of Christ. See Little's *Religious Poverty and the Profit Economy in Medieval Europe* (Ithaca, N.Y.: Cornell University Press, 1983), p. 52.

22. A copy of the broadside is reproduced by Simon Wiesenthal in *Every Day Remembrance Day: A Chronicle of Jewish Martyrdom* (New York: Henry Holt, 1987), p. 239.

A sad legacy of persecution links these Jews to another Jew who was tortured to death on a cross outside of Jerusalem. What had happened? The earliest church communities avoided courts of law. The earliest Christians were persecuted for efforts to follow their Lord, one who had proclaimed liberty for the captives. And yet by 1300 C.E., church courts and prisons and inquisitions struck terror into the hearts of many, and the Jubilee had been transformed into a Roman carnival.

The Early Church

If we bear in mind that the word *myth* is *not* a synonym for "false," it makes sense to speak of "the myth of the pre-Constantinian church." By their very nature, myths prize a story's spiritual and parenetic value more highly than its empirical historicity. The currency of myth is truth rather than fact. Of course, that is not to say that myths are devoid of facts. I personally believe that the myth of the pre-Constantinian church presents a historical characterization that, even though inaccurate in detail, is nonetheless fair. The radical discipleship of the early Franciscans and the early Anabaptists, of the Confessing Church in Germany and the Catholic Workers in America — these have all harked back to the reality and the vision and, yes, the myth of the early church.

We ought not to labor under the illusion that the early church was free from fallibility. As Dale Brown notes, "One has only to be aware of the issues involved in Paul's correspondence with the Corinthian church to recognize that the early church was not constituted by morally pure, doctrinally sound, well-ordered members."[23] Still, Brown observes that the fallibility of the early church does not preclude the possibility of finding normative models for faith and faithfulness within the story of the early church community. There is a sense in which looking to one's roots constitutes not only a historical investigation but also a search for direction. Our understanding of the roots of the faith community has as much to do with the future as with the past.

It is clear that the early church had special concerns for prisoners,

23. Brown, *The Christian Revolutionary* (Grand Rapids: William B. Eerdmans, 1971), p. 31.

partly because of the admonitions expressed in the Hebrew Scriptures and in the logia of Jesus, but also because many members had personal acquaintance with prisoners and prisons. In the pre-Constantinian church, the visitation of prisoners was a responsibility shared by all believers, not only deacons and church leaders. In view of the periods of imperial intolerance toward Christianity, visiting a believer in prison involved no small risk, but the risks were taken because the imprisoned faithful were respected and the visits served as a conduit for relaying their letters and teachings back to local congregations. It was not that the imprisoned were viewed as inherently possessing more wisdom than others, but a biblical tradition dating all the way back to Joseph (Gen. 39:20-21) and Jeremiah (32:26; 33:1) held that God's revelations were often communicated through prisoners. In the annals of the early church (Acts 5:18-20; 12:6-9; 23:11), prisoners were visited by angels and given the gift of the Spirit. The prison diaries of two women martyred at Carthage — Perpetua in 203 C.E. and Quartillosa in 259 C.E. — tell of the horrors of prison life. But Perpetua and Quartillosa also wrote of the dreams and visions that filled them with courage and certainty of a life beyond their own impending deaths.[24]

So visitors brought the writings of prisoners back to local congregations, but the visits also served as a means for churches to provide food and other support for the imprisoned. In his "Apology," Justin Martyr specifically mentions the prisoners along with the widows, the orphans, and the sick as those who should be supported by church offerings.[25] Bishop Dionysius of Corinth appealed to churches for supplies to send "to the mines," a reference to the fact that the Romans sentenced many prisoners

---

24. For a description of Perpetua's prison diary, see Robin Lane Fox, *Pagans and Christians* (New York: Alfred A. Knopf, 1987), p. 401. On the diaries of both Perpetua and Quartillosa, see Peter Brown, *The Body and Society: Men, Women and Sexual Renunciation in Early Christianity* (New York: Columbia University Press, 1988), pp. 141-42. Brown comments that "in the legacy of courage, at least, men and women were remembered as equal within the Christian Church."

25. Justin Martyr, "Apology," in *Readings in Christian Thought*, ed. Hugh T. Kerr (New York: Abingdon Press, 1966), p. 26. One early critic of Christianity sought to provide evidence of the gullibility of believers by telling the story of a certain prisoner who was supposedly living a life of leisure due to the abundance of food and gifts provided by the church. See Lucian of Samosata, "The Story of Peregrinus," in *The Fathers of the Primitive Church*, ed. and trans. Herbert A. Musurillo (New York: New American Library, 1966), pp. 109-10.

to hard labor in stone quarries and mines.[26] The distribution of food to prisoners became such a hallmark of the church that the Emperor Lucinius imposed sharp restrictions on the practice.[27]

The work of the church involved not only visiting and feeding but also actually procuring release for prisoners by paying ransom or bail.[28] The writings of Tertullian and Clement of Rome and the "Apostolic Constitution" contain references to those who set about the work of freeing prisoners, often at great self-sacrifice. Clement refers to some individuals within the church who sold themselves into slavery in order to feed the hungry or ransom prisoners.

Were these services of visiting, feeding, and ransoming prisoners offered by churches to their own members only, or were they also extended to nonbelievers and so-called "common criminals"? The cases most often reported by the early church seem to deal with Christians ransoming other Christians, but that is hardly unusual, since at various times large numbers of believers were imprisoned.[29] There is ample evidence to indicate, however, that the whole array of services provided by the early church was by no means restricted to members. The Emperor Julian, in an attempt to revive paganism, instituted a program of imperial charities to counter the "disgraceful" fact that the church communities "support not only their own poor, but ours as well." The ransoming of prisoners continued even after the reign of Constantine, and this later ransoming was clearly *not* a matter of procuring release for those jailed for their faith. Ambrose of Milan melted down gold in order to ransom "criminals" held prisoner, an act that caused grumblings in the local community.[30]

---

26. Dionysius of Corinth is quoted by George H. Williams in "The Ministry of the Ante-Nicene Church (c. 125-325)," in *The Ministry in Historical Perspectives*, ed. H. Richard Niebuhr and Daniel D. Williams (New York: Harper, 1956), p. 34. Norman Johnston notes that both classical Greece and Rome established prison camps in mines and quarries ("The Human Cage," in *Correctional Institutions*, 2d ed., ed. Robert M. Carter, Daniel Glaser, and Leslie T. Wilkins [Philadelphia: J. B. Lippincott, 1977], p. 3).

27. See Adolf Harnack, *The Mission and Expansion of Christianity in the First Three Centuries*, trans. and ed. James Moffatt (New York: Harper, 1961), pp. 163-64.

28. Paul Johnson, *A History of Christianity* (New York: Atheneum, 1979), p. 62.

29. During the Diocletian persecution, e.g., a regular church was formed at the prison camp of the Phaeno mines (Harnack, *Mission and Expansion*, p. 164).

30. Gerald Austin McHugh, *Christian Faith and Criminal Justice: Toward a Christian Response to Crime and Punishment* (New York: Paulist Press, 1978), p. 18. Pope

In the pre-Constantinian church, believers on the whole refused to work as judges, magistrates, or prison guards. (There is a long-standing debate about a few cases in which individual church members may have held these positions, but these would have been rare exceptions to the rule.) The legal apparatus of the Roman Empire was virtually an arm of the military. Garrisons served as prisons, and soldiers served as prison guards. Believers refused to become soldiers, especially because of the biblical admonitions against all forms of violence but also because the soldiers' oath of allegiance to the emperor was regarded as idolatrous. Thus, Hippolytus's "Apostolic Tradition" has these instructions for the catechumenate: "Anyone who has the power of the sword or the magistrate of a city who wears purple, let him give it up or be dismissed." In "De Pallio," Tertullian declares that the Christian is "no judge, no soldier." Clement of Alexandria notes that believers refused to assume official positions in courts of law in addition to heeding the Pauline admonitions against taking others to court.[31]

Even though the early church community declined participation in the official functions of the state, and even though the state was often a persecutor of the church, it is not accurate to say that the church held a totally negative attitude toward governing authorities. Its attitude might better be characterized as dialectical, holding in tension Romans 13 and Revelation 13. Polycarp affirmed that the magistrates are ministers of God, and Hippolytus reminded believers that the empire was the beast, but the two likely would have agreed with each other. Perhaps Tertullian best captured the irony of the church's dialectical attitude. While many church leaders called for prayer for public officials on the basis of the biblical admonition to do so, Tertullian called for prayer for the state on the basis of the biblical admonition to pray for one's enemies. Clearly, the early believers shared none of the later proclivity for identifying the law of the state with divine law. With reference to human

---

Pelagius I (556-561) was known for ransoming prisoners of war, and the "Roman Penitential" (c. 830) directs that some of the money collected from penances "be spent for the redemption of captives" (William A. Clebsch and Charles R. Jaekle, *Pastoral Care in Historical Perspective: An Essay with Exhibits* [Englewood Cliffs, N.J.: Prentice Hall, 1964], p. 152).

31. See Jean-Michel Hornus, *It Is Not Lawful for Me to Fight: Early Christian Attitudes toward War, Violence, and the State* (Scottdale, Pa.: Herald Press, 1980), pp. 159-60.

law, the second-century Christian philosopher Tatian asserted that "all law is relative"; while it should be noted that Tatian later became a Gnostic, his identification of the state's law as relative was shared by many within the church.

Of course, loyal Romans viewed all this as insolence. In the second century, the philosopher Celsus wrote a work entitled *True Doctrine* in which he charged Christians with "revolution" and "sedition." The refusal of Christians to be involved with the military and the magistracy showed their true identity as "enemies of humanity." If Christians were really concerned about the public welfare, wrote Celsus, they ought to "accept public office in our country . . . for the sake of the preservation of the laws of piety." In *Octavius*, a third-century dialogue between a pagan and a Christian, Minucius Felix depicted the pagan as being offended by the irresponsibility of Christians, who, he said, simply "do not understand their civic duty."[32]

Unfortunately, beginning in the fourth century, Christians not only came to understand "civic duty," but they also helped to enforce it.

Christendom

It was either late on the day of 28 October 312 or early the next morning that Maxentius's body was located among the hundreds of corpses floating in the Tiber River. Amid confusion and carnage, he had apparently fallen off the Milvian Bridge and drowned. After his body was fished out of the Tiber, it was decapitated and his head was impaled on the end of a lance. Thus displayed, the head of Maxentius was carried through the streets of Rome and subsequently shipped to northern Africa as proof that he was indeed dead and that Constantine was the sole ruler of the western region of the Roman Empire.[33] As it was shipped here and there, the severed head of Maxentius not only announced the reign of Constantine but also foreshadowed the birth of Christendom.

While Galerius was firmly established as ruler in the eastern portion of the empire, the western struggle between Constantine and Max-

---

32. Celsus and Minucius, quoted by Robert L. Wilken in *The Christians as the Romans Saw Them* (New Haven: Yale University Press, 1984), pp. 117-18.

33. A. H. M. Jones, *Constantine and the Conversion of Europe*, rev. ed. (New York: Collier Books, 1962), p. 72.

entius had been brewing for several years. When war came in 312, thousands were killed in battles in and around the towns that lined Constantine's path to Rome. Both Maxentius and Constantine put great stock in the superstitions of their day, and, as the decisive battle for Rome approached, both sought to avail themselves of magical assistance. For his part, Maxentius consulted the oracles and was apparently oblivious to the ambiguity of the message he received: "On this day the enemy of the Romans will fall." As Maxentius marched out of Rome to do battle with Constantine, owls were perched on the city walls.[34] The signs were not auspicious.

There is less clarity about the magical assistance sought by Constantine. He was an adherent of Apollo, and throughout his life (even after the events of 312) he gave public homage to Apollo's sign, the Sun.[35] Indeed, in March 321, he issued a law that all work should cease on "the venerable day of the Sun" — Sunday.[36] But something is reported to have happened on the eve of the battle at Milvian Bridge. It was not something that significantly altered his faith in Apollo and the Sun, but it did lead him to include Jesus in a sort of solar pantheon. One story has it that, prior to the battle, Constantine and all his troops saw a cross superimposed over the sun along with the words "In this conquer" written across the sky. But this particular version of the event first appeared after the death of Constantine in an account written by Eusebius, a notoriously obsequious Christian biographer. A different story claims that Constantine had a dream in which Christ promised him the victory. Whatever the source of the conviction, Constantine came to believe that his victory was attributable to the Christian God — sort of. Erected in 315, Constantine's triumphal arch bore the inscription "Because under the impulse of divinity and by the might of his own spirit, using just weapons, he has vindicated the common weal against the tyrant and his faction."[37] So, three years after the event, the identity of the "divinity" who provided the impulse remained vague.

34. Hans Lietzmann, *A History of the Early Church*, vol. 3, trans. Bertram Lee Woolf (New York: Meridian Books, 1961), pp. 74-75.

35. Ramsay MacMullen, *Christianizing the Roman Empire, A.D. 100-400* (New Haven: Yale University Press, 1984), p. 44.

36. Jones, *Constantine and the Conversion of Europe*, p. 88.

37. Cited by Hermann Dörries in *Constantine the Great*, trans. Roland H. Bainton (New York: Harper & Row, 1972), p. 31.

In many respects, imperial Rome was little changed by the reign of Constantine. Citizens could still marvel at the imperial court intrigues that left several of Constantine's relatives dead under what might generously be called "suspicious circumstances." The worst of Roman institutions were still maintained, including slavery and the legislation that demanded that slaves who attempted escape should be mutilated and imprisoned in the mines.[38] Rome remained militarily adventurous, seeking to expand its frontiers against "barbarian" threats. When Constantine "converted" to Christianity and gave official recognition to the church, much within the empire was unchanged.

It was the church that underwent dramatic changes that can fairly be called "the Constantinian fall of the church." Only two years after Milvian Bridge, Constantine took it upon himself to deal with the Donatist controversy within the church by calling for a conciliar meeting at Arles. Besides addressing the potential schism, the 314 Council at Arles took tentative but significant steps in the direction of affirming a Christian role in the maintenance of the newly tolerant state. In a ruling that can only be described as contorted by anguished compromise, the Council ruled that members of the church could take up the sword as soldiers, but they should not use the sword, but they also should not put the sword down in times of peace. In other words, Christians could perform police functions in times of peace as long as they did not shed blood in the process, and they could also march with troops into battle as long as they themselves did not do any of the battling. An equally incredible compromise was reached with regards to the magistracy: Christians could assume public office as long as their bishops determined that their official functions and decisions were in accord with church standards; if conflicts arose, Christian magistrates should either surrender their office or be dismissed from the church.[39] Of course, such a tortured sense of balance could not be maintained for long. It was only a short time until the ranks of the military and the magistracy were filled by the churched (with the exception of church officials, who were granted a special exemption by Constantine). There was soon enough the spectacle of soldiers marching into the river and being baptized while holding their right hands out of the water; by remaining

38. Dörries, *Constantine the Great*, p. 92.
39. Dörries, *Constantine the Great*, pp. 111-12.

unbaptized, those hands could still wield the sword. By 438, the Theodosian Code declared that *only* Christians could be soldiers, since the presence of those who believed in pagan gods might jinx the fortunes of the army.[40]

With the Constantinian era, accounts begin to appear of Christian involvement in the imprisonment of others. Constantine's "conversion" and tolerance rendered some believers less suspicious of the state's system of "justice." With the official recognition of the church, there was a nearly simultaneous hardening of the church's definition of orthodoxy — this at the urging of Constantine, who apparently hoped that an official religion with a single creed might enhance the chances for unity in his empire. Alongside such credalism, the fourth century marked the advent of what has come to be known as "canon law." In order to enforce the new definitions of orthodoxy and canon law, some church leaders developed a theology of "immanent judgment," which held that the church could serve as an instrument of God's wrath by imposing imprisonment or other punishments on heretics. Actually, one of the earliest forms of punishment administered by the new, official church was not imprisonment but exile. There was a problem, however, with the practice of sending heretics and apostates into exile. The Constantinian church had acquired pretension to being a universal church to match the universal nature of the Roman Empire. If heretics were exiled, the heresy would go with them; if heretics were imprisoned, their dissent might be contained.[41] And so one of the earliest accounts of Christian involvement in the imprisonment of others has to do with the imprisonment of rival bishops by Athanasius, bishop of Alexandria and defender of "orthodox" Christianity against Arianism.

Early in the fifth century, Augustine provided the church with a philosophical basis for participation in the imprisonment and punish-

---

40. Roland H. Bainton, *Christendom: A Short History of Christianity and Its Impact on Western Civilization*, vol. 1 (New York: Harper & Row, 1966), p. 103.

41. Even later, banishment was most often utilized as a form of punishment by the civil authorities rather than by the church. In medieval history, when there were overlapping civil and ecclesiastical judicatories, civil courts were likely to banish dissidents and some other criminals, while church courts imposed sentences involving penitential acts, imprisonment, or even death, to be administered at the hands of secular authorities. See Richard Kieckhefer, *Repression of Heresy in Medieval Germany*, Middle Ages series (Philadelphia: University of Pennsylvania Press, 1979), p. 76.

ment of others. In his struggles with Manichaeism and the question of theodicy, Augustine maintained that moral evil springs from free will rather than from any independent forces of evil. Free will can be met by coercion. If coercive techniques are utilized by governmental officials for the divinely ordained purposes of the state, certainly the church can likewise avail itself of that authority for its own goals. Augustine, you will recall, was one of the first to identify the kingdom of God with the earthly church.[42] In an interesting use of Scripture, Augustine found not only justification but a virtual mandate for the church's use of coercion in the parable of the banquet in Luke 14: when the invited guests failed to show, the host sent servants out to "compel" the poor, the blind, and the lame to come to the banquet (14:23). Indeed, Augustine even saw an endorsement of coercion in the account of Paul's conversion on the road to Damascus: "You also read how he who was at first Saul, and afterwards Paul, was compelled, by the great violence with which Christ coerced him, to know and to embrace the truth."[43]

Unlike some later theologians, however, Augustine did not endorse the death penalty, and he grew squeamish at some of the torture techniques common to state prisons. He thought it best to examine heretics "not by stretching them on the racks, nor by scorching them with flames or furrowing their flesh with iron claws, but by beating them with rods." Augustine believed that church and state should be allies in holding back the chaos that would result from unpunished lawlessness. Punishment would serve to spoil the "sweet taste of sinning."[44]

While the pre-Constantinian church declared that its members should not be magistrates, by the Middle Ages, the most influential magistrates were bishops of the church. A long line of popes had their primary training in the law.[45] In many areas of Europe, canon law and secular law were indistinguishable from one another, and, with juris-

42. See "Kingdom of God," in *The Oxford Dictionary of the Christian Church* (New York: Oxford University Press, 1957), pp. 768-69.

43. For a discussion of the alarming implications of this statement, see Frederick A. Norwood, *Strangers and Exiles: A History of Religious Refugees*, vol. 1 (New York: Abingdon Press, 1969), p. 107.

44. Augustine, quoted by Johnson in *A History of Christianity*, pp. 116-17.

45. Joseph R. Strayer, *Western Europe in the Middle Ages* (New York: Appleton-Century-Crofts, 1955), pp. 105-6.

dictional disputes raging, it was often a combination of circumstance and chance that determined whether an offender was tried in a civil or ecclesiastical court.[46]

Penal accoutrements were devised to accompany the courtly ways of the medieval church. Some of the earliest prisons of the church were located in monasteries, a development that was influenced by the communal style of various orders and by the very architecture of the monasteries. The sixth-century Benedictines at Monte Cassino stressed the corporate nature of their monastic life. Living quarters were arranged with groups of ten to twenty monks staying in the same large dormitory rooms. Short of excommunication, the most severe form of punishment

---

46. Among some twentieth-century believers committed to reforming the modern court system, there has been an unfortunate tendency to romanticize both the efficacy and the compassion of ecclesiastical courts in the Middle Ages. Such a tendency is discernible in "Toward a Christian Approach to Criminal Justice," an address delivered by Marlin Jeschke to "The Church and Criminal Justice" Conference sponsored by Mennonite Central Committee Offender Ministries Program, Evanston, Illinois, 18-20 September 1980. Jeschke correctly notes that the dual system of ecclesiastical and civil courts eventually gave rise to a medieval version of (it must be emphasized) *limited* protection from double jeopardy: "Pope Sixtus IV in 1484 demanded that if somebody was absolved in the confessional, that decision was binding upon the secular courts. So if a person had committed an offense and then ran to the priest, made confession and did repentance, whether it was always genuine or not, and the priest absolved him, that person could not thereafter be seized by the secular courts and punished, which treatment usually was much more harsh."

Jeschke then seeks to apply the lessons of the Middle Ages to the modern system: "We might suppose that a uniform criminal code would be more just than a dual church and state system, although the variations from state to state in American law are just about as extreme as those two ways in the Middle Ages. But at least the Medieval system offered one thing that is not available in all of today's American criminal justice process — the opportunity for repentance, amendment of life, and forgiveness. In that regard the Medieval system was much more Christian than our practice, where repentance, if it is offered at all, is offered by the church or chaplaincy *alongside* the legal process but is hardly ever an *alternative* way of dealing with offenders."

Certainly Jeschke's critique of the modern system is more compelling than his praise of the medieval system. The offenses addressed by medieval ecclesiastical courts included theological and political dissent, and, whether for these or other offenses, the confessions and penitential attitudes of the accused were not infrequently elicited by means of torture. In fact, the punishments meted out by medieval church courts were often more severe than those imposed by the civil authorities. And, as we have seen, when church courts reckoned that offenders were not sufficiently repentant or that they had lapsed back into their sinful ways, they might be handed over to the state for execution. Double jeopardy: torture by the church, execution by the state.

administered to disobedient Benedictine monks was flogging.[47] Other orders placed a greater emphasis on solitude, however, and provided individual cells for nuns and monks. In these convents and monasteries, the architecture was conducive to the practice of punishing disobedient sisters or brothers by confining them for periods of penitential solitude in their cells. As early as 600, special cells were set aside to confine those who were being punished. Some of these cells were underground and could be entered only by means of a ladder lowered through a hole cut into a vaulted ceiling.[48] As special cells were set aside for punishment, what had started as fairly brief periods of penitential confinement turned into long periods of imprisonment — including the possibility of life imprisonment for monks and nuns who had committed major infractions.[49]

At an early stage in the development of the monastic prison cells, some of the people imprisoned there were not monks; they were slaves and children. Some orders were not averse to owning slaves in an effort to bring monastery land into agricultural production. The Bavarian Laws of the eighth century (c. 745) provided penalties for anyone who killed one of these "church slaves" or for anyone who "persuades a church slave or maidservant to flee."[50] Slaves who showed a propensity

47. See *The Rule of St. Benedict,* trans. Anthony C. Meisel and M. L. del Mastro (Garden City, N.Y.: Doubleday, 1975), pp. 70-73.

48. Johnston, "The Human Cage," p. 5. Johnston observes that "in Eastern Europe, especially Austria and Russia, monastic prisons with a larger number of underground cells continued to be used well into the 20th century."

Throughout history, many tyrants who reckoned that they were in need of extra prisons took note of the suitability of convent and monastery architecture. Under Robespierre's reign of terror, a list of prisons in Paris reveals that many of them were situated in confiscated monasteries and convents (Olivier Blanc, *Last Letters: Prisons and Prisoners of the French Revolution, 1793-1794,* trans. Alan Sheridan [New York: Farrar, Straus & Giroux, 1989], pp. 217-18). Of course, the seizure of monastic property was motivated by more than just architecture. In the anticlerical spirit of Robespierre's reign, many priests and nuns and monks were imprisoned in confiscated convents and monasteries (Simon Schama, *Citizens: A Chronicle of the French Revolution* [New York: Alfred A. Knopf, 1989], pp. 633-35).

49. E.g., the rules for the Order of Knights Templar stipulated that any member guilty "of grievously killing a Christian man or woman" or "of the crime of sodomy" could be sentenced to "perpetual imprisonment" (Barber, *The Trial of the Templars,* p. 255).

50. *Laws of the Alamans and Bavarians,* trans. Theodore John Rivers (Philadelphia: University of Pennsylvania Press, 1977), pp. 119-20.

to escape were confined in cells when they could not be kept under direct supervision. But slaves were not the only unwilling guests of monasteries and convents. Early in church history, "unwanted" children (often the children of parents who could not afford to support them) were abandoned at church meeting houses or monasteries. By the sixth century, the practice was formalized into a procedure known as "oblation," whereby children were literally donated to monasteries. In the words of the Rule of Benedict, these children were "offered to God's service," and the offering was accompanied by a ceremony in which children's hands were symbolically fettered.[51] These oblates provided a valuable source of labor, and, by the seventh century, both ecclesiastical and civil legislation ruled that the children were not permitted to leave the monasteries. Since "the piety of their parents" had led them to be donated, they were to remain in the monastery even after they had grown to adulthood.[52] If any oblates attempted escape, they were confined in monastic cells. Slaves and children formed a historical bridge between the use of monastic cells to confine disobedient monks and nuns and the later use of monasteries to imprison large numbers of heretics, dissidents, and other "criminals."

While monasteries were some of the earliest prisons of the church, they were soon joined by dungeons and prisons of popes and bishops. Mont St. Michel in France (built between the eleventh and fourteenth centuries) was originally an ecclesiastical prison that was later used as a civil and military prison.[53] The prisons of the church were designed not merely as holding tanks for those awaiting trial but as facilities for long-term imprisonment. In the thirteenth century, following the dispute between the papacy and Emperor Frederick II, one of Frederick's sons was imprisoned in a papal dungeon for a period of forty-five years. Indeed, in some areas of Europe during the various inquisitions of the thirteenth century, the sentence most frequently pronounced by the church against "heretics" was not death but life imprisonment. When an inquisition was launched in a certain region, the bishop's prisons as well as the prisons of the civil authorities were often filled. In the crusade against the Beghards

51. *The Rule of St. Benedict*, p. 95.
52. See John Boswell, *The Kindness of Strangers: The Abandonment of Children in Western Europe from Late Antiquity to the Renaissance* (New York: Pantheon Books, 1988), pp. 232-35.
53. Johnston, "The Human Cage," p. 5.

in northern Europe, there are records of inquisitors confiscating the houses of executed Beghards and converting them into prisons for the next batch of dissidents.[54] There were other punishments for the accused who abjured their heresy. One bishop in Bavaria suggested that the penance for reformed heretics should be a period of submitting to regular beatings by the parish priest and lying in front of the church meeting house door so that the faithful could walk on them after worship.[55]

As the medieval church became increasingly involved in judicial and penal matters, some within the church maintained a commitment to ransoming and feeding prisoners. Founded in 1198, the Order of Trinitarians has provided a remarkable witness over the years by ransoming many, often by way of Trinitarian monks exchanging themselves for captives. Cervantes was among those freed by the efforts of Trinitarians, and in more recent times, Trinitarians worked with some success at procuring the release of black people who had been enslaved — this even during periods when the larger church was unwilling to issue a clear renunciation of slavery.[56] But apart from the work of the Trinitarians and some other individuals, the services extended by the medieval church to prisoners seem like crude parodies of those offered in the pre-Constantinian situation. While the early church had ransomed prisoners of lowly means, accounts from the Middle Ages record special ecclesiastical interest in ransoming lords and princes taken prisoner during war. In 1298, for example, when the nobleman John de St. John was held prisoner in France following hostilities between France and England, the monastery at Gloucester participated in his ransoming.[57]

---

54. Kieckhefer, *Repression of Heresy in Medieval Germany*, p. 37.

55. Kieckhefer, *Repression of Heresy in Medieval Germany*, p. 65.

56. "Trinitarians," *Oxford Dictionary of the Christian Church*, p. 1375. It should be noted that medieval Jewish communities were also active in ransoming captives, often Jews who had been taken prisoner by Christians or Muslims. See Gabriel Sivan, *The Bible and Civilization*, New York Times Library of Jewish Knowledge (New York: Quadrangle, 1973), pp. 97-98. When Moses Maimonides was in Egypt, political unrest from 1169 to 1171 resulted in hundreds of Jews being seized and sold into slavery. In the rabbinic tradition of *pidyon shebuim* (the delivery of captives), Maimonides raised funds and organized committees for the ransom of the captives. See Jacob S. Minkin, *The Teachings of Maimonides* (Northvale, N.J.: Jason Aronson, 1987), pp. 68-69.

57. William E. Lunt, *Papal Revenues in the Middle Ages*, 2 vols., Records of Civilization: Sources and Studies, no. 19 (1935; reprint, New York: Columbia University Press, 1962), 1:170-73. It is clear that some prisoners of war as well as some other

It had been a full millennium earlier that the church was busy feeding prisoners; during the time of the medieval inquisitions, the bishop was expected to provide bread and water in special cases of poverty, but most prisoners were required to provide their own food either through the support of their families or through direct payments for board to the appropriate church judicatories.[58]

In the civil prisons of the Middle Ages, prisoners seem to have fared no better nor worse than those in the prisons of the church. State penal standards were often based on the examples provided by church prisons. During periods of social and political unrest, there were dramatic expansions in the numbers of people imprisoned by various states, but, ironically, periods of upheaval were also marked by expansions in state-sponsored relief and social welfare programs. The institution of harsher criminal penalties along with the simultaneous expansion of welfare programs points to social control as the primary function of both criminal law and relief. The state's primary concern was (and, we might add, is) for social order, not for the victims of either crime or poverty.[59] During periods of labor shortage, civil authorities not only curtailed state welfare programs but also occasionally outlawed private charity. In 1349, after the Black Plague had depleted the labor force in England, the Statute of Laborers provided a prison sentence for anyone who gave alms to beggars.[60]

In the prisons of the church, custody over prisoners was exercised at several levels of ecclesiastical administration. Popes, bishops, and inquisitors all had prisons, and a prison was even maintained by the camera, the papal financial administration. The camerarius (minister

---

captives were intentionally held with an eye to extracting ransom. In 1074, Pope Gregory VII wrote, "Pilgrims going to or returning from the shrines of the Apostles are captured, thrust into prison, tortured worse than by any pagan and often held for a ransom greater than all they have" (*The Correspondence of Pope Gregory VII: Selected Letters from the Registrum,* trans. Ephraim Emerton [New York: W. W. Norton, 1969], p. 40). Gregory's description of conditions in France here may have been somewhat exaggerated, however, given the fact that he made no secret of his rancor toward the French King Philip I.

58. Johnson, *A History of Christianity,* pp. 254-55.

59. For historical examples that illustrate this point, see Frances Fox Piven and Richard A. Cloward, *Regulating the Poor: The Functions of Public Welfare* (New York: Vintage Books, 1971), pp. 8-22.

60. Piven and Cloward, *Regulating the Poor,* p. 36.

of finance) initially had criminal jurisdiction over the camera staff, papal debtors, and situations with potential impact on papal finance. But there was a gradual expansion of the juridical powers of the camera; in 1363, it was given jurisdiction over pirates and later over common civil suits that had no direct relationship to the papal treasury.[61]

The camera received reports from the regional treasurers of the church on all income derived from prisoners' payments for board.[62] Accounts of expenditures were also forwarded to the camera, as in the following report which appears in the Vatican Archives:

> And first, on Wednesday, 5 December 1414, I, Stephen, bishop of Volterra, gave from the moneys of the register, at the order of the lord vice-camerarius, to the proctor of the convent of the order of Preachers of Constance for enclosures and implements of iron for strengthening the prisons of the said convent for holding John [H]us, heretic, and the hiring of watchers for the said John [H]us and the keeping of him, up to the festival of St. Matthew the apostle; in all he had 15 gold florins of the camera.[63]

In terms of attitudes toward law and order and punishment of wrongdoers, the changes brought by the Protestant Reformation were less than dramatic. Some church historians have noted that the impetus for the Reformation had as much to do with the emerging nationalism in northern Europe as with theology. The respect that both Calvin and Luther demonstrated for lawyers, magistrates, and civil law betrays something of their alliances with the aristocracy and nationalist princes. In contrast, the common folks were less beguiled by the charms of those who wrote and enforced the laws. The popular ballads and fables that circulated on the eve of the Reformation indicate that many peasants viewed magistrates and law enforcers as their oppressors. The Robin Hood legends that began circulating in England as early as the thirteenth century show that many people thought their interests were better served by outlaws than by law enforcers. An animal epic called "Reynard the Fox" originated in Germany and was told and retold throughout most of Europe. In one section of a 1498 version, Reynard the Fox comments on justice: "Thus

61. Lunt, *Papal Revenues in the Middle Ages*, 1:21-22.
62. Lunt, *Papal Revenues in the Middle Ages*, 2:18.
63. Cited by Lunt in *Papal Revenues in the Middle Ages*, 2:508.

our king the lion has sitting in council with him a select band of robbers, whom he holds in great honor and makes the greatest among his nobles. But let the poor wretch Reynard take a chicken, and you'll see them pounce upon him and scream, 'To the gallows with him!' Little crooks are hanged; big crooks govern our lands and cities."[64]

John Calvin's attitude toward law and order was partially shaped by his training as a lawyer. During his studies at Bourges and Orléans, he published a commentary on Seneca's essay on clemency,[65] a work that doubtless influenced his admonitions to magistrates in the *Institutes*. Calvin warned magistrates not to "favor undue cruelty," but he seemed even more concerned that the magistrates would fall into a "superstitious affectation of clemency, fall into the cruelest gentleness." He warned that "it is indeed bad to live under a prince with whom nothing is permitted; but much worse under one by whom everything is allowed."[66]

In theocratic Geneva, clearly not everything was allowed. Church and civil authorities were allied in holding back lawlessness. Calvin always stressed the prevalence of human wickedness and the need for strong governing authorities who could restrain it. But while he was thus keenly aware of how the fall had given rise to human sinfulness, it was almost as if he believed that human laws and governments were immune from its effects. In his commentary on Romans, Calvin maintains that even blatant tyranny teaches helpful lessons about obedience and serves the vital purpose of conserving society.[67]

64. Excerpts from "Reynard the Fox," in *Manifestations of Discontent in Germany on the Eve of the Reformation*, ed. and trans. Gerald Strauss (Bloomington, Ind.: Indiana University Press, 1971), p. 91.

65. William J. Bouwsma, *John Calvin: A Sixteenth-Century Portrait* (New York: Oxford University Press, 1988), p. 10.

66. Calvin, *Institutes of the Christian Religion*, Library of Christian Classics, vols. 20-21, ed. John T. McNeill, trans. Ford Lewis Battles (Philadelphia: Westminster Press, 1960), 2:1498-99 (4.20.10). It is worth noting how Calvin's desire to avoid both "undue cruelty" and "cruelest gentleness" worked itself out in the case of Michael Servetus. Calvin had Servetus arrested and found guilty on charges of heresy. The town council sentenced Servetus to be executed by burning. Since Calvin saw a need for zeal in the defense of orthodoxy, he agreed with the death sentence, but he thought that burning was too cruel a mode of execution for Servetus. Calvin notwithstanding, Servetus was burned. See Bouwsma, *John Calvin*, pp. 27, 244n.115.

67. For an excellent summary of this aspect of Calvin's thought, see Michael Walzer, *The Revolution of the Saints: A Study in the Origins of Radical Politics* (Cambridge: Harvard University Press, 1965), pp. 30-38.

Calvin did not believe that reconciliation is the goal of human justice. In view of human wickedness, he thought that reconciliation smacked too much of utopia, "a foolish fantasy the Jews had."[68] Nor did Calvin subscribe to the contention of the medieval church that punishment could serve as a form of penance and that wrongdoers might escape God's wrath later by suffering punishment now. Indeed, Calvin viewed judicial punishment not as a means of escaping God's wrath but as an *expression* of God's wrath. The magistrate "carries out the very judgments of God," he wrote.[69] But this immanent divine punishment by the magistrates should in no way lead the wicked to assume that they will escape a second dose:

> If the judgments of God are so dreadful on this earth, how dreadful will he be when he shall come at last to judge the world! All the instances of punishment that now inspire fear or terror are nothing more than preludes for that final vengeance which he will thunder against the reprobate. Many things which he seems to overlook he purposely reserves and delays till that last day. And if the ungodly are not able to bear these chastisements, how much less will they be capable of enduring his glorious and inconceivable majesty when he shall ascend that awful tribunal before which the angels themselves tremble![70]

As a means of maintaining what little righteousness remained in the community, Calvin placed great stock in the avoidance of pollution.[71] The reprobate should be punished with execution or imprisonment or exile not to extract a penance for sins but in order to defend the community from their polluting influence. Besides which, magistrates were not permitted to refuse to inflict the punishments of God to which, in a sort of divine double jeopardy, God would add still more punishments later.

Like most other Protestant reformers, Calvin drew no significant distinctions between "crime" and "sin." The Reformation in England was marked by a stiffening of criminal laws against such behaviors as

68. Calvin, quoted by Walzer in *The Revolution of the Saints*, p. 47.

69. Calvin, *Institutes*, 2:1497 (4.20.10).

70. Calvin, *Commentary on Isaiah*, quoted by Bouwsma in *John Calvin*, p. 42.

71. Bouwsma cites examples of what he calls Calvin's "obsessive pollution imagery" (*John Calvin*, p. 36). There is, notes Bouwsma, a certain contradiction in Calvin's stress on human wickedness and simultaneous concern for the avoidance of pollution.

fornication, drunkenness, foul speech, and "Sabbath breaking."[72] Martin Luther bemoaned the fact that theft was punished with more severe criminal penalties than the "more grievous" sin of adultery.[73]

The consistency of Luther's two-kingdoms theology was put to a test when he sought to address matters of crime and punishment. On the one hand, Luther said that heresy was a spiritual matter and that it should not be opposed by the power of the sword (he was doubtless aware of those in the Roman Church who were leveling charges of heresy against him). Yet he argued that Anabaptists such as Thomas Münzer should be restrained by the state, since these particular "heretics" constituted a threat of rebellion. Cutting his distinctions still finer, Luther also granted the governing authorities the power to regulate the outward manifestations of faith (e.g., rebaptism) but not interior matters of belief. While Luther tried to maintain a comprehensible dividing line between spiritual and temporal kingdoms, Lutheran churches were actually governed by councils on which state officials had substantial representation.[74]

Luther's delicate distinctions between his two kingdoms were also evident in the ethical guidance he offered to individual believers. In effect, he called on believers to maintain allegiance to both an individualized biblical discipleship and corporate civic obligations. Luther believed that the state had a responsibility to punish lawbreakers so that a modicum of order could be maintained. Christians should turn the other cheek to those who had wronged them personally, said Luther, but Christians were also duty-bound to participate in the state's prosecution of criminals. "If you see that there is a lack of hangmen, constables, judges, lords, or princes, and you find that you are qualified," he wrote, "you should offer your services and seek the position, that the essential governmental authority may not be despised and become enfeebled or perish. The world cannot and dare not dispense with it."[75]

72. Joy Cameron, *Prisons and Punishment in Scotland from the Middle Ages to the Present* (Edinburgh: Canongate, 1983), pp. 18-19.

73. William A. Mueller, *Church and State in Luther and Calvin: A Comparative Study* (Garden City, N.Y.: Doubleday, 1965), p. 50.

74. See A. G. Dickens, *The German Nation and Martin Luther* (New York: Harper & Row, 1974), p. 69.

75. Luther, "Temporal Authority: To What Extent It Should Be Obeyed," in *Luther: Selected Political Writings,* ed. J. M. Porter (Philadelphia: Fortress Press, 1974), p. 58.

In assisting with the maintenance of temporal order, the hangman is giving expression to love of neighbor. Of course, Luther confessed that the state is fallible, but even though a person be wrongly imprisoned, freedom is an element of the spiritual kingdom and not of earthly circumstance.[76]

The Anabaptists rejected Protestant endorsements of Christian participation in the legal system. Anabaptism represented a return to the early church's dialectical attitude toward the magistracy. When called before the courts, Michael Sattler and others addressed the magistrates as "servants of God." Still, the Schleitheim Confession admonished believers against assuming the position of magistrate. Felix Manz, arrested on charges of sedition, explained that "no Christian could be a magistrate, nor could he use the sword to punish or to kill anyone, for he had no Scripture for such a thing."[77] Manz was imprisoned in an Augustinian monastery in Zurich.

Anabaptists also revived the early church tradition of service to the imprisoned. Their efforts in this area flowed from biblical leadings but also from concern for the many Anabaptists who were imprisoned. There is a record of two Sulingen Brethren, John Weck and Clemens Knepper, visiting two imprisoned Brethren at Juelich Fortress and offering to take their place in prison; the general in charge declined the request, saying that he was only the servant of the judge.[78]

---

76. Luther, "Admonition to Peace: A Reply to the Twelve Articles of the Peasants in Swabia," in *Luther: Selected Political Writings,* p. 82. Despite publishing some rather fearsome opinions concerning how the state should deal with outlaws, Luther retained an awareness of biblical concerns for prisoners. In "The Fourteen of Consolation" (1520), he cites as one of the "duties" of the works of mercy to "endeavor to set free the prisoners" (see Clebsch and Jaekle, *Pastoral Care in Historical Perspective,* p. 211).

77. Manz, quoted by William R. Estep in *The Anabaptist Story* (Grand Rapids: William B. Eerdmans, 1975), p. 29.

78. See Donald F. Durnbaugh, *European Origins of the Brethren* (Elgin, Ill.: Brethren Press, 1958), p. 259. Records show that later Brethren service to those being persecuted by the civil authorities was not limited to other Brethren. During the American War of Independence, Martin Urner, a Church of the Brethren preacher from Chester County, Pennsylvania, was arrested for giving breakfast to escaped prisoners of war. Urner was suspected of British sympathies, a not uncommon charge against the Brethren, who then were struggling with a question prompted by Romans 13: Who constituted the governing authorities? The British or the Americans? Urner wrote from his prison cell, however, that he had fed the escaped prisoners "not because they were British" but because they were people (Richard K. MacMaster, *Christian Obedience in*

One of the most vociferous critics of the Anabaptists was John Calvin. In an essay entitled "Brief Instruction for Arming All the Good Faithful against the Errors of the Common Sect of the Anabaptists," Calvin seems to place greater distance between himself and the Anabaptists than between himself and Rome. Lest one doubt the intensity of Calvin's attack, it is worth noting the epithets he uses to describe the Anabaptists in just one section of this essay: blasphemers, frantic people, scatterbrains, poor fools, these giddy people, silly, wretches, perverse.[79] Calvin wrote that just "as a drunk after belching loudly throws up foul broth," so also the Anabaptists, "having reviled this holy calling which our Lord so esteemed, vomit finally at the top of their voice far more disturbing blasphemies."[80]

Besides hurling epithets, Calvin sought to refute the Anabaptists by arguing points of Scripture. Predominating in his biblical arguments is an effort to demonstrate that, if the Anabaptists were correct in discerning biblical admonitions to refrain from reliance on the sword and the magistracy, then there were several points at which the Bible contradicted itself. If the Anabaptists were to understand the Bible correctly, said Calvin, it would become obvious to them that "our Lord did not want to change anything about the government or the civil order, but without reviling it in any way, He made His office, for which He came into the world, that of forgiving sins."[81] Ultimately, however, Calvin's arguments against the Anabaptists are based not so much on the Bible as on social and political necessity:

> Besides, if it is not lawful for a Christian man to enter into litigation with anyone in order to settle quarrels regarding possessions, inheritances and other matters, then I ask these good theologians, what will become of the world? . . .

Revolutionary Times: The Peace Churches and the American Revolution [Akron, Pa.: Mennonite Central Committee Peace Section, 1976], p. 25). Actually, with many prisoners of war on both sides, escapes were not uncommon. The Americans relied on makeshift prisons, while the British commandeered churches to use as prisons in New York and elsewhere (Charles H. Metzger, *The Prisoner in the American Revolution* [Chicago: Loyola University Press, 1971], p. 46).

79. Calvin, *Treatises against the Anabaptists and against the Libertines*, ed. and trans. Benjamin Wirt Farley (Grand Rapids: Baker Book House, 1982), pp. 80-91.

80. Calvin, *Treatises against the Anabaptists and against the Libertines*, p. 89.

81. Calvin, *Treatises against the Anabaptists and against the Libertines*, p. 83.

Thus it is easy to see that these miserable fanatics have no other goal than to put everything into disorder, to undo the commonwealth of property in such a way that whoever has the power to take anything is welcome to it. Though they firmly deny this with vigor! But let all trials and arbitration be taken from the world, according to their wish, and what will happen . . . except wholesale robbery?[82]

It would "ruin the world" if reprobates went unpunished, so Calvin hoped that magistrates and lords would not fall prey to the teachings of Anabaptists, for "the devil speaks through their mouths in order to lead princes astray and to hinder them from doing their duty."

Finally, wrote Calvin, by advocating a path that would lead to the dissolution of civil order, the Anabaptists had revealed themselves to be "the enemies of God and of the human race."[83] Calvin may have been unaware that the Roman philosopher Celsus had used those same words for exactly the same reasons to denounce the early church.

Prison Reform/Prison Entrenchment

In its very origins, the title *chaplain* bespeaks something gone awry. The word *chapel* derives from the late Latin *cappella* meaning "cape," in this case the cape of Martin of Tours.[84] Martin was a soldier who lived in the fourth century, but upon converting to Christianity, he believed that his new faith did not permit him to kill or inflict injury on anyone. He left the army, founded a monastery, and devoted himself to monastic life and service of the poor. After his death, the attribution of miracles to Martin led to his canonization and eventual sainthood. Articles that had once belonged to him were revered as relics, among them his cape. In the seventh century, there is reference to the chapel as the structure that housed Martin's cape when it was carried (of all places!) into battle. The kings of France believed that the cape had special powers that would help them to defeat their enemies, and "chaplains" were assigned to carry the cape of this nonviolent man into war.

The irony of their work was apparently lost on the chaplains of

---

82. Calvin, *Treatises against the Anabaptists and against the Libertines,* p. 85.
83. Calvin, *Treatises against the Anabaptists and against the Libertines,* p. 91.
84. See "Chapel," in *Oxford Dictionary of Christian Church,* p. 263.

the seventh century, or, if they felt it, they kept it to themselves. Today, prison chaplains who are serious about their faith and their work cannot help but feel that they are in a position characterized by similar irony — or, more precisely, characterized by an impossible balancing act. Out of church, state, prison, guards, prisoners, themselves, and the Lord who calls them to ministry and to discipleship, to whom are they responsible? To all of the above? And if to all, what happens when the inevitable conflict arises between two or more of those allegiances? What happens if confidential contact with prisoners gives the chaplain information that the guards "ought" to know? Who pays the chaplain, and why would the prison administration even permit a chaplain's presence unless he or she were viewed as "part of the team"? No matter what the other "rehabilitation" or "treatment" responsibilities of the staff, the primary duty of a prison staff is to see that the prisoners remain imprisoned. Is security also the chaplain's concern?

Chaplains figured prominently in the prison reform movements that swept Europe and the United States in the eighteenth and nineteenth centuries. But chaplains were not so much the instigators of reform as they were the beneficiaries. The movements to reform prisons were also movements to reform prisoners, and many of the major reform advocates believed that the placement of chaplains in all prisons would provoke the reformation of both the institutions and the offenders. It was due primarily to these reform movements that the chaplaincy has become a regular part of prisons in Western Europe and the United States.

But the prison chaplaincy itself antedates the reform movements of the eighteenth century. One antecedent of the prison chaplaincy lies in the role played by clerics in the church prisons of the Middle Ages. At a time when many prisoners were confined on charges of heresy, clergy who were concerned for the spiritual welfare of the prisoners understood it as their responsibility to convince the imprisoned of the seriousness of their errors. Priests were usually authorized to offer communion to those who had been sentenced to prison after having renounced their heresy, but clergy were expected to help elicit the confessions of those who had not yet confessed their guilt. In fact, ecclesiastical rules stated that a prisoner could not be considered to have been tortured properly unless a cleric was present.[85]

85. Barber, *The Trial of the Templars*, p. 114.

The Protestant Reformation produced an additional influx of "heretics" who had to be convinced of their errors. It was from the professional soldiers of the Roman Church, the Knights of St. John, that King Louis XIV of France learned the art of developing a galley fleet and using prisoners to power the oars. From the middle of the seventeenth century to the early eighteenth, a significant number of Huguenots were imprisoned on French galleys. The Catholic priests on board these ships served as both military and prison chaplains, and their ecclesiastical superiors gave instructions that their work with the prisoners should focus on efforts "to provoke abjurations." The efforts to provoke conversion were as likely to rely on brutality as on kindness. Until Louis XIV himself called a halt to the practice in the early eighteenth century, galley prisoners received one hundred lashes for failure to doff their caps when in the presence of the communion bread and cup. One chaplain priest, Jean-François Bion, renounced his Catholicism and became a Protestant due to his disgust with the floggings administered at the behest of chaplains.[86]

The sufferings of Protestants gave rise to martyrologies, the most influential of which was a "Book of Martyrs" written by John Foxe and first published in English in 1563.[87] To hear Foxe tell it, after the pre-Constantinian Romans, the papacy was the source of all persecution. He clearly did not believe that the Catholics who were being persecuted in England during his own time qualified as martyrs. As Catholics were led to the gallows, Protestant clergy usually rode by their side and harangued them about their dying opportunities for repentance and conversion. An especially fearless seminary priest named John Hewett, executed 5 October 1588, entered into theological argument with the Protestant chaplains as he stood on the gallows.[88] In sixteenth-century England, many Catholic priests were executed under charges of treason

---

86. Paul W. Bamford, *Fighting Ships and Prisons: The Mediterranean Galleys of France in the Age of Louis XIV* (Minneapolis: University of Minnesota Press, 1973), pp. 120-21.

87. The work by Foxe (or Fox) remains in print and continues to be influential in some Protestant circles. See *Fox's Book of Martyrs: A History of the Lives, Sufferings and Deaths of the Early Christian and Protestant Martyrs*, ed. William Byron Forbush (Grand Rapids: Zondervan, 1967).

88. John Bellamy, *The Tudor Law of Treason: An Introduction* (Toronto: University of Toronto Press, 1979), p. 193.

in ways a good deal more grisly than simple hanging. With Protestant chaplains haranguing on the sidelines, the condemned priests were strapped to boards. The executioner would cut off their genitals, slit them up the abdomen, and remove their intestines. Not infrequently, the victim was still conscious as these organs were burned. Finally, the executioner would remove the heart and burn this as well. The execution of a priest named Edmund Jennings caused some stir when his prayers to St. Gregory continued even after his heart had been removed. Jennings's executioner was said to have exclaimed, "God's wounds! His heart is in my hand and yet Gregory is in his mouth."[89]

The grisly treatment at the hands of executioners was nearly matched by the horrid conditions inside the gaols of England. During the period of the English Revolution, radical representatives of groups such as the Levellers, Diggers, and Seekers responded to prison conditions not with a call for reform but with a call for abolition. In an anarchist work entitled *The Law of Freedom in a Platform* (1652), Gerard Winstanley noted that it was only covetousness that motivated criminal penalties for theft, and since only the Giver of life could justifiably take life away, the execution of murderers was itself murder.[90] One of Winstanley's contemporaries, William Erby, noted that prisoners and the poor were "chief among the oppressed," while "clergymen and common lawyers are the chiefest oppressors."[91] During the same period, John Warr wrote *Administrations Civil and Spiritual*, a philosophy of law that was virtually based on the emerging Quaker idea of the "inner light." Warr suggested that the legal "Forms" of this world must be swept away to make room for God's holy "confusion." If we could put aside the structures of legalism, rulers would lose the very foundation of their might, and it would become clear that "God favours all weak things."[92]

As with the early Christians and the Anabaptists before them, the concern of the Society of Friends for prisoners grew quite naturally out of Quaker experiences with imprisonment. In the mid-seventeenth century, George Fox was held captive at a number of prisons in England.

89. Bellamy, *The Tudor Law of Treason*, p. 205.

90. Christopher Hill, *The World Turned Upside Down: Radical Ideas during the English Revolution* (New York: Penguin Books, 1975), pp. 134-35.

91. Erby, quoted by Hill in *The World Turned Upside Down*, p. 270.

92. For a helpful summary of Warr's writing, see Hill, *The World Turned Upside Down*, pp. 272-76.

He often preached to other prisoners, and he addressed crowds outside Lancaster Gaol through his prison window.[93] Other Friends were imprisoned in colonial North America, and Fox appealed for contributions to send assistance to them.[94] Several Quakers in New England were hanged, and it was only after petitioning from English Quakers that a royal decree ended the hangings.[95] In April 1659, 164 Friends appeared in the chambers of Parliament and asked to take the place of other Quakers who were suffering in prison, a request that Parliament denied.[96] Quakers and others in the Free Church tradition were more effective in procuring the release of debtors from prison. A Baptist pastor named Thomas Lambe (d. 1686) used his personal wealth and the contributions of others to free hundreds of debtors.[97]

But one of the earliest and most renowned of the prison reformers was John Howard, who was neither a Quaker nor an especially radical nonconformist. Born in 1726, Howard was a member of the Congregational Church, but he eventually joined the Church of England. He was a man of no small wealth whose own concerns for prison conditions grew not from being a prisoner (though he was briefly held captive by the French in 1756) but from being appointed High Sheriff of Bedford in 1773. What Howard saw at Bedford Prison horrified him.

While all prisons in eighteenth-century England were ostensibly the property of the king, the gaols scattered throughout the country included many that were in effect under the private control of an assortment of lords, bishops, and other gentry. While these individuals

93. J. Arthur Hoyles, *Religion in Prison* (New York: Philosophical Library, 1955), pp. 2-3.

94. The text of a letter Fox wrote in 1662 appealing for such assistance is reproduced in *Every Need Supplied: Mutual Aid and Christian Community in the Free Churches, 1525-1675*, ed. Donald F. Durnbaugh, Documents in Free Church History Series (Philadelphia: Temple University Press, 1974), pp. 195-96.

95. For a description of the martyrdom of these New England Quakers, see David D. Hall, *Worlds of Wonder, Days of Judgment: Popular Religious Belief in Early New England* (New York: Alfred A. Knopf, 1989), pp. 186-89. Hall notes that these early Quakers went to the scaffold with a belief in "the inversion of the meaning of punishment." While Calvin had viewed earthly punishment as a mere prelude to the greater wrath that God would inflict on the reprobate, the Quakers understood their own punishment as a sign that the greater wrath of God would fall not upon themselves but upon the magistrates who sentenced them.

96. *Every Need Supplied*, p. 201.

97. *Every Need Supplied*, p. 176.

who operated prisons were theoretically responsible to the king, there were instances in which even county sheriffs or royal representatives were denied entrance for prison inspections. There was considerable pecuniary interest in operating a gaol, since prisoners were required to pay not only their board but also an array of seemingly arbitrary fees and taxes. In some prisons, prisoners who received from relatives or friends any extra money over the amount required for board would be subject to a sort of "luxury tax" imposed by the gaoler. Some gaolers made additional money by charging passers-by for the opportunity to gaze through the gaol windows at the imprisoned.[98] Robert Hughes has described how the Bishop of Ely turned a profit in the prison he operated:

> On entering the Bishop of Ely's lockup, a prisoner was chained down to the floor with a spiked collar riveted round his neck until he disgorged a fee for "easement of irons." Any jailer could load any prisoner with as many fetters as he pleased and charge for their removal one at a time. The "trade of chains," though often denounced as a national disgrace, survived well into the 1790s.[99]

With the exception of debtors, offenders in eighteenth-century England were usually not incarcerated as a result of having been sentenced to prison. The gaols were places where the accused awaited trial, transport, hanging, whipping, or other punishment. In practice, however, it was not uncommon for people to remain imprisoned for life because they lacked the money to gain release. At prisons in Clerkenwell and Leicester, for example, special release fees were levied, along with an additional fee for "turning the key" at the time of discharge. If a prisoner was unable to pay these fees, he or she would not be let out even if a court had already ordered the release.[100] The fees structure of the English gaols went with settlers to colonial North America. And so in Massachusetts, for example, even as the late seventeenth-century judicial and religious persecution of women known as the "Salem witch trials" ground to a tenuous halt, several women continued to languish

98. D. L. Howard, *John Howard: Prison Reformer* (London: Christopher Johnson, 1958), pp. 16-17.

99. Hughes, *The Fatal Shore* (New York: Alfred A. Knopf, 1987), p. 37.

100. Howard, *John Howard*, pp. 16-17.

in prison. Though Massachusetts Governor William Phips granted a reprieve and "jail delivery" for the accused who had escaped the executions of 1692, these women were not released until they had paid their jailers for board and what amounted to rental for the shackles that had bound them. Sometimes relatives were unable or unwilling to come to the financial aid of "witches." Mary Watkins and a Caribbean woman named Tituba were released only when they agreed to remain indentured servants of the strangers who paid their jail fees. Others remained locked up for years. Sarah Daston died in jail.[101]

The churches of England bore complicity in the horrid conditions of the gaols. In fact, when the Protestant Reformation came to England, the jails and prisons that had been run by the Roman Catholic Church were merely transferred to Protestant ownership. In some towns, the church building itself served as the jail. Some prisoners were shackled to "the jougs," chains and iron rings anchored into the walls of churches. In the Scottish towns of Dundee, Edinburgh, Inverness, and Perth, church steeples served as prisons. Offenders were chained to the inside walls of steeples, and one or two of them would occasionally be brought down on Sundays to sit on "stools of repentance" before the righteous. There are several reports of prisoners who hanged themselves in the steeples, but it was not the suicides that eventually led some church members to object to the penal use of the steeples. St. Giles in Edinburgh stopped jailing offenders in the steeple because parishioners complained that the prisoners dropped pebbles on them during worship.[102]

But as some churches were busily chaining prisoners to jougs and steeples, others were engaged in charitable efforts. Even prior to the flurry of reform activity in the eighteenth and nineteenth centuries, some churches in England took up collections specifically for hungry prisoners. Begging grates were a common feature of gaols, and the offerings begged at these grates combined with the collections from the churches provided the sole means of sustenance for some of the poorer prisoners. At Christmastime in the cities, prisoners were grouped into long lines and chained to one another so they could be led through the streets to beg.[103]

101. Marion L. Starkey, *The Devil in Massachusetts: A Modern Enquiry into the Salem Witch Trials* (Garden City, N.Y.: Doubleday-Anchor Books, 1969), pp. 230-31.

102. Cameron, *Prisons and Punishment in Scotland from the Middle Ages to the Present*, p. 33.

103. Hoyles, *Religion in Prison*, p. 49.

John Howard's contribution was to move beyond charity to question the whole fees structure of the English prison system. The reforms he successfully urged on Parliament included the abandonment of the fees structure, the appointment of salaried officials for the administration of prisons, and the imposition of guidelines for improved sanitation. Howard's reform efforts won respect partially because of his extensive experience in visiting and evaluating prisons throughout England and elsewhere in Europe. He vigorously proceeded with his visitations despite the considerable risk of contracting "gaol fever" — a risk that prompted numerous gaolers to refuse to accompany Howard into the wards of their own prisons. Howard provided accounts of his prison visitations in *The State of the Prisons* (1777) and *Account of the Principal Lazarettos in Europe* (1789), two books that remain indispensable for their descriptions of European prisons in the eighteenth century.

While the last officially sanctioned use of the rack in English prisons was in 1726, Howard's travels included visits to other European prisons where torture was still commonplace. Except for the use of torture, Howard considered the prison system in Holland to be enlightened. At the Dutch prison in Deventer, however, Howard noted that torture was used to induce confessions of guilt from prisoners who had already been tried and convicted but who were still maintaining their innocence. Howard denounced the torture he found in northern and central Europe, including the practice in a Munich prison of holding two crucifixes in front of prisoners who were being tortured. In Spain, Howard intended to visit the prisons of the inquisition, but he was granted admission only to a limited number of "interrogation" rooms.

It would be misleading to mention the humanitarian nature of Howard's reform efforts without also stressing the theological motivation behind these efforts. Indeed, some of Howard's observations indicate that he saw spiritual deprivation as a form of abuse more harmful than physical maltreatment. Consequently, after he visited slave ships at Naples, Howard made no comment on the morality of slavery or the practice of chaining people to each other and to the ship, but he praised the presence of chaplains and the frequent opportunities for worship. Likewise, after his visit on board the pope's prison galleys at Civita Vecchia, Howard approvingly noted the presence of priests to serve the spiritual needs of the prisoners.[104] In *The State of the Prisons,* Howard wrote that every prison should have a chaplain "who is in principle a Christian; who will not content himself with officiating in public, but will converse with the prisoners; admonish the profligate; comfort the sick, and make known to the condemned that mercy which is revealed in the Gospel."[105]

Howard's work eventually received enthusiastic support from John and Charles Wesley, both of whom visited prisoners and preached among them, as did a Methodist named Sarah Peters whose work among prisoners led to her death by "gaol fever." Howard, the Wesleys, and others involved in the eighteenth-century reform movement were convinced that faith could have a rehabilitative impact in the lives of prisoners. There was, in effect, a dual thrust to much of their work: reform of the system and spiritual regeneration of the individual.

The British prison reformers of the eighteenth century were clearly innovative and humanitarian, but in important respects they also reaffirmed the penology of their own age. Their advocacy of public administration of prisons made ecclesiastical prisons and jails in steeples and gaols run by bishops things of the past. But these efforts demonstrate the reformers' belief that the church had played the *wrong* role in prisons, not that it should have *no* role. In fact, these reformers believed that religion held the best hope — perhaps the only hope — for the transformation of prisoners. Genuine biblical concerns led them to challenge the harsh treatment of caged people but not the caging itself. Unlike the seventeenth-century Levellers and Diggers and Seekers, the eighteenth-century reformers were not outraged by the prison walls. They believed that Christians were not called to challenge the walls or those who built them but rather to challenge the prisoners inside the walls. It was a popular

104. By the time of Howard's visit, the temporal power of the papacy was already in decline, and some of the penal trappings of an earlier era were fading with it. But the decline did not continue unabated. Early in the nineteenth century, Pope Leo XII (1823-1829) reasserted the juridical power of the church in what amounted to a reign of terror in the papal states of Italy. Censorship was imposed, Jews were confined to ghettos, and police-state tactics were employed to sniff out sedition. Thousands were imprisoned, and executions were not uncommon. The repression was continued by two of Leo's successors, and it was not until the pontificate of Pius IX (1846-1870) that an amnesty was declared (Cheetham, *Keepers of the Keys,* pp. 254-57).

105. Howard, quoted by Howard in *John Howard,* p. 57.

belief among wealthier Christians that poor people constituted a "criminal class" and that poverty and criminality were both indicative of defects
in character. In a sense, each individual was viewed as a microcosm of the
larger society, and just as it was believed that society would collapse into
chaos without proper governance, so too it was believed that each individual was responsible for exercising governance over his or her "will"
and "passions."[106] Once individuals lost governance of their own passions, religious conversion offered the only hope for rising up from
poverty or criminality. In one model, the profligate might be won to
conversion by hearing of the horrible wrath of God: if nothing else, fear
might motivate them to regain governance of their passions. In a different
model, the poor and the criminals were encouraged to give over control
of their passions to a loving God who would bring order into lives that
had been allowed to slip into disorder. What was the problem? The
criminal class. What was the answer? Religious conversion.[107] As Europe
was exploring lands previously unknown to white people, missionaries
encountered many who were ripe for proselytism. But as prison chaplain
John Clay later noted, "Whatever may be the claim of the swarthy uncon-

106. Philip Greven notes that similar beliefs were prominent among Protestants
in early America. Writing to her son in 1780, Abigail Adams emphasized that "the due
Government of the passions has been considered in all ages as a most valuable acquisition" (*The Protestant Temperament: Patterns of Child-Rearing, Religious Experience, and
the Self in Early America* [New York: Alfred A. Knopf, 1977], p. 210).

107. It should be noted that these convictions were hardly limited to eighteenth-
and nineteenth-century England. American evangelicalism has also exhibited a tendency
to act as though the poor were both especially prone to sin and especially ripe for
conversion. On middle-class biases in the development of American evangelicalism, see
George M. Marsden, *Fundamentalism and American Culture: The Shaping of Twentieth-
Century Evangelicalism, 1870-1925* (New York: Oxford University Press, 1980). American
evangelicals have also tended to view the "religious conversion" of prisoners and those
of lower socioeconomic standing as the answer to crime. The nineteenth-century prison
ministry of organizations such as the "Prison Discipline Society" and individuals such
as Phoebe Palmer (a Methodist evangelist) tended to focus on the distribution of Bibles
and tracts to prisoners. See Whitney R. Cross, *The Burned-Over District: The Social and
Intellectual History of Enthusiastic Religion in Western New York, 1800-1850* (Ithaca, N.Y.:
Cornell University Press, 1982), p. 236; and Timothy L. Smith, *Revivalism and Social
Reform: American Protestantism on the Eve of the Civil War* (New York: Harper & Row,
1965), p. 169. The point here is not to criticize these evangelists, who were at least
showing active concern for prisoners; the point is to question the assumptions that the
poor are more inclined to criminality than the rich and that those who violate the laws
of the state are in more urgent need of conversion than are law-abiding citizens.

verted natives of an opposite hemisphere, it is not a *better* claim than that of our own countrymen."[108] Prisoners were heathens in the very belly of Christendom.

Heathens are best converted at a distance. While some Christians have shown a proclivity for supporting proselytism on foreign shores, that has not necessarily been an indication that the unwashed would be welcome in the neighborhood. Prisoners are heathens too close. And so began the shipment of prisoners out of Europe. As the European powers explored lands that were deemed ripe for colonizing, the establishment of penal colonies became a way of laying claim to the land. The prisoners were canaries in the mines. If, through forced labor, the prisoners were able to establish settlements and raise crops and survive the onslaught of "savages," then more genteel settlers could be certain that the air was safe to breathe. The Portuguese sent prisoners to Brazil, the French to New Hebrides, and the British to everywhere, or so it seemed. There were British penal colonies in North America and in the Caribbean and, most notorious of all, in Australia. The British prisoners were rejected by their homeland and deemed unfit to live in England, but their British identity helped to establish England's claim to a far-flung empire.

In the early days, the prisoners who were transported from England had all been convicted of capital crimes, and the transportation was in lieu of hanging. Of course, for poor people in eighteenth- and nineteenth-century England, it took no more than adolescent pranks or minor thievery to bring a sentence of death. Elizabeth Powley was sentenced to hang for stealing bacon, flour, butter, and raisins; her death sentence was suspended, and she was shipped to Australia. In 1786, Thomas Gearing stole a communion plate from Magdalen College Chapel, and he too was scheduled to hang but got transported instead.[109] When a court sentenced prisoners to death, they were taken to a separate holding area of the prison, and there was a cruel waiting period before they would be informed whether their sentences had been confirmed or suspended. For those who were actually going to be killed, it was the responsibility of the prison chaplain to read to them the confirmation of their sentence. But prisoners who were spared from the

---

108. Clay, quoted by Philip Priestley in *Victorian Prison Lives: English Prison Biography, 1830-1914* (New York: Methuen, 1985), p. 99.

109. Hughes, *The Fatal Shore*, pp. 72-73.

noose only to face transport hardly had cause for joy. Not infrequently, transport was a different kind of death sentence. While British public officials and clerics spoke of how the natural beauty and honest labor in Australia would have a beneficial impact on the wayward, many knew that the prisoners who were sent there faced a hellish life. When prisoners faced hanging or transport as the result of a conviction for theft, the victims of their crimes would sometimes seek to intervene on their behalf.[110]

The decision of whether to hang or transport a prisoner was influenced by considerations other than a judge's estimation of the seriousness of the crime or the character of the prisoner. In the seventeenth century, decisions about whether to transport specific prisoners to Jamaica were clearly influenced by reports on the waxing and waning need for laborers on Jamaican sugar plantations.[111] But the late eighteenth- and nineteenth-century transport to Australia was a larger enterprise. It was unthinkable that the sons and daughters of rich people would be banished to Australia for stealing apples, but not so for the daughters and sons of the poor. "The final aim of the transportation system," notes Robert Hughes, "... was less to punish individual crimes than to uproot an enemy class from the British social fabric. Here lay its peculiar modernity."[112] Also uprooted were the aboriginal people of Australia. Some died of diseases introduced by Europeans, some were hunted and gunned down, and some were intentionally poisoned like vermin.

Where the prisoners went, the chaplains went too. One of the earlier chaplains in New South Wales was the Reverend Samuel Marsden (1764-1838). Marsden seems to have held animosity for prisoners who did not share his Church of England affiliations, and he had a particular dislike for Irish Catholics. With women in the penal colony, he devised a system of registry that labeled all women who were wed under the auspices of the Church of England as "married" and all other women as "concubines," no matter that many of these women were in marriages recognized by other churches or by synagogues.[113] Marsden combined his chaplain duties with a position as magistrate at Parramatta, New

---

110. Hughes, *The Fatal Shore*, p. 136.
111. Dalzell, *Benefit of Clergy in America and Related Matters*, pp. 48-49.
112. Hughes, *The Fatal Shore*, p. 168.
113. Hughes, *The Fatal Shore*, p. 247.

South Wales, and his propensity for inflicting physical punishment earned him the nickname "The Flogging Parson."[114]

But Marsden's approach was totally different from that of the Christians who set about reforming the gaols of England. The reformers believed that prisoners were changed by conversion instead of whips. By bearing in mind this confidence in the transforming power of Christian conversion, one is better able to understand the work of the Quaker reformer Elizabeth Fry (1780-1845). Fry offered not so much a systematic proposal for prison reform as a style for prison visitation. Her approach to helping prisoners was to sit with the women at Newgate Gaol and read to them from the Bible. Fry thought that crime could be prevented by means of Christian education for the poor, and in her memoirs she wrote of the "extreme importance of the influence of the higher on the lower classes of society, by their example and precept."[115] She recommended that wealthier people should provide an example for the poor by avoiding the theater and late hours. From a later vantage point, it might seem tempting to dismiss Fry as a maternalistic woman of wealth, but her visitations involved sacrifice, and they had the beneficial impact of exposing prison conditions to public scrutiny.

Even during her lifetime, Fry had numerous critics who dismissed her as disruptive of the evangelistic work that properly fell within the purview of the prison chaplains. One of her critics was the chaplain at Reading Gaol, the Reverend J. Field, who said that the ministry already present at Reading (a ministry that involved prisoners in the compulsory memorization of lengthy biblical texts) was adequate.[116] While some of the criticism aimed at Fry was likely due to a certain territoriality among chaplains, some of the unkind reception accorded her was also due to her status as a layperson, a member of the Society of Friends, and a woman. It was not until later, during the Moody and Sankey revivals of the 1870s, that Anglican clergy gave favorable recognition to lay evangelism.

Like Howard before her, Fry was concerned for the quality of spiritual guidance available for prisoners. The typical worship service in a nineteenth-century prison chapel was not necessarily an uplifting or

114. Hughes, *The Fatal Shore*, p. 187.

115. Fry, quoted by John Kent in *Elizabeth Fry* (London: B. T. Batsford, 1962), p. 39.

116. Kent, *Elizabeth Fry*, pp. 59-60.

docile event. Guards roamed the chapel aisles, and the worship was often punctuated by their shouting for prisoners to "Stop talking!" Prisoner Stuart Wood noted that "chapel was just part of one's punishment. If one looked either to the right or the left or attempted to whisper to another fellow, it meant three days' bread and water in close confinement."[117] In an effort to minimize talking or even visual contact between prisoners, some chapels were so designed that prisoners sat in individual boxes from which they could only look forward toward the chaplain in the pulpit. Still, some prisoners were able to communicate with each other during hymns. Some became quite proficient at singing loudly on the first word or two of a line and then using the remainder of the line to communicate more quietly with their neighbors. In prisons where total silence was imposed as part of the daily regimen, singing in chapel provided quite a release. Later in the century when the Moody and Sankey revival introduced some hymns of an upbeat nature, some prisoners apparently engaged in a bit of whooping and hollering. Most chaplains quickly banned the new hymns in favor of more somber standards.[118]

Attendance at chapel was compulsory. The services were Anglican, but Jewish and Catholic services were eventually scheduled as well. In the mid-nineteenth century, a Muslim prisoner named Henry Harcourt was told by prison officials, "we have no Mahommedan [sic] religion here," and "you will have to go to church or chapel, and if you refuse to do so you will be flogged."[119] Some resisted the compulsory nature of this religious indoctrination. In a move that was both principled and risky, an elderly prisoner named Joseph Wells wrote on his drinking cup: "yor order is for me to go to chapel, but mine is that I'll go to Hell first." When prison officials told him that the writing was inappropriate, Wells laughed.[120] Chaplains were viewed as (and in fact were) part of the prison system, and the presence of a chaplain was by no means guaranteed to elicit respect from prisoners. In one incident at the prison in Millbank, there was a prisoners' plot brewing to murder the chaplain during worship. On 3 March 1827, a riot broke out in the chapel at Millbank, and on another

117. Wood, quoted by Priestley in *Victorian Prison Lives,* p. 93.
118. Priestley, *Victorian Prison Lives,* pp. 94-95.
119. Cited by Priestley in *Victorian Prison Lives,* p. 91.
120. Noel McLachlan, "Penal Reform and Penal History: Some Reflections," in *Progress in Penal Reform,* ed. Louis Blom-Cooper (London: Oxford University Press, 1974), p. 9. I know nothing of Wells's fate, but that he was punished is certain.

occasion, the reference during worship to "give us this day our daily bread" gave rise to prisoner protests for more and better food.[121]

In addition to preparation for worship services, a major responsibility of the chaplain was to attend to condemned prisoners. Elizabeth Fry was consistently opposed to the death penalty, but such was not the case with many of the chaplains she encountered. Much of Fry's work centered on the prison at Newgate, where the chaplain was the Reverend Horace Salisbury Cotton. Cotton's contemporaries testified to the fact that he was not well loved by the prisoners; in fact, he was often ridiculed by them. At one point, Cotton was called before a committee of Parliament to talk about his work. During the testimony, he gave an extensive description of the "condemned sermon" that he and other chaplains preached before each execution. For Cotton's version of the condemned sermon, the prisoner who was about to be hanged was seated facing a table upon which an open coffin had been placed. Half of the people attending the service were prisoners, and the rest of the available space was open for the public. Cotton defended the practice of admitting the public to hear the sermon on the grounds that executions would serve as a warning for them to remain virtuous. In any case, it was a popular preaching event. Cotton noted that "the anxiety of the people to come and hear the condemned sermon is wonderful."[122] And so, with gallows humor, the prisoners noted that the condemned died "with Cotton in their ears."[123]

Part of Fry's opposition to the death penalty was based on her conviction that, given the proper guidance and opportunities, all prisoners were capable of reform and conversion. She believed that work facilitated the reform process, while idleness and sloth were the enemies of a virtuous life.[124] Some of the English prison reformers were so

121. Hoyles, *Religion in Prison*, pp. 21-23.
122. Kent, *Elizabeth Fry*, p. 64.
123. Hughes, *The Fatal Shore*, p. 32.
124. Fry was by no means alone in this emphasis on the value of productive work. Max Weber provides ample evidence of the influence of this notion in Protestant theology, citing, among others, Count Zinzendorf ("One does not only work in order to live, but one lives for the sake of one's work") and Richard Baxter (sloth and idleness are potential "destroyers of grace"). These reverent attitudes toward the benefits of work were also influential throughout the history of prison reform movements. See Max Weber, *The Protestant Ethic and the Spirit of Capitalism*, trans. Talcott Parsons (New York: Scribner's, 1958).

convinced of the value of work in curbing crime that they tended to celebrate the child labor in the growing industrial centers and mills of England as a cure for juvenile delinquency. Fry proposed that looms be provided so that prisoners could be engaged in productive work, but some of her critics protested that such an approach amounted to coddling criminals. If prisons were intended to punish people, why should prisoners be able to see the fruits of their labors? In criticism of Elizabeth Fry, the Reverend Sidney Smith wrote that "hers is not the method to stop crimes." Instead, Smith suggested that prisons require "some species of labour where the labourer could not see the results of his toil" and "where it was as monotonous, irksome and dull as possible."[125] Smith had his way. The treadmill and the crank were used in many of England's prisons until the end of the nineteenth century. Theoretically, both machines might have had utility in tasks such as grinding grain, but prisoners were compelled to operate the machines for no purpose other than the toil. The treadmill was rigged so that the stepping and climbing accomplished nothing but the turning of a large fanlike contraption. The crank was a box with an outside handle attached to a paddle on the inside; for the purposes of prisoners' work, the box was filled with stones, and prisoners were typically required to do 14,400 turns of the crank each day.[126] And so to the delight of Smith and others, prisoners' work accomplished nothing.[127]

While Fry's proposal for prison labor met with limited support, she was more successful at pressing other reforms. She spoke out in

125. Smith, quoted by Cameron in *Prisons and Punishment in Scotland from the Middle Ages to the Present*, p. 49. In the penal colony in Australia, some agreed that it was more important that the work of prisoners be irksome than that it be productive. Lt. John Cuthbertson, commandant at Macquarie Harbor, instructed his assistants to engage the prisoners in constant toil: "You must find work and labour, even if it consists in opening cavities and filling them up again" (quoted by Hughes in *The Fatal Shore*, p. 372).

126. Cameron, *Prisons and Punishment in Scotland from the Middle Ages to the Present*, p. 95.

127. I know of very few people who believed that there are prisons in heaven (!), but one such was the mid-nineteenth-century spiritualist Henry Horn. He wrote of his visions in a work entitled *Strange Visitors* (1869), describing the prisons as having cells made out of a transparent substance akin to crystal. Since "idleness is the mother of crime," said Horn, even the heavenly prisoners toiled at "making articles of curious workmanship" (quoted by McDannell and Lang in *Heaven: A History*, p. 299).

favor of the segregation of women prisoners from men, and she was instrumental in introducing "matrons" into the prisons, changing the system of male keepers for female prisoners. In those jails where women were segregated, however, Fry noted that they often faced worse conditions than men. At the County Gaol in Carlisle, for example, the women were separated at the expense of needing to spend day and night in a small, crowded room where they were required to do their own cooking and washing; the sole luxury afforded was a bit of straw upon which to sleep.[128]

In the 1840s, the reform impetus gave rise to new prison models, the most notorious of which was Pentonville. In response to the calls for segregation of prisoners by gender, age, and crime, Pentonville utilized a system of individual, isolated cells. It is typical of the history of prison reform that later reformers (including Charles Dickens) protested the horrors of Pentonville, itself a product of reform. Chaplains played a prominent role in these "reformed" prisons. An 1868 list of salaries from one prison shows that, behind the prison governor and resident surgeon, the chaplain was the third highest-paid prison official; also on the payroll were visiting Episcopalian and Roman Catholic clerics and a "Scripture Reader" whose salary exceeded that of the guards.[129] When Oscar Wilde was imprisoned at Reading Gaol (1895-1897), he described the chaplain

> addressing his shorn and grey-garbed flock, telling them how wicked they all were, and how thankful they should all be that they lived in a Christian country where a paternal Government was as anxious for the welfare of their souls as for the safekeeping of their miserable bodies; . . . and that the community against which they had previously sinned, was fattening calves to feast them, if they would but undertake to return to the fold and become good citizens. . . . I long to rise in my place and cry out, and tell the poor disinherited wretches around me that it is not so; to tell them that . . . society has nothing to offer them but starvation in the streets, or starvation and cruelty in prison.[130]

128. Kent, *Elizabeth Fry*, p. 46.

129. Cameron, *Prisons and Punishment in Scotland from the Middle Ages to the Present*, p. 109.

130. Wilde, quoted by Priestley in *Victorian Prison Lives*, p. 100.

In an essay entitled "The Soul of Man under Socialism," Wilde commented, "As one reads history, not in the expurgated editions written for schoolboys and passmen, but in the original authorities of each time, one is absolutely sickened, not by the crimes that the wicked have committed, but by the punishments the good have inflicted."[131]

It was good people who devised the penitentiary system in America. Quakers in Pennsylvania were anxious to avoid the brutality of the public stocks and whippings of Calvinist New England and so, guided by humanitarian and religious impulses similar to those of the reformers in England, they invented the penitentiary in Philadelphia. With its emphasis on the reformation of prisoners through the nurturing of penitence, the penitentiary was related to the Quaker belief in "the light within." An 1842 observer of the Philadelphia penitentiary wrote, "Alone in his cell, the convict is handed over to himself; in the silence of his passions and of the world that surrounds him, he descends into his conscience, he questions it and feels awakening within him the moral feeling that never entirely perishes in the heart of man."[132] In the quiet solitude of the halls of the Philadelphia penitentiary, people were slowly driven mad.

The Philadelphia system was soon joined by the model prison in Auburn (which emphasized work to accompany the solitude and silence) and the Elmira Reformatory (which included work and education and a form of indeterminate sentence). Each system claimed a theological foundation, and each made liberal use of clerics and the Bible. Prison inspectors reported in 1831 that

> when, as punishment to a sturdy and disorderly convict, the Warden has ordered the light of his cell to be closed, a little time has elapsed with the most hardy before a prisoner has been found broken down in his spirit, and begging for hard work and his Bible to beguile the tedium of absolute idleness in solitude . . . work and moral religious books are regarded as favours and are withheld as punishment.[133]

Of course, depriving prisoners of Bibles and placing them in solitary confinement were not the only disciplinary measures that were

---

131. Wilde, quoted by Priestley in *Victorian Prison Lives*, p. v.
132. Cited by Michel Foucault in *Discipline and Punish: The Birth of the Prison*, trans. Alan Sheridan (New York: Random House, 1979), p. 238.
133. Quoted by McHugh, *Christian Faith and Criminal Justice*, pp. 38-39.

utilized. While Quakers had envisioned penitentiaries as replacements for corporal punishment, American prisons actually became not a replacement for but the setting for physical torture. Many mid-nineteenth-century prison personnel administered discipline with whips. Unruly prisoners were stuck in straitjackets or hung by their wrists from hooks embedded in ceilings or walls. One prison in Kansas devised a "water crib" into which a prisoner in need of discipline would be immersed; the prisoner experienced the sensation of drowning until, in the words of one guard, "he wilts and says he will be good."[134]

But even as some Christians were busily devising prisons for America, others were advocating prison abolition. The earliest American prison abolitionists were also actively advocating the abolition of slavery; in fact, they saw a link between these two forms of captivity. Charles K. Whipple and Adin Ballou, members of the nineteenth-century New England Non-Resistance Society, advocated replacing the police with individuals trained in nonviolent restraint. In his Declaration of Sentiments for the Society, William Lloyd Garrison reiterated the biblical call to refrain from taking offenders to court: "We cannot sue any man at law to compel him by force to restore anything which he may have wrongfully taken from us or others; but if he had seized our coat, we shall surrender up our cloak rather than subject him to punishment."[135]

But prison abolitionists have always been a small minority. In the mainstream of Christendom, church and state have been and remain prison collaborators.[136] Many Christians today remain convinced that

---

134. David J. Rothman, *Conscience and Convenience: The Asylum and Its Alternatives in Progressive America* (Boston: Little, Brown, 1980), p. 20.

135. Garrison, in *The Power of the People: Active Nonviolence in the United States,* ed. Robert Cooney and Helen Michalowski, from an original text by Marty Jezer (Philadelphia: New Society Publishers, 1987), p. 25. Some members of the New England Non-Resistance Society were later involved with the work of what became known as the "Underground Railroad." But as Charles L. Blockson reminds us, the railroad depended less on the support of white Christians than on the efforts of black churches (*The Underground Railroad: First-Person Narratives of Escapes to Freedom in the North* [Englewood Cliffs, N.J.: Prentice Hall, 1987], p. 229).

136. Because of the formal (if not actual) separation of church and state in America, the collaboration here remains more subtle than elsewhere. In 1982, when celebrity Sophia Loren was sentenced to a brief term in prison for Italian tax evasion, she was sent to a women's prison in Caserta, Italy. A former convent, the prison is run by nuns (*New York Times,* 6 June 1982, p. 3).

the gospel message for prisoners is one of condemnation rather than liberation. For its part, the state appreciates the support. Alexander Paterson, the British Prison Commissioner during the 1930s, applauded "the importance which the State attaches to religion as a necessary part of prison administration."[137] Central to the church/state compact is the chaplain. A manual for chaplains published in Philadelphia during the 1970s emphasized that "the prison chaplain supplements and reinforces other professional treatment."[138] And as the 1959 American Correctional Association's Manual of Standards says, "It is felt . . . that the teaching of the church can be put into operation in any institution and need never impose upon the institutions a program in conflict with good correctional management."[139] And perhaps that is still true today. "Correctional" management may be perfectly comfortable with the teachings of the contemporary church. But it is likely that the teachings of Jesus would wreak havoc.

From the blatant power politics of medieval popes to the sincere reform efforts of Pennsylvania Quakers, many factors have contributed to the complicity of Christians with the imprisonment of others. But perhaps one of the more interesting and dangerous justifications was given by the Reverend F. H. Wines in his concluding address to the Congress of the National Prison Association in Cincinnati in 1870. Wines urged the prison officials gathered there to go out and continue their work to "fulfill the high mission assigned to us by Providence — the regeneration and redemption of fallen humanity."[140] In the zeal of his address, Wines forgot what many of us tend to forget: prisoners have already been redeemed along with the rest of fallen humanity on a hill named Golgotha.

137. Paterson, quoted by McLachlan in "Penal Reform and Penal History," p. 10.
138. Cited by McHugh in Christian Faith and Criminal Justice, p. 58.
139. Cited by McHugh in Christian Faith and Criminal Justice, pp. 58-59.
140. Wines, quoted by Jessica Mitford in Kind and Usual Punishment: The Prison Business (New York: Alfred A. Knopf, 1973), p. 33.

Chapter V

Prisons and Discipleship

Whoever takes away what is yours, do not demand it back.

Luke 6:30

Biblical discipleship is marked by several identifying characteristics or qualities.[1] It is not my intent here to offer a complete listing of marks of discipleship or to arrange them in any particular order of importance — except for the first: I would stress that, by its very nature, biblical discipleship is Christocentric.

1. These characteristics of discipleship fall within the purview of what is called "Christian ethics." For discussions of greater detail, see two books that have become known as "modern classics" in Christian ethics: James M. Gustafson's *Christ and the Moral Life* (New York: Harper & Row, 1968) and Paul L. Lehman's *Ethics in a Christian Context* (New York: Harper & Row, 1963). But Joachim Jeremias provides a helpful reminder that we must exercise some caution in our use of the phrase "Christian ethics." After observing that the Sermon on the Mount is gospel, not law, Jeremias writes, "For this is indeed the difference between law and gospel: The law leaves man to rely upon his own strength and challenges him to do his utmost. The gospel, on the other hand, brings man before the gift of God and challenges him really to make the inexpressible gift of God the basis for his life. These are two different worlds. In order to make the difference clear, one should avoid in New Testament theology the terms 'Christian ethic,' 'Christian morality,' 'Christian morals,' because these secular expressions are inadequate and liable to misunderstanding. Instead of these, one should speak of 'lived faith' *(gelebter Glaube)*. Then it is clearly stated that the gift of God precedes his demands" (*The Sermon on the Mount*, trans. Norman Perrin, Facet Books Biblical Series, no. 2 [Philadelphia: Fortress Press, 1963], p. 34).

1. The call to discipleship is a call from Jesus and a call to follow Jesus. Any other claims about what the call to discipleship is or is not are totally groundless unless they are grounded in the one who calls. There is no biblical call to follow a particular social or political reform program, nor is there a call to follow any other person. The call is *only* to follow Jesus. But to say that the call is "only" to follow Jesus is not to imply that this is a call without content. The content of discipleship is provided by the identity of Jesus himself. The worst perversions of discipleship occur whenever anyone ignores the biblical proclamation about who Jesus is. To say merely that "Jesus is my personal Savior" is to say substantially more about me than about Jesus ("*my* personal Savior" shows that *I* am at the center of this particular arrangement — *I* have chosen Jesus for *my own* salvific benefit). Once the name *Jesus* is emptied of biblical content, it can be evoked for purposes ranging from attaining "health and wealth" to bludgeoning enemies. The call to discipleship is not a call to follow an empty name. It is a call to follow Jesus the Prisoner. It is a call to follow Christ crucified. It is a call to "take up your cross" (Matt. 16:24; Mark 8:34; Luke 9:23). It is a call from one who chooses to be with and actually to *be* "the least of them" (Matt. 25:31-46), so that anytime and every time we inflict injury rather than suffering it, it is Jesus whom we crucify anew. It is precisely as Mother Teresa said to the keepers of death row prisoners: "Remember, what you do to these men, you do to God."[2] Jesus did not choose "the least of them" because the least are good but because if the gospel of redemption is not also announced to and for the least, then it is announced to no one at all. And in addition to Christ crucified, the call to discipleship is a call to follow Christ resurrected. There is no longer any recourse to death threats or reliance on the power of death, for death has been totally and irrevocably defeated. All punishments (capital or otherwise) based on the threat or the spirit of death are left behind in the call to follow the resurrected Christ. Before it is anything else (and it is only on this basis that it is anything at all), discipleship is a call to follow Christ crucified and risen.

2. Mother Teresa, quoted by Ian Gray and Moira Stanley (for Amnesty International U.S.A.) in *A Punishment in Search of a Crime: Americans Speak Out against the Death Penalty* (New York: Avon Books, 1989), p. 93. She said this during a visit to San Quentin's death row in 1987.

2. Biblical discipleship seeks to reflect the love that God has first shown to us. The Song of Solomon and other sections of Scripture indicate that erotic love is *not* biblically condemned; in fact, it is a celebrated gift. But erotic love is reciprocated love, and such is not the case with the agape love that God has first shown to us. Indeed, agape love means to "love someone who does not deserve it."[3] According to the Bible, that is who the people of God are: people who are undeserving but loved nonetheless. The way of discipleship involves granting forgiveness when it is not merited. It is no forgiveness at all to embrace sisters and brothers after they have acknowledged wrongdoing and agreed to become the type of people we expect. True forgiveness is what Jesus asked God to grant his crucifiers — not because they had confessed and vowed to change their ways but in spite of the fact that their zeal for law and order had rendered them incapable of even knowing what they were doing (Luke 23:34). Such love and such forgiveness go beyond the bounds of reason. As the community of discipleship, the church is to have *no* concern — none whatsoever — for its own survival. Instead, the church is called to expend itself wildly in the service of God and in the love of the undeserving — indeed, in the love of the enemies of the church.[4] It is a love described by Sister Helen Prejean, an opponent of the death penalty who ministers to prisoners on death row *and also* ministers to the families of victims of murder. Says Helen Prejean, "the Church must stand on both sides of the Cross."[5]

3. Biblical discipleship is a life of eschatological celebration and expectation, which is to say that discipleship celebrates the very real presence of God's kingdom and hopes for the ultimate revelation of that kingdom. Jesus leads along this path by both establishing the kingdom in our very midst and praying "thy kingdom come." So, eschatological hope is the very antithesis of passive waiting. The powers are

3. Wendell Berry, "Manifesto: The Mad Farmer Liberation Front," in *Collected Poems, 1957-1982* (San Francisco: North Point Press, 1985), p. 151.

4. Will Campbell and James Holloway cite the words of a friend: "Howard Moody says the Church is an instrument of God literally to be used up in his service, a service to those not even within it. There is little evidence at this point in God's economy of the Church going out of business through such usefulness" (*Up to Our Steeples in Politics* [New York: Paulist Press, 1970], p. 45).

5. Prejean, in an interview with Gray and Stanley in *A Punishment in Search of a Crime*, p. 99.

already unmasked, and the victory is already won. There is no need to wait for "better times" to celebrate the upside down reality of the Sermon on the Mount. The mark of discipleship is "to live in such a way that one's life would not make sense if God did not exist."[6]

4. Biblical discipleship is marked by freedom — freedom from the law, freedom from responding in the habitual ways in which the world tells us we must respond, and, even more, freedom from necessity. When all justifications and foundations for the power of death are wiped away, necessity is the final excuse. But in the biblical view, necessity is no excuse. Still, as Karl Barth suggested, this "freedom from" has importance only insofar as it is also "freedom to" and "freedom for" — freedom to be reconciled to God and freedom for service to the least.[7] If we deny Jesus' proclamation of freedom for slaves and prisoners, then we deny God's freedom for the rest of us as well. If it is not true for them, it is not true for any of us.

5. Discipleship is marked by prayerful repentance and metanoia. At its best, conversion is something that happens not once in a lifetime but every day and perhaps more often than that. No matter what our concrete actions, all of our actions must be judged by the presence of God's kingdom and by the "not yet" of the kingdom and by the Spirit who is in our midst. Whether we are executioners or prison abolitionists, all of our actions are sinful, provisional, inadequate (Luke 17:10). The point is not to arrive at "the answer" or to establish our own righteousness. The point of discipleship is to follow the righteous one who calls.

6. Biblical discipleship is marked by community rather than individualism. Through Jesus, God has acted "for *us* and thus only in this way for *me*."[8] It is the servant community of faith that is called to respond to the needs of those who have been victimized by crime or other hardship. When victims turn to institutional responses instead, it is a sign that the community of believers has been unfaithful. It is a sign that the church has not been loud enough in saying, "We exist for *no* other reason than that Jesus calls us to serve the suffering.

6. Cardinal Suhard, quoted by Robert Ellsberg in *By Little and by Little: The Selected Writings of Dorothy Day*, ed. Robert Ellsberg (New York: Alfred A. Knopf, 1984), p. xv.

7. Barth, *The Humanity of God* (Richmond: John Knox Press, 1960), pp. 69-96.

8. Barth, *The Humanity of God*, p. 63.

We are not called to judge you. We are not called to 'save' you. We do not want to be above you. In fact, we ask that you permit us to be your servant."

But we must not carry community to a certain point and then drop it. It would be wrong to pretend that service and faithfulness are reflected through communities while crime and sin are purely the products of individuals. If Barth is correct that God's love is first "for *us* and thus only in this way for *me*," so too with God's judgments. To view individual responsibility for crime in its proper light, we have to give precedence to a confession of corporate responsibility. To focus on the individual culpability and ignore the corporate responsibility is to delude ourselves. It is to pick up stones because we fancy ourselves to be "without sin" (John 8:1-11).

Our Shared Criminality

It is perhaps a bit too boldly that Charles Colson and Daniel Van Ness announce that "criminals, not society, are the cause of crime."[9] At the most fundamental level, it is *only* society that creates crime, by empowering elected representatives to define what is or is not crime. Thus, for example, the Nuremberg Laws of Nazi Germany created crime by defining what activities were illegal for Jews and by further defining who was and was not Jewish. Clearly, the "cause" of these crimes was societal and governmental decisions, not Jewish criminals. Examples from contemporary America may be of a different magnitude than those of Nazi Germany, but it is no less true that our society (indeed, any society) creates crime through legislative definition. Our definitions of crime outlaw the inner city crack house but not the Wall Street cocktail lounge. They make killing a crime in some circumstances and not in others. Legislative bodies have as their very purpose the creation of crime via definition.

It is illusory to assume that the business of defining crime occurs in a vacuum. As an American Friends Service Committee report observes,

9. Colson and Van Ness, *Convicted: New Hope for Ending America's Crime Crisis* (Westchester, Ill.: Crossway Books, 1989), p. 60.

The selection of candidates for prosecution reflects inequality in the larger society not only because of bias on the part of police or prosecutors, but because the substantive content of the law affects those who are not social equals in quite different ways. A wealthy industrialist has little difficulty in having his opinions on political questions heard at the highest levels of government. . . . But who speaks for the unemployed, the welfare mother, the habitual drunkard, the inmate, the drug addict, the recidivist? Laws forbidding armed robbery and burglary have very different impact for a millionaire and for an unemployed twenty-year-old black male in a ghetto where the unemployment rate is 25 percent.[10]

This is not to imply that poor people commit more crime but rather to suggest that the content of the law is more often weighted against them than against the wealthy.

There is, however, a less direct (but no less real) way in which society causes crime. While it is usually assumed that the offender is rejecting social values, the exact opposite is frequently the case. The offender is often embracing the very values that the society puts forth as exemplary. As Alex Comfort has asserted, "To some extent the prohibition of delinquency is the reaction of those who have a deep-rooted community of desire with the delinquent."[11] Not infrequently, offenders' offenses have less to do with the values they are embracing than with the manner and circumstances of the embrace. American culture identifies "success" with the acquisition of money and the things it can buy while simultaneously denying or restricting some people's access to the legal means for acquiring such "success."[12] In fact, thieves affirm the manner in which the culture defines and values success. And, as

10. *Struggle for Justice: A Report on Crime and Punishment in America,* prepared for the American Friends Service Committee (New York: Hill & Wang, 1971), p. 15.

11. Comfort, "Power Attracts Delinquents: A Contemporary Study," in *Patterns of Anarchy: A Collection of Writings on the Anarchist Tradition,* ed. Leonard I. Krimerman and Lewis Perry (Garden City, N.Y.: Doubleday-Anchor Books, 1966), p. 307. David Greenberg also notes the manner in which an offender's "values coincide with those of society" (*The Problem of Prisons* [Philadelphia: American Friends Service Committee, 1970], p. 8).

12. See Robert K. Merton, "Anomie," in *The Criminal in Society,* vol. 1 of *Crime and Justice,* ed. Leon Radzinowicz and Marvin E. Wolfgang (New York: Basic Books, 1971), pp. 442-73.

Gerald Austin McHugh has observed, so do others: "Stripped of cultural differences, both the ambitious Wall Street lawyer and the street corner pimp are engaged in a self-destructive quest to be thought of as a 'big man.'"[13] It is the same quest, fueled by the same motivations, in pursuit of the same goals.

If it is true that a society gets the leaders it deserves, it is equally true that a society gets the criminals it deserves. The mayhem on the streets of America is marked not by a revolt against societal values but by an affirmation of cultural icons and idolatries. A few examples illustrate the point:

a. America is under the sway of the idolatry of violence. I do not mean merely that Americans occasionally view violence as efficacious (a trap into which all people have fallen) or that Americans occasionally resort to militarism (a trap into which all nations have fallen). I mean that America is *possessed* by the spirit of violence, that violence has become an idol more palpably real than any golden calf. Violence is worshiped; it is glorified as the divine source of security, and sacrifices both material and human are offered up to it. Anyone who doubts this can check the national military budget or explore the desk drawers and gun cabinets of millions of American homes or (simplest of all) turn on the television.[14] A society that busily legitimizes violence and extols its supposed virtue cannot hope to control or circumscribe the various guises in which violence manifests itself. Even though Durkheim believed that crime is a normal phenomenon that cannot be

13. McHugh, *Christian Faith and Criminal Justice: Toward a Christian Response to Crime and Punishment* (New York: Paulist Press, 1978), p. 182.

14. There are six acts of physical violence in an average hour of "prime time" programming and eighteen in an average hour of children's programming. Much of this televised violence (that inflicted by "the good guys") is depicted as necessary and/or legitimate. I do not advocate censorship, but I do advocate that we stop pretending that our assorted legitimizations and justifications for violence exact no human toll. In a study of battery by men in domestic relationships, there was no difference in the rate of assault by men of various income levels. Major differences emerged, however, between those men who did and did not consider "physical aggression" to be legitimate in the face of insult or uncontrollable anger or infidelity. Those men who believed that physical aggression is legitimate in such cases perpetrated much more assault in their domestic relationships than those who did not legitimize physical aggression. These findings by sociologist Beth Vanfossen were reported by Fritz Longabaugh in "Problems of Valuing Violence," in *Justicia* (Newsletter of Genesee Ecumenical Ministries Judicial Process Commission), March 1988, pp. 4-5.

eradicated from any society, he nonetheless granted that murder rates are altered according to the ways in which life is valued or not.[15] It is quite simply a ruse when politicos claim that current levels of violence in America are the result of drugs. The per capita rates of hard drug use in some nations of Europe are comparable to those in the United States, but their rates of violence are far lower than in America. Like the rest of us, drug users in America have been taught to value violence. Violent offenders are not rebelling against the values of America; they are affirming them.

Indeed, theologians and philosophers dating back to Erasmus and Thomas More have hypothesized that nations engaging in warfare run the risk of experiencing increased rates of violent crime at home. Recent studies have given support to the theory. In a cross-national study, Dane Archer and Rosemary Gartner compared the postwar rates of homicide in combatant nations with the rates of homicide in a control group of nations not involved in the various wars covered by the study. They found that the warring nations were much more likely to experience increases in homicide rates than were the nations not involved in the conflicts. They also found that those nations that were "victorious" in war (i.e., those for which the resort to violence had proven to be most effective) were more likely to have increased rates of homicide than were the defeated nations. Whether one believes that the United States won or lost the war in Vietnam, it is worth noting that U.S. murder rates doubled during that war; the increase was particularly alarming in view of the fact that violent crime rates in the U.S. had been declining for a number of years prior to the war.[16] There was an 8 percent increase in U.S. violent crime in 1991, the year of the "Desert Storm" war in the Persian Gulf. "Even though social scientists have in the past amassed impressive experimental evidence that violence can be produced through imitation or modeling," note Archer and Gartner, "they have in general neglected the possibility that government — with its vast authority and resources — might turn out to be the most potent model of all."[17]

15. See Durkheim, "Crime as a Normal Phenomenon," in *The Criminal in Society*, pp. 391-95.

16. Archer and Gartner, *Violence and Crime in Cross-National Perspective* (New Haven: Yale University Press, 1984), p. 68.

17. Archer and Gartner, *Violence and Crime in Cross-National Perspective*, p. 94.

b. Materialism is another American icon that some offenders have learned to value. Indeed, since the basic necessities of life have already been provided for America's sizable upper and middle classes, and since there seems to be scant inclination on our part to provide necessities for those in the world who cannot afford them, the strength of the American economy is dependent on the creation of sufficient levels of materialism. That is the sole purpose of the advertising industry: to convince us that we need things that in fact we do not need. As Paul Wachtel has observed, "An economy primarily driven by growth must generate discontent. We *cannot* be content or the entire economic machine would grind to a halt."[18] Curiously, materialism both over-values and undervalues the material world. Too much importance is loaded onto material when it is viewed as the source of happiness or the sign of success. But then when material possessions inevitably fail to yield the happiness they are supposed to provide, they are tossed aside in favor of new ones. When adults move through possessions like children move through toys, material is cheapened and the creation suffers. But the economic powers that be need to generate discontent, and they do. Thieves are not rebelling against American materialism; they are affirming it.

c. Our history of patriarchy is affirmed by those who commit crimes against women. Rape is not common to every society. In her study of ninety-five tribal societies, anthropologist Peggy Reeves Sanday found that 47 percent of these societies were free of sexual assault. Tribal societies in which rape is nonexistent are characterized by an abhorrence of interpersonal violence and by a familial and communal style of decision making in which women have an equal share.[19] In contrast, a 1988 survey of junior high school students in Rhode Island found that many of the students believed that there are circumstances in which male force against women is justified — for example, if the man is married to the woman, if the man has previously had sexual intercourse with the woman, or even if the man has covered the expenses for a

18. Wachtel, *The Poverty of Affluence: A Psychological Portrait of the American Way of Life* (Philadelphia: New Society Publishers, 1989), p. xi.

19. The Sanday study is cited by Fay Honey Knopp in "Community Solutions to Sexual Violence: Feminist/Abolitionist Perspectives," in *Criminology as Peacemaking*, ed. Harold E. Pepinsky and Richard Quinney (Bloomington, Ind.: Indiana University Press, 1991), p. 189.

date.[20] Such attitudes (certainly not confined to Rhode Island students) serve to legitimize violence against women.

I could cite additional examples, such as the manner in which the use of drugs (illegal or otherwise) actually affirms cultural preoccupations with escapism and with the notion that there should be a convenient technological fix for every problem. In view of the fact that some criminal offenders are so affirming of social and cultural values, we might well join with those who ask, "So what could the 'prisoners' freed do to us that we are not already doing to ourselves? Murder us? Pervert us? Steal from us? Use us? Lie to us?"[21]

Those who boldly absolve the larger community of any responsibility in crime ignore the manner in which the wrongs done by any of us (criminal offenders included) are complex realities often woven out of *good* intentions (Rom. 7:18-23). Biblical faith evaporates our attempts to draw any ultimate distinctions between "criminals" and the rest of us. "Frequently people will refer to crimes as 'inhuman acts,'" notes Gerald McHugh. "In fact, given the . . . sinfulness of all human beings, the opposite is true. Nothing could be more human than crime. Human beings will always fail, and inevitably the community must deal with that failure. Outrage over crime is partly frustration over our own fallen humanity."[22]

But we must exercise care when we speak simultaneously of "crime" and "sin." Luther, Calvin, and other Christians before and since have demonstrated an unfortunate tendency to equate the two. The equation falls apart when we recognize that many crimes are not sins and many sins are not crimes. Some young men, for example, have justifiably committed the crime of refusing to register for the draft in order to renounce the sin of war. On the other hand, even though the prophets railed against the sins of those who cast widows out of their homes, modern bankers can do precisely that without committing any crime at all. Even though sin and crime may coincide at some points,

20. The survey results are cited by Susan Caringella-MacDonald and Drew Humphries in "Sexual Assault, Women, and the Community: Organizing to Prevent Sexual Violence," in *Criminology as Peacemaking*, pp. 101-2.

21. Will D. Campbell and James Y. Holloway, "The Good News from God in Jesus Is Freedom to the Prisoners," in *And the Criminals with Him*, ed. Will D. Campbell and James Y. Holloway (New York: Paulist Press, 1973), p. 150.

22. McHugh, *Christian Faith and Criminal Justice*, p. 182.

the laws of society often pick at specks while ignoring beams. There is an incongruity to punishing petty theft when the middle-class life-style of most Americans represents a grand-scale theft from the planet. There *are* enough resources to provide all people with food and shelter, but it would simply be impossible to provide six billion people with a middle-class American life-style. What remains of the natural integrity of the creation is already under severe strain. We cannot continue to view the earth as one giant "resource" from which we may extract at will. We share the planet with other creatures that have also been given the gift of life, and we share the planet with other people. We have limits, and today those limits mean that the acquisition of possessions invariably *dis*possesses others. Climbing up the social ladder is stealing. It is stealing from future generations, and, more immediately, it is stealing from the earth and from those sisters and brothers who are currently living on the fringes of survival. It is an example of how some of the most deadly sins are perfectly legal. The point is not to criminalize sin but to stop pretending that law-abiding citizens are holier than common criminals. Quite literally and directly, climbing up the social ladder is stealing — and it is time for us to climb on down.

Alternatives to What?

For purposes of review and clarification, it may be helpful at this point to summarize some of what I have and have not said about prisons and the people involved in the penal system. First, it is important to emphasize that I am not claiming that police, judges, prison guards, and others working in the juridical system are evil people. In fact, these people are hired and paid by the rest of us, and we ought not to presume that they have any guilt that the rest of us do not bear as well. More often than not, the police and prison guards are victimized by the same system that victimizes prisoners. While we must not dismiss the seriousness of the racism and other violence inherent in tragedies such as the notorious 1991 videotaped beating of Rodney King in Los Angeles, to focus solely on individual instances of alleged or real police brutality is to ignore the larger crisis. The police do not carry guns because they are brutal people; they carry guns because the power of the gun is the only power of which the fallen state avails itself. When the "already" but "not yet" kingdom of God is fully revealed, the state will understand that it might have instead resorted to love, forgiveness, and reconciliation (and this is what we need to tell the state today!). But in its refusal to confess the defeat of death, the state continues to resort to the power of the gun as its ultimate power. The problem is the spiritual crisis of the state, not evil police or prison guards.

Likewise, I am not claiming that lawbreakers are basically good people. Rather, my position is that so-called criminals are our sisters and brothers, subject to the same tendencies toward greed and hatred and sinfulness as the rest of us. Lawbreakers share our strange nature as human beings: neither monsters nor angels.

Having emphasized that, however, I would also emphasize that corporate responsibility does not absolve any of us individually. To use corporate responsibility and/or the assurance of forgiveness as an excuse for victimizing people through criminal activity or victimizing people through police or prison work or victimizing people through passively paying taxes for more prisons is to embrace what Bonhoeffer called "cheap grace." Forgiveness is *never* an excuse for actions; forgiveness is love in the face of inexcusable actions. In all aspects of our lives, we do well to remember and to avoid the excuses of Hitler's "good Germans": I was just doing my job. I was just taking orders. I didn't know what was happening. What could one person do to make a difference?

So, I have not been claiming that some people are evil or that some people are righteous or that any of us may resort to justifications for victimizing others. Instead, I have tried to elucidate the following points:

a. Cages, chains, pits, dungeons, jails, and prisons are biblically identified with the power and spirit of death. They are totally and irrevocably renounced. It is Jesus who announces the fall of the prison with his Jubilee proclamation of liberty for the captives. It is Jesus the Prisoner who breaks the power of the prison through resurrection.

b. God's kingdom is not yet *and* it is present now in our very midst. We are called to live in its hope *and* in its presence. Jesus' call to discipleship is a call to be guided by the presence of the kingdom rather than by the lowest common denominator of the situations or people who might threaten us.

c. The gospel is good news of *freedom*. Realistically, the thought of throwing open the prison doors is frightening because we have first-hand knowledge of the pervasiveness of sin. We are not even sure that we can trust ourselves not to lash out, let alone trust "common criminals." But the biblical proclamation of liberty for the captives is a call to freedom in the face of fear and in the face of our obsessive quest for security. It is freedom *from* enslavement to the habitual responses that are always depicted as necessary. But it is also freedom *to* respond with nonviolent creativity. It is freedom *for* sisters and brothers who are suffering. It is freedom *to* be reconciled to God and neighbor. It is not only prisoners but also the rest of us who are held captive by the power of the prison. As a million prisoners attest, we have not been free not to imprison people. The gospel is good news of freedom.

d. Regarding the ideologies that stand behind the prison system, the penal understandings of deterrence, rehabilitation, and retribution are nonbiblical and sometimes blatantly antibiblical. People must never be used as a means to the supposedly utilitarian goal of deterrence. There is absolutely nothing to which we could possibly rehabilitate offenders other than to our own sins and our own self-righteousness. It is a violent form of hypocrisy to call for the infliction of some theoretically "just" desert on others when God has spared us from the penalties we so justly deserve. Jesus points to the way — the *only* way — for ending the vicious cycles of retribution and retaliation. Even unto the cross, he lived and lives that way: not "retribution has to end with you" but "retribution has to end with me." In Jesus, retribution has ended.

e. The biblical identification of prisons with the power of death tells us that the problem is not that prisons are ineffective at curbing crime and violence and victimization but rather that prisons are part of the reality they claim to combat. This identification is biblical *realism*, a realism that demythologizes all of our supposed social necessities and would-be solutions. Biblical realism unmasks the naiveté of modern mythologies. It is as Mark Olson describes it: "Evil begets evil. And prisons are among the greatest begetters of evil we have going. To think that slamming people behind bars, breaking their spirits and destroying their souls could do anything other than lead to more evil is the ultimate in naiveté."[23]

f. The police are victimized by those of us who ask them to wield the gun on our behalf. The fact that I do not own a gun or that I do not threaten others with physical violence or that I do not imprison

23. Olson, "The God Who Dared," *The Other Side*, 26 (May-June 1990): 15.

others does not mean that I seek to be a nonviolent follower of the Prince of Peace if I am at the same time relying on others to wield the gun for me. If we believe that death is conquered and that it is against God's will to carry guns and threaten violence, then we must not ask the police to sin on our behalf while we pretend to remain guiltless.

g. The Bible does not present crime as the problem of a few evil individuals within the society, nor does it suggest that the answer to crime is to apprehend and lock up all the bad people. We cannot pretend that the problem is a hundred or a thousand or a million bad people. The Bible links crime with a crisis in the fabric of society. We are corporately responsible. More often than not, offenders are merely reflecting the idolatrous values of the larger community. Any of us who pretend that prison bars separate the good from the bad need to be reminded of the manner in which Jesus equated anger with murder and sexual objectification with rape and oaths with perjury (Matt. 5).

h. To rely on court systems and the power of guns and prisons is to ignore the community God has given us. The body of Christ is God's gift for reconciliation and service. And that is why Jesus (Matt. 5:39) and Paul (1 Cor. 6:1) called upon believers to refrain from taking others to court, even if wrongs were suffered as a result. If the police are called and charges are filed, the concern becomes a matter for the mechanical deliberations of the court. But the point is not to suggest that the church is wiser or more proficient at legal proceedings than are the courts. Rather, the biblical community which proclaims the Lordship of Jesus recognizes that the important concern is neither legality nor the shuffling of property but reconciliation. Jesus taught, "whoever takes away what is yours, do not demand it back" (Luke 6:30). The real concern is not the restoration of property but the restoration of right relationship among people and between people and God.

i. In its origins, the church community is a prison community. These are our sisters and brothers who are in prison, and the paradigm for our relationship with them is the service rendered by the early church — visiting, feeding, ransoming. The church is called to use itself up in service to those who have been victimized, not limited to but including both those who have been violated by crime and those who have been violated by the machinations of the juridical process.

j. In the biblical understanding, all lives are equally precious — a truth that is established not by talking about the worth and dignity of the powerful and the wealthy but by Jesus' identification with "the least of them." The lives of the great and powerful are precious and sacred only because Jesus has established it to be so for the least, whether least in terms of money, power, righteousness, or any of the other distinctions that people value. The lives of police and prison guards are no more or less sacred than the lives of offenders and prisoners.

Our review of the biblical renunciation of prisons points to the history of Christendom as a history of faithlessness. More than it is a judgment on any other people or principalities or powers, the biblical renunciation of prisons stands as a judgment on Christendom. Some scholars of biblical Greek hypothesize that *ekklēsia*, the word for "church," derives from a combination of *kaleō* (to call) and *ek* (out of). If such were the case linguistically, it would coincide with the biblical identification of the church as the community that is called out of the world. But the church is not called out of the world for the sake of remaining separate from the world in some social or spiritual utopia. Rather, the church is called out of the world only for the sake of being sent back into the world (Matt. 28:19) as a community that no longer follows the lords of the world or the standards of the world or the bad news that the world seeks to pawn off as good. The church is sent back into the world with a new Lord, a new calling, a new service. If such is not the case, then the church has no service whatsoever to offer to the world. If the church is guided by the standards of the world, then the church merely tries "to sanctify what the world was going to do anyway, however reluctantly and with or without our support."[24]

Ever since the church first unconditionally surrendered to Constantine, the history of Christendom has been a history of doing what the world was going to do anyway. That is not to suggest that there has not been faithful witness offered by churches and individuals and movements of discipleship, but such witness has often come as the result of standing outside of or even against the mainstream of Christendom. As we have seen, Christendom itself has been busy not only blessing the wars of the world but also helping to initiate and fight them — not only blessing the prisons of the world but also helping to form and reform them.

Does the biblical proclamation of the fall of the prison mean that the church must break ties with any prison reform movements or formal

24. Campbell and Holloway, *Up to Our Steeples in Politics*, p. 66.

prison chaplaincy? History itself would suggest this as an option. The history of Christendom is a history of chaplains who helped to oppress prisoners and of reforms that helped to entrench the prison system. In writing about the prison system, George Bernard Shaw observed that "its worst features have been produced with the intention, not of making it worse, but of making it better."[25]

The church has been unfaithful to the call to be "in the world but not of it" and has frequently ignored Paul's admonition "Do not be conformed to this world" (Rom. 12:2). But the call itself points to the possibility that Christians can minister to those inside the prison without inevitably affirming the prison itself — that they need not be of the prison while in it as servants. Unfortunately, there are prison chaplains who see themselves as part of the "treatment team," but there are others who refuse to become cogs in the wheels of the prison and who openly resist the standard operating procedures of incarceration (sometimes to the point of being fired) so that they might be advocates for and servants of prisoners. Unfortunately, there are death row chaplains who see it as their responsibility to elicit cooperation from condemned prisoners and to help the killing ritual run smoothly, but there are others who boldly speak out against capital punishment and forthrightly announce that the sins of prisoners who have perpetrated cold and calculating murder are only matched by the colder and more calculating executions of "justice."[26] So it has proven possible for some believers to serve as chaplains without affirming the prison.

Likewise, it may be possible for those in the faith community to join in the advocacy of some changes in the juridical system that aim toward "decarceration" or "excarceration" rather than toward legitimizing and supposedly improving prisons.[27] With a million Americans in jail or prison, a growing number of people are showing interest in

---

25. Shaw, from *The Crime of Imprisonment* cited in *The Wit and Wisdom of Bernard Shaw*, ed. Stephen Winsten (New York: Collier Books, 1962), p. 321.

26. For a description of chaplains facilitating the execution process, see Norman Mailer, *The Executioner's Song* (New York: Warner Books, 1979), pp. 844-45. For interviews with two death row chaplains who actively oppose the death penalty, see Gray and Stanley, *A Punishment in Search of a Crime*, pp. 147-56.

27. For a discussion of this distinction, see Fay Honey Knopp et al., *Instead of Prisons: A Handbook for Abolitionists* (Syracuse: Prison Research Education Action Project, 1976).

looking elsewhere for possible means to address crime. Despite the quickened pace of new prison and jail construction, there is an increasing awareness that, in the words of Sharon LaFraniere, "there is no way to build our way out of the current situation."[28] But there should be no assumption that the American prison system will collapse of its own weight. A decade ago, prison overcrowding was viewed as an acute crisis that had to be resolved; the crowding is even more severe today, but it has come to be viewed as a chronic problem that has to be managed.[29]

Even though they have rates of incarceration that are much lower than those in the United States, countries elsewhere in the world are beginning to turn away from the notion that prisons offer an antidote to crime. In 1991, Britain's Conservative government adopted new sentencing laws that could reduce the British prison population by half within five years. In contrast, U.S. Attorney General William Barr expressed the following sentiment in a 1992 meeting with California district attorneys: "The choice is clear. More prison space or more crime."[30] What has in fact been clear for quite some time now is that Americans have been subjected to *both* more prison space *and* more crime.

Caution must be exercised by people within the faith community and others as we consider advocating changes that might help to move us away from reliance on prisons. On the one hand, to endorse nothing short of immediate prison abolition risks ignoring opportunities to alleviate the current suffering of both offenders and victims of crime. On the other hand, endorsing any interim steps short of prison abolition risks ignoring the persistent way in which history has demonstrated that "innovations that appeared to be substitutes for incarceration became supplements to incarceration."[31] We have to ask some hard questions before we endorse any interim or intermediate proposals: Will these proposed changes alleviate violence, suffering, and coercion? Will these

28. LaFraniere, quoted by Annette Jolin and Brian Stipak in "Drug Treatment and Electronically Monitored Home Confinement: An Evaluation of a Community-Based Sentencing Option," *Crime and Delinquency* 38 (April 1992): 158.

29. See John M. Klofas, Stan Stojkovic, and David A. Kolinich, "The Meaning of Correctional Crowding: Steps Toward an Index of Severity," *Crime and Delinquency* 38 (April 1992): 172.

30. Both the British sentencing laws and the Attorney General's remarks are cited in "The Talk of the Town," *New Yorker*, 13 April 1992, p. 27.

31. David J. Rothman, *Conscience and Convenience: The Asylum and Its Alternatives in Progressive America* (Boston: Little, Brown, 1980), p. 9.

changes foster social and economic justice? Rather than serving as "supplements" to legitimize the current system, will these changes represent movement toward abolition?[32] Clearly, none of these questions can be answered affirmatively when posed with regard to some of the newer tools of American penology such as electronically monitored home confinement. If changes only serve to expand state surveillance and control and to continue emphasis on punitive rather than reconciling measures, then even though the prison walls tumble, the spirit of the prison will have carried the day.

We could effect an immediate and dramatic reduction in America's prison population by decriminalizing several types of offenses and making the decriminalization retroactive. The offenses most often mentioned as candidates for decriminalization are the so-called "victimless crimes" — actions that do not inherently harm other people, such as prostitution and the possession and use of drugs. While these activities might be considered sinful or unhealthy or offensive to personal morality, the imposition of sanctions for actions that are sinful or unhealthy leaves us all eligible for punishment. Some contend that these offenses are not actually "victimless." With drug use, for example, there is the risk of the devastation of addiction that not only harms drug users but has an impact on their families and friends as well. That is an important and legitimate concern, but it is a concern that also properly pertains to the use of such legal drugs as alcohol. If the concern is for families and friends, we cannot ignore the fact that the imprisonment of drug users also has a devastating impact on their families and friends.

Today, over half of all prisoners in the U.S. federal prison system are drug offenders; with federal legislation mandating minimum sentences for a variety of drug offenses, estimates are that the number will increase to almost seventy percent by 1995.[33] In addition to representing a grand-scale warehousing of human beings, such figures represent a huge expenditure of financial resources. What have we bought with the investment? Criminal sanctions raise the price of illegal narcotics, making drug trafficking an attractive enterprise for organized crime syndicates. In a society that legitimizes violence and offers easy access to weapons, disputes over drug deals and turf are likely to be settled

---

32. Similar questions are raised by Knopp et al. in *Instead of Prisons*, pp. 101-2.
33. "The Talk of the Town," *New Yorker*, 13 April 1992, p. 27.

with guns. Drug users turn to property crimes to satisfy costly addictions. The criminalization of drug use may very well be contributing to increased levels of other categories of crime.

Even some elected, public officials (e.g., Baltimore Mayor Kurt Schmoke) are calling for the decriminalization of the possession and use of certain categories of currently illegal drugs. The resultant hundreds of millions of dollars in savings on court and penal costs could be used for drug education and treatment programs that stand a chance of being more effective in preventing and addressing addictions than the current punitive approach. An anonymous prisoner notes that there is more than a little irony to the fact that

> while I was at liberty on the streets and sought a residential treatment program for my cocaine addiction I was told there was a waiting list for such programs. . . . Now as a prisoner of the state, I am not only given such a residential program — long after the exigencies of my former condition have subsided due to over four years incarceration — but I am compelled to partake of such a program.[34]

The retroactive decriminalization of certain "victimless" offenses would result in a substantial reduction in America's prison population. There would be an additional mass exodus from jails if bail requirements and pretrial detention were abolished. Already in 1833, Alexis de Tocqueville noted in *Democracy in America* that the U.S. bail system favored the rich and penalized the poor. Current studies show that defendants who are incarcerated at the time of their trials are more likely to be convicted and sentenced to harsher penalties than defendants who are not confined. In addition, several studies have indicated that defendants who are released on their own recognizance have lower rates of nonappearance than defendants who post bail, and, contrary to common expectation, the rate of nonappearance declines as the seriousness of the charges increases.[35]

The abolition of pretrial detention and the retroactive decriminalization of "victimless" offenses could free as many as half of all people incarcerated in American jails and prisons. But then what about those

34. Cited by Russ Immarigeon in "Beyond the Fear of Crime: Reconciliation as the Basis for Criminal Justice Policy," in *Criminology as Peacemaking*, p. 76.

35. See Knopp et al., *Instead of Prisons*, pp. 110-12.

who would remain behind bars? Some prison abolitionists suggest that one possible step along the path of "excarceration" would be to negotiate parole contracts with prisoners.[36] In such negotiations, the financial resources that would otherwise be used to cage people could be used instead to guarantee good jobs and educational opportunities for offenders; in return, offenders could contract to pay restitution to any people who have been victimized by their offenses and/or to participate in community service programs. Indeed, some commentators who are concerned about the burgeoning prison population note that there is evidence that "intermediate sanctions" such as fines or sentences to probation or community service "are at least as effective as imprisonment in reducing crime."[37]

While the imposition of intermediate sanctions is more humane than confinement, we should be cautious about this alternative on several counts. Currently, the imposition of fines is the most widely utilized intermediate sanction, but fines inevitably have a greater punitive impact on the poor than on the wealthy. Both corporate executives and bosses of organized crime have been known to view fines as merely part of the cost of doing business. For the poor, a small fine can have a devastating impact on family finances, but some Wall Streeters convicted of insider trading are not much fazed by millions of dollars in fines.

An additional caution regarding intermediate sanctions pertains to questions of noncompliance. What happens with those offenders who are unable or unwilling to pay fines or perform community service or comply with probation guidelines? As long as the prison system remains intact, the judicial establishment inevitably reverts to incarceration as the backup to try to force compliance with lesser sanctions. By definition, intermediate "sanctions" are still punitive, and punitive measures are typically enforced by holding in reserve more onerous and coercive punishments.[38]

36. Knopp et al., *Instead of Prisons*, pp. 96-98.
37. "The Talk of the Town," *New Yorker*, 13 April 1992, p. 28.
38. David Rothman notes the manner in which, historically, "the need for one more sanction" and for "coercive backup" has operated even inside the prison system: "If the inmate will not behave at the minimum security camp, we have the threat of the maximum security penitentiary, and if he will not behave there, we have the threat of administrative segregation, and if that will not do, solitary, and if that does not break

Too frequently, discussion of responses to crime that might serve as alternatives to imprisonment dissolves into talking about alternative models of punishment rather than alternatives to the punishment model.[39] A commitment to making "war on crime" arises from the belief that evil must be restrained by inflicting pain rather than by practicing love and reconciliation. In the "battle" against evil, the same war rhetoric is applicable domestically and internationally; we are told that the "deterrence" of either nuclear strike or criminal activity depends on our ability to "retaliate" swiftly and that we must not "handcuff" our police or military officers as they seek to win the war against criminals or Iraqis or Vietnamese.[40]

Wars and crimes are both manifestations of conflicts that can produce devastating damage and harm.[41] In current military and judicial practice, the response to such conflicts is to inflict still more damage in the belief that evil is thereby restrained. But our response to conflict need not be a call to battle. Instead, a healing response to conflict would entail the pursuit of peace and reconciliation and repair of damage.[42]

Some mediation programs offer approaches that seriously seek to foster reconciliation. One example is the Victim Offender Reconciliation Program originally started by a group of Mennonites in Elmira,

---

him, bread and water, or physical punishment. Is there any point short of brutality to stop? A system of incarceration seems incapable of maintaining decency throughout *all* its sectors" (*Conscience and Convenience*, p. 420).

39. This point is also made by Howard Zehr in *Changing Lenses: A New Focus for Crime and Justice* (Scottdale, Pa.: Herald Press, 1990), pp. 93-94.

40. For other examples of the rhetorical and actual equivalence between the war on crime and other military conflicts, see M. Kay Harris, "Moving into the New Millennium: Toward a Feminist Vision of Justice," in *Criminology as Peacemaking*, pp. 90-91. In the same volume, see also Robert Elias, "Crime Control as Human Rights Enforcement," pp. 252-53.

41. In books such as *Criminology as Peacemaking*, some criminologists are beginning to call for a new understanding of the very concept of "crime." Instead of defining it as activity that violates laws, this new understanding maintains that crime should be defined as activity that produces harm and damage to other people. In this understanding, war is crime, and governments could stand indicted for no small number of offenses.

42. J. Peter Cordella notes that the redefinition of conflict as crime occurs in settings where "the societal eclipses the communal." In a helpful article, Cordella contrasts society's retributive response to conflict with the reconciling approach practiced in intentional communities such as the Amish and Hutterites. See "Reconciliation and the Mutualist Model of Community," in *Criminology as Peacemaking*, pp. 30-46.

Ontario.[43] This program began outside the judicial system, although it now receives occasional referrals from courts. It brings victims and offenders together in a safe environment. The aim is not to ask questions like "What should be done to the offender?" but rather "What can be done to make things right?"[44]

One clear advantage of the mediation approach is its potential for assisting victims of crime. Under the current system, several states have instituted "victim assistance programs," but some authors have commented on the manner in which such programs can assist prosecutors more than victims.[45] Current "victim assistance" includes transportation to and from the court; in cases in which victims do not report crimes or refuse to cooperate with the prosecution, various forms of assistance can be denied. In short, the focus still remains on the offender and on securing a conviction. It is not a given that the interests of prosecutors and victims coincide. Russ Immarigeon observes that the prosecutors may be interested in convictions and stiff penalties, "while the victim's main concern, to use a simple example, is that she get her purse and its contents returned to her."[46]

In the mediation process, the needs of victims are central. Many victims of crime speak of the need to talk about what has happened to them and to give voice to their pain, fear, and anger.[47] The expression "forgive and forget" is an oxymoron. True forgiveness requires remembrance.[48] Victims frequently need to bear witness to the injustices they have suffered and the ways in which they have been violated. Family,

---

43. For a description of the program and a brief history, see Howard Zehr and Earl Sears, *Mediating the Victim-Offender Conflict* (Akron, Pa.: Mennonite Central Committee, 1982); and Zehr, *Changing Lenses*, pp. 158-74.

44. Zehr, *Changing Lenses*, p. 186.

45. See, e.g., Marilyn McShane and Frank P. Williams III, "Radical Victimology: A Critique of the Concept of Victim in Traditional Victimology," *Crime and Delinquency* 38 (April 1992): 258-71.

46. Immarigeon, "Beyond the Fear of Crime," p. 72. Immarigeon also cites the case of the murder of a community volunteer in Tennessee (p. 73). The victim was an opponent of capital punishment, and in a 1989 letter to the prosecutor, the victim's family called for compassion and noted that "God's forgiveness and love . . . is the only response to violence." The prosecutor asked for the death penalty.

47. Zehr, *Changing Lenses*, pp. 19-29.

48. A similar point is made by Susan Jacoby (*Wild Justice: The Evolution of Revenge* [New York: Harper & Row, Publishers, 1983], p. 1), but I differ with her description of remembrance as "a form of revenge."

friends, and other supportive people need to listen and to share in the grief, but some victims are also helped by being able to express their pain and anger to the people who have wronged them. By bringing the victim and offender together, mediation makes that possible. If the victim and the perpetrator did not know each other before the offense, mediation gives the opportunity to ask some of the questions that often plague victims — questions like "Why did this happen to me?"

While judicial sentences frequently ignore the needs of victims, mediation often results in some form of restitution. The restitution might be financial, but some mediation sessions have resulted in agreements that offenders would provide restitution in the form of services or work for victims. When poor people have been victimized by crime, financial restitution can be vital to their well-being, but in these and other cases, restitution can also serve an important symbolic function.[49] It is a symbol that someone has been wronged and that steps are being taken to make things right. Such steps are movements toward reconciliation, and, as indicated by the words of Jesus in Luke 6:30, the most meaningful restoration is not property but right relationships.

For the offender, mediation offers the possibility of constructively working through the guilt engendered by his or her action.[50] Our judicial system maintains that the offender owes a "debt to society," an abstract notion that is likely to elude even the most repentant of offenders. In mediation, however, the offender meets a real person who has been harmed. Moreover, the offender can understand what specific measures might help to repair the damage resulting from his or her actions. By focusing on the *actions* that have hurt and the actions that might help to heal, we can avoid the harmful and counterproductive practice of labeling and stigmatizing the offender as an evil person.

Victim Offender Reconciliation Programs report that over 80 percent of all restitution contracts resulting from mediation are fulfilled and that over 90 percent of all victims and offenders who participate express satisfaction with the mediation process.[51] A popular misperception is that crime victims favor harsher punishments than the public at large. In fact, recent surveys have shown that crime victims are more

49. Zehr, *Changing Lenses*, p. 192.
50. Zehr, *Changing Lenses*, p. 50.
51. Zehr, *Changing Lenses*, pp. 164-65.

likely than others to favor restitution and rehabilitative "help" for the offender rather than imprisonment.[52] Also recommending the mediation approach are studies that show lower rates of repeat offenses among offenders who participate in programs of restitution and reconciliation.[53]

There are, of course, situations in which victims may be unwilling to meet with offenders or vice versa. Victims of sexual assault or other forms of violence may be frightened or repulsed by the prospect of meeting their assailants. In such instances, it may still be possible to proceed with indirect mediation through a trusted third party. Restitution in cases such as these can come in the form of reparations for therapy and medical care and time off from work. Programs have been devised in both Canada and England that involve meetings between offenders and surrogate victims of violence.[54]

So far, mediation has been utilized most frequently in cases of property crimes, but the judicial system itself occasionally allows for mediation for a range of criminal offenses. In New York, some felonies are referred to local dispute resolution centers.[55] One Victim Offender Reconciliation Program in Batavia, New York, successfully mediated a case of rape,[56] and another program in Winnipeg, Manitoba, has worked with cases of serious violence up to and including homicide.[57]

I do not mean to gloss over the fact that there are some people in our society who have committed acts of heinous brutality and are fully capable of doing so again. But I would point out that the prison system makes these few people the norm for how we should respond to all offenders.[58] Are there any alternatives to imprisonment for those who must be viewed as truly dangerous?

It was in the 1850s that a Boston shoemaker named John Augustus persuaded some judges to grant him custody over several juvenile of-

---

52. See Zehr, *Changing Lenses*, p. 193.

53. Immarigeon, "Beyond the Fear of Crime," p. 70.

54. Zehr, *Changing Lenses*, p. 206.

55. Maria R. Volpe, "Mediation in the Criminal Justice System: Process, Promises, Problems," in *Criminology as Peacemaking*, p. 201.

56. Harold E. Pepinsky, "Peacemaking in Criminology and Criminal Justice," in *Criminology as Peacemaking*, p. 312.

57. Zehr, *Changing Lenses*, p. 163.

58. See Zehr, *Changing Lenses*, p. 180.

fenders.[59] Augustus believed that these young people would be harmed by jail or prison, and he thought that he could provide them with new opportunities in life. He assumed responsibility for their room and board and for seeing that they posed no threat to the community. Some prison abolitionists have cited the example of John Augustus as one possible approach to the restraint of those who might present a threat to others. Would it not be possible for church communities or intentional communities actively involved with concerns of peace and justice to voluntarily assume care and responsibility for those who could pose a threat? "Feminist values suggest that we should move toward conceiving restriction of liberty as having less to do with buildings, structures, and walls and more to do with human contacts and relations," writes M. Kay Harris. "Few if any creatures are dangerous to all other creatures at all times, especially to those with whom they are directly and closely connected on an ongoing basis."[60] Harold Pepinsky cites a successful Massachusetts program of close supervision of violent offenders in the community.[61]

But in addition to holding out the promise of an alternative, the example of John Augustus raises another caution. Augustus was a compassionate man with a creative vision, but his vision was eventually co-opted by the judicial system to become what we now call "probation." Instead of freeing people from the punitive power of the state, probation brought more people under state control. Instead of replacing incarceration, probation became a supplementary sanction for which imprisonment was the backup.

That example is a good reminder and warning to those of us who might be tempted into the facile concoction of "alternatives" to prisons. And it is a warning that is even more requisite for those who might be tempted into reform of the "criminal justice system" or of prisons. Those who seek to pursue prison reform should be reminded that modern prisons are totally the product of reform and that "God's good news in Jesus to the prisoners calls us to the reality that Jesus means *freedom*, not *reform*."[62]

---

59. Rothman, *Conscience and Convenience,* p. 44.
60. Harris, "Moving into the New Millennium," p. 95.
61. Pepinsky, "Peacemaking in Criminology," p. 310.
62. Campbell and Holloway, "Freedom to Prisoners," p. 148.

Our technological society does so love an institutional fix. And so in response to the latest social crisis, committees are appointed, position papers are issued, reforms are proposed, and institutional flow-charts are shuffled. Institutional fixes are responses that focus on what "they" ought to do. "They" usually refers to politicos on federal or local levels who may in fact be less in control of institutions than controlled by them. Institutional fixes are responses that look to the power of the state and invest confidence in the ability of the state to reform itself. But as Dorothy Day and Peter Maurin noted, to look to the state to respond to human needs is to ask the question of Cain, "Am I my sister's or brother's keeper?" Instead, Day and Maurin spoke of the need for "personalist revolution." By "personalist," they were not referring to individualism; in fact, both Day and Maurin were members of the Catholic Worker Community, and their emphasis was communitarian. But instead of raising questions about how institutions must be rearranged or how "they" ought to do this or that, the personalist revolution addresses different questions: Who am I called to be? And in community together, who are we called to be?[63]

It is really a question of *being* more than a question of *doing*. Campbell and Holloway:

> A friend of ours, Tom Merton, liked to remind us that "Bonhoeffer himself said it was an 'Anglo-Saxon failing' to imagine that the Church was supposed to have a ready answer for every social problem." . . . "What can we, as Christians, do to help?" is the perennial question that the oppressor demands of his victim. "Before you do a damned thing," Tom would comment, "just *be* what you say you are, a Christian; then no one will have to tell you what to do. You'll know."[64]

Unfortunately, dissatisfaction with the prison system often gives rise to questions like "What system can be devised to replace the prison?" There are assumptions and dangers inherent in such questions. One of the assumptions within the question is that prisons have served a good purpose (even if inadequately) and that, if we are to eliminate prisons, we must devise institutional structures and systems that better serve the purposes prisons have served. But if these supposedly good purposes have

---

63. For a summary of some aspects of the personalist revolution, see William D. Miller, *Dorothy Day: A Biography* (New York: Harper & Row, 1982), pp. 227-48.

64. Campbell and Holloway, *Up to Our Steeples in Politics*, pp. 152-53.

to do with keeping bad people away from good people (deterrence) or imposing compulsory change (rehabilitation) or satisfying society's need to punish (retribution), then the only possible alternative to prisons would be prisons with a different name. If we believe that good ends justify evil means and that prisons are designed to pursue good ends, then there is no reason even to pose the question of alternatives. If we assume that prisons serve good purposes, then the question itself is an oxymoron because the alternative to prisons can only be prisons — perhaps reformed and modernized, but prisons nonetheless.

But the question about alternatives makes even less sense when our understanding of prisons is demythologized by the biblical perspective. The biblical identification of prisons with death unmasks the pretenses. Prisons are not resisting violence; prisons *are* violence. Prisons are not resisting stealing; prisons steal people away and rob them in body and spirit. Prisons are not resisting immorality; short of the barrel of the gun, prisons are the ultimate bastion of support for a system of immorality that casts modern-day widows and orphans out of their homes. From such a perspective, the question of alternatives makes no more sense than questions like "What are alternatives to slavery?" or "What are alternatives to concentration camps?" The only alternative is to stop. The only alternative is Jesus' proclamation of liberty for the captives.

But Jesus' proclamation brings with it new and more meaningful questions — questions that direct us away from devising plans for what "they" ought to do and toward the discipleship to which we are called. How can we be of service to those who are victimized? How can we nonviolently respond to violence when it is directed toward ourselves or others? How can we witness to the presence of the kingdom and to Jesus' proclamation of liberty while taking adequate account of the dangers that confront our sisters and brothers and ourselves? Even if imperfectly, it is vital that we all attempt to grapple with those questions.

Seeking to Live the Fall of the Prison

During the late 1960s and early 70s, when the American war in Southeast Asia was raging at its bloodiest level, some people appeared at peace rallies bearing signs with the words, "THE WAR IS OVER!" Of course, no one could claim that the killing had stopped or that a truce had been signed. Empirically, the war was not "winding down," and the lights at the end of the tunnel were merely the hallucinations of America's leaders. And yet, some announced in all seriousness that the war was over. The announcement was not a call to ignore the suffering and killing. Instead, the announcement was a way of saying, "We declare peace, and where peace has already been declared, we can no longer cooperate with this nation's war plans. This nation may no longer have our silence or our tax dollars or our bodies to be used as killing machines or cannon fodder. This nation's enemies are not our enemies, and we will proceed to give them food and medical supplies. Where Jesus has already declared peace, we will not wage war."

Jesus' proclamation of liberty for the captives marks the fall of the prison. It is precisely in our own age, when we are bombarded with evidence of the empirical reality of prisons, when prisons are proliferating and overflowing — it is precisely now that we need to hear Jesus' proclamation that prisons are unreal, that they have already been defeated, that they have already fallen. Why cooperate with the prison system or look to prisons to provide security for "good" people and corrections for "bad" when the prison has already fallen? It is not that we can nurture any illusions that all suffering has ended. Indeed, with the fall of the prison, our attention is directed *toward* the needs of those who are suffering and those who have been victimized and *away from* the cops-and-robbers motif of chasing down and apprehending and prosecuting and caging people in the mistaken belief that that will help either the victims or the caged. To proclaim that the prison has fallen is not to pretend that God's will is fully incarnate in the world; rather, it is to witness to the presence of God's kingdom and to allow that presence to demythologize us. In the shell of our old world, a new reality is present, and we are called to live the new within the shell of the old.

There are stories that witness to the fall of the prison. There are stories of communities and individuals offering persistent love and nurture that have helped to contribute to healing for victims of assault and rape, whereas in contrast, the courtroom pursuit of "justice" only compounded the trauma. There are stories of people who pay bail for prisoners and develop the kinds of friendships in which the lives of both friends are changed. There are amazing stories of how people have effectively responded to dangerous situations by relying on the power of nonviolence.

In an excellent videotape entitled *Nonviolent Response to Personal Assault* produced by Pax Christi USA in 1986, Angie O'Gorman and Maggie Pharris tell precisely such stories of their own encounters with situations of potential violence. In 1982, Angie O'Gorman was living alone in a Catholic Worker House that had been closed for repairs. One night she was asleep in a third-floor bedroom and was awakened to the spectacle of a large man kicking in her bedroom door, yelling something, and moving toward her bed. Rather than cowering in fear or engaging in what would have been fruitless screaming, O'Gorman was struck with the sudden awareness that both she and the man who had burst into her room shared a dilemma; either they both got through the situation safely or they would both suffer — she from whatever he was about to do to her and he from the very experience of victimizing someone and also from prison if he was apprehended. O'Gorman doesn't know where the question came from, but she describes it as a "moment of grace" when her first words to the man who had come crashing through her door were, "What time is it?" Amazingly, the simple question elicited a human response. That is a vital moment in any situation of potential violence. It is the moment when, in the words of Dorothy Samuel, "attacker confronts not victim, not a mere thing; attacker confronts living, feeling, autonomous human being. Attacker must himself become a living, feeling human being — or flee."[65]

The man who had invaded Angie O'Gorman's room looked at his watch and said that it was 3:15. O'Gorman looked over to her clock and pointed out to the man that her clock said 3:30. In this most precarious of situations, O'Gorman and the man actually had a discussion about whose timepiece might be awry. The human link was established. O'Gorman notes that, "I never felt so vulnerable in my life, but I knew that if I came out with fear or anger, it was going to explode." Most often, expressions of fear or anger evoke responses of fear or anger. Instead, O'Gorman's question about the time introduced enough surprise to cause the man to pause, and in this pause there was an opportunity to redirect his focus and his actions. Angie O'Gorman went on to ask the man to tell her about himself. They talked, and the threat of impending violence slowly diminished. When she found that the man

65. Samuel, *Safe Passage on City Streets* (New York: Abingdon Press, 1975), p. 40.

was without a place to stay, O'Gorman invited him to spend the night on the couch downstairs in the Catholic Worker House.

In the same videotape, Maggie Pharris tells a story that also involved establishing a human link and responding to a situation of potential violence in a way that evoked surprise and wonder. Pharris was jogging one evening in Minneapolis when a man came up alongside her, grabbed her arm, and pinned her against a tree. Pharris's first awareness was of fear and of feeling totally blocked from any ability to respond. Within moments, another man came along — a small man who was walking his dog. Pharris became aware that this third person could be endangered by being drawn into the situation, and she acted to redirect the scenario. She took her assailant by the arm and said, "Come on, we're going this way," motioning her assailant away from the man with the dog. Her assailant moved with her but paused to ask, "What are you doing?" Maggie Pharris responded, "I can tell by looking at your eyes that there's a lot of hurt, and maybe it would be better for us to talk than to do anything else." The human link had been established. Pharris mentioned her family and asked the man about his family. The man talked about his painful remembrances of having killed people in Vietnam. They talked for an hour, but Pharris still wasn't sure that she was free to leave. She mentioned that it was a cold evening and asked the man if he would walk her home. On the way, he asked her to name her favorite flower. The next morning, she found some daisies at her door along with a note: "Thank you for being my friend."

Both Pharris and O'Gorman freely admit that the stories sound "pie in the skyish" and that some people might attribute the outcome to "luck." But a far more significant factor than "luck" in these cases was the manner in which moments of grace enabled both women to evoke a disarming sense of wonder or surprise in their assailants and to present themselves to the assailants as real people and not just faceless victims. Pharris notes, "I wanted to quickly become a person to him."

The experiences of O'Gorman and Pharris are echoed in other stories. Terry Dobson has written of an encounter with a drunken laborer who boarded a train in a Tokyo suburb.[66] The man was out of

---

66. Dobson, "The Art of Reconciliation," in *What Would You Do? A Serious Answer to a Standard Question,* by John H. Yoder et al. (Scottdale, Pa.: Herald Press, 1983), pp. 96-99. Dobson's article first appeared in *Reader's Digest,* December 1981.

control, swaggering about, and cursing at no one in particular. When the drunken man swung his fist at a woman holding a small child, Dobson moved to intervene. Dobson confesses that he saw the situation as an opportunity to put his intensive akido training into practice: "I planned to take this turkey apart, but he had to make the first move. I wanted him mad, so I pursed my lips and blew him an insolent kiss." This totally enraged the drunken man, but a fraction of a second before he could leap at Dobson, the attention of everyone in the train car was drawn by a loud and happy shout: "Hey." It was a small, elderly Japanese man smiling and calling to the man who was about to attack. "Hey, c'mere." All smiles, the elderly man boisterously asked the drunken man to talk, and he was happily oblivious to the response: "Why the hell should I talk to you?"

> The old man continued to beam at the laborer. "What'cha been drinkin'?" he asked, his eyes sparkling with interest.
>
> "I been drinkin' sake," the laborer bellowed back, "and it's none of your business!" Flecks of spittle spattered the old man.
>
> "Oh that's wonderful," the old man said, "absolutely wonderful! You see, I love sake too. Every night, me and my wife (she's 76, you know), we warm up a little bottle of sake . . ."[67]

And then the old man proceeded to tell of how they took the sake into the garden and sat on a bench and watched the sunset and saw how the persimmon tree was growing. And aren't persimmons delicious? Through his drunken fog, the laborer strained to follow the meanderings of the old man's talking. And when the old man asked about the laborer's family, the laborer began to cry as he talked of the death of his wife and his own homelessness. As Dobson disembarked the train, the old man was gently cradling the laborer, who lay with his head resting in the old man's lap. Said Dobson, "what I wanted to do with muscle had been accomplished with kind words."[68]

These stories all testify to the importance of establishing human contact in situations of potential violence, of introducing a surprise that evokes not fear or anger but wonder. Similar elements are present in a story related by Dorothy Samuel:

67. Dobson, "The Art of Reconciliation," p. 98.
68. Dobson, "The Art of Reconciliation," p. 99.

In a large city, a woman who had devoted her life to the peaceful resolution of conflict at all levels of living found herself overtaken by two young men. They came up from behind and separated significantly at her shoulders. Her arms were loaded with shopping bags, and she was far from any residence where she was known.

Before they could enclose her, before they could speak a word, she beamed from one to the other, thrust out her packages, and told them how glad she was that they had come along.

"I was rather nervous on this street — and these bags are so heavy. Would you help me?"

Instinctively, they took the packages. The three then walked along together while the woman cheerily thanked them and told them how good they were to help.[69]

The element of surprise in these stories entails evoking wonder or a respectful response from potential assailants. This is totally different from a "surprise" that would evoke anger or fear. A homeless man named Bobby was one of the hospitality guests staying at our community house in Baltimore in 1977. While Bobby was with our community, his grandfather was murdered in his own home by an unarmed intruder. When he heard the intruder, Bobby's grandfather grabbed a gun out of a drawer and tried to confront the man who had broken into his home. A scuffle ensued and Bobby's grandfather was killed with his own gun. The police later apprehended the intruder, who reported that his purpose in breaking into the house had been to steal money, not to commit murder. While not wanting to blame the murder victim in this or any other case, I think it is important to note that confronting someone with a gun can evoke a very powerful and primal "fight or flight" response. If someone is held at gunpoint in such a way as to preclude flight, the ensuing fight can have tragic consequences.

Of course, there are many ways of evoking surprise in potential assailants, and there is a whole range of responses between the horror of a gun on the one hand and the loving, humanizing responses of Angie O'Gorman and Maggie Pharris on the other. Dorothy Samuel reports instances in which robbery and assault were turned aside by surprising responses that were breathtakingly naive ("You can't do that. It's against the law")[70] or righteously indignant ("You can't bother me! This is my

69. Samuel, *Safe Passage on City Streets*, p. 89.
70. Samuel, *Safe Passage on City Streets*, p. 34.

neighborhood!")[71] or even simply disinterested ("I'm sick. I couldn't move if I had to").[72] While I personally believe that the ideal (and less dangerous) responses are those which avoid the possibility of evoking anger in potential assailants, I must confess that my own responses have sometimes fallen short of the ideal. In at least one instance, indignant anger was the surprise with which I confronted a man wielding a knife.

Manna House was the free kitchen staffed by our Advaita community in Baltimore. Our community members shared responsibilities at the kitchen, but there was a period in 1978 when I was left alone with the work as other community members were either out of town or busy with other responsibilities. After a period of six days consumed with very little but preparing and serving meals and washing dishes and floors, I was ready for a break. Kim, one of our community members, returned to town and generously suggested that she take care of Manna House while I take a day off.

I did a bit of work around the community house and then planned to devote the rest of the day to reading. I had barely settled into a book when the phone rang. It was Kim.

"Lee, Butch is high on something. He has a knife and he's ranting and raving around the kitchen and threatening people. He won't give me the knife." I told Kim I'd be right there. It took about five minutes to walk to the kitchen.

I was thankful Kim had called. In our community, we agreed to call on each other in times of trouble, and I had made such calls myself. But as I hustled my way out the door and down the street, I felt a growing sense of anger — not at Kim, certainly, but at Butch. Butch came into the kitchen regularly, but we had rarely spoken. Nonetheless, I decided then and there that I didn't like him. As I hurried down the street, I must confess that my mind was not primarily engaged with thoughts of concern for the people in the kitchen. I wish I could say that I was saying a prayer for the safety of Kim and the others, but that was not the case either. I confess to thinking, "This is my day off. Who the heck does Butch think he is?" By the time I reached the kitchen, the surprise I had to offer Butch was not fueled by either compassion or bravery but rather by simple indignation.

71. Samuel, *Safe Passage on City Streets*, p. 35.
72. Samuel, *Safe Passage on City Streets*, p. 63.

I flung open the kitchen door and paused a second to locate the culprit. Butch was standing near the center of the room. In response to my melodramatic entry, he turned to face me, knife in hand. I walked directly toward him, and, stepping well within his knife's reach, I blurted, "This is my day off. Now give me the damned knife, Butch."

I do not recommend my action or my words as a wise or particularly "nonviolent" response to someone who is holding a weapon. The fact that Butch was obviously under the influence of some drug made his response even less predictable. Glassy-eyed, he looked at me for a tense moment and then said, "Lee, I like the way you talk to me," and he handed me the knife. I was relieved to have the knife away from him, but I was perturbed by his comment. Something in the tone of his voice made the scene appear to be some sort of showdown between two hombres on the village square. Something in his remark made me wonder if Butch had refused to give the knife to Kim because she was a woman and if perhaps I had just played a role in some macho standoff. I exchanged only a few words with Kim, and then, my indignation unabated, I slammed my way back out of the kitchen. I was muttering to myself as I stomped my way up Calvert Street toward home. I had gone a full block before becoming aware that other people on the street were looking at me in horror. There I was in full public view, stomping and muttering and carrying a large knife in my right hand.

While my response to Butch is certainly no model for nonviolent response to a potential assailant, the story still illustrates the value of responding in such a way as to evoke wonder and redirect attention. When Butch and I talked several days later, he told me that he had been drunk on the day that he had brought the knife into the kitchen and that he had been interested in confronting some people who had been "disrespecting" him. When I asked why he had given me the knife, Butch explained that he had never seen me angry before and that that had surprised him, but also, "Do you remember what you said to me? I think you said something about a day off. It started me to thinking that you were going nuts. Could you kindly tell me what having a day off had to do with anything?"

Following the incident with the knife, Butch and I started talking more frequently. He visited our community home, and he established friendships with several members of our community. In the years that followed, Butch started helping with the work at the kitchen, and I distinctly remember a later encounter with him at Manna House. We were both standing in the food preparation area swapping ideas about nonviolence and the gospel. I was up to my elbows in soapy dish water. Once again Butch had a knife in his hand, but this time he was using it with no small agility to chop up vegetables for the next batch of soup.

Of course, it would be naive to assume that attempts to respond nonviolently inevitably turn assailants into friends. At times, victims of crime are left with feelings of powerlessness. At times, the question is not whether the assailant's life will be changed but whether the victim's life will be spared.

It was on a warm, summer evening in 1976 when the doorbell rang at Jonah House in Baltimore. Most of our community members were gone for the evening. Phil Berrigan and Liz McAlister were in a room on the basement level of the house, and I was on the first floor making a batch of bread. I opened the inside door and saw two men standing on the other side of the screen. "Is John home?" As I pushed open the screen door, I started to explain that there was no John living at the house. Time started moving in slow motion from the instant I saw the gun.

As I was pushed back through the doorway, my mind was stuck on their asking about "John." Was there some John who owed them money or who had crossed them in a drug deal? My attempt to explain that "No, really, John doesn't live here" was met with a sharp "Shut up." I was ordered to sit on the couch, and as I did so, the man with the gun adopted a stance he must have seen in dozens of TV pictures. Standing a few feet in front of me, he crouched slightly and grasped the gun with both hands. Extending his arms to their full length, he placed his finger on the trigger and pointed the gun directly toward my eyes. He did not speak, nor did I. For what seemed like an interminable period, my world was silent. A few moments earlier at the doorway, I had experienced intense fear, but in those moments on the couch, staring into a gun held by a man in executioner's pose, I experienced something beyond fear. I felt the strange calm of knowing that I was going to die.

The silence was broken by the other intruder, who was standing off to the side. "Empty your pockets." The words broke my calm certainty of death, and so in a way I was relieved by the order. Perhaps robbery was their intent. If they wanted to kill me because they thought that I was "John" (my mind was still trying to make sense of it all) or for whatever reason, the wallet in my pocket would not be very relevant. So that none of my movements could be interpreted as threatening, I very slowly emptied my pockets of wallet, pen, and key ring and placed them on a coffee table by the couch.

"All right. Stand up and face the wall," ordered the man with the gun. I did so. As his partner went through my wallet, the man with the gun came up behind me and put me in a choke hold with his arm around my neck. Simultaneously, he placed the barrel of the gun tight against the back of my head. In that position, he slowly led me through the first floor of the house and into the kitchen where the bread was still rising.

"Do you have any guns?"

I explained that we were opposed to guns and to violence in any form.

"Lower your voice," he said.

In a whisper, I continued, "You don't need your gun either. We will freely give you whatever money we can give." That was my only opportunity to say anything meaningful to the two brothers with the gun.

"Is there anyone else in the house?"

I don't believe in lying, but I wanted so much to lie. Instead of answering, I paused as I mentally rehearsed scenarios. Had Liz and Phil heard the intruders? Did they know what was happening up here? Why involve them in this terror? But what if they hadn't heard what's happening? What if I say that I'm alone and then there's suddenly the sound of people talking downstairs? Or what if the intruders want to lead me around the whole house and we end up making an unexpected encounter?

"Answer me. Is there anyone else in the house?"

I did not lie. Gun at my head, they led me to the top of the basement stairs.

"Tell them we're coming down."

Feeling like I was betraying dear friends, I called, "Liz. Phil. They have a gun and we're coming down."

The only courage in the house that night was displayed by Phil and Liz. They had in fact been listening since the doorbell rang. They could have chosen to leave through the back, but they stayed, hoping to find an opportunity to secure my safety. As we reached the base of the stairs, neither Liz nor Phil showed any sign of fear.

"Give us money," the man with the gun said. As Liz slowly reached for her purse, the gunman released his grip on my neck. Freed of his grip for the first time since I stood up from the couch, I started to feel an easing of tension. I stepped over to stand alongside Phil and Liz.

But quite suddenly, the terror built again. Perhaps the intruders were sensing a threat from Phil, or perhaps they were wondering if Liz had a weapon in her purse, or perhaps they were thinking that they should not have released their grip on me. For whatever reason, one of the intruders grabbed Liz and threw her to the floor. Phil and I were thrown to the floor in quick succession, and the gunman trained his weapon on us. Sounding as if he were in a panic, his partner yelled, "Kill 'em! Kill 'em!" For the second time in fifteen minutes, I fully expected to die — this time, along with my friends. I experienced the scene as a whirl of terror and of bodies falling to the floor. I was brought into focus by the touch of a hand on my arm. In the falling, I had landed with my head on Liz' shoulder. In the midst of all the terror, she was reaching out to touch my arm in a reassuring manner.

The man who was yelling changed tenses: "You should have killed 'em. You should have."

When the present places the future in doubt, it helps to hear the past tense used with death threats. As we stayed on the floor, one of the intruders rifled through a desk, and then the gunman said, "If you don't want to die, you'll stay where you are for half an hour." They went up the stairs, and we could hear them heading out of the house. Fearless as always, Phil waited barely half a minute before he was in pursuit. Concerned that others in the neighborhood might also be victimized, Phil headed out the front door to try to catch a glimpse of where the two men might be headed. But the intruders had vanished into the night.

We did not call the police. Instead, we called our neighbors. Up and down the streets of our neighborhood, word spread about the potential danger. Over the following weeks, bonds among neighbors were strengthened and renewed as people talked about looking out for one another.

Terror leaves its mark. For weeks after those two brothers had brought their gun to our home, I was on edge every time I heard the doorbell ring. Totally independent of my will or control, my body would jerk at the sound of any sudden noise. Whether in rural or inner-city environs, I had never before felt frightened about being on the street during day or night, but I suddenly found myself embroiled in paranoia. I studied faces: "That man coming toward me on the sidewalk — was he one of the men?" It is not unusual for crime victims who have experienced violence or the threat of violence to feel something akin to the post-battle stress suffered by soldiers.

Several factors helped me to cope with the stress. Certainly the support of my community was vital, and the simple passage of time served to dull some anxieties. But the new spirit in our neighborhood played a crucial role in preventing me from giving in to any temptation to imprison myself behind locked doors. Getting to know concerned people in the neighborhood helped to restore some feelings of confidence and safety. Ironically perhaps, my feelings of safety were not enhanced by the presence of police cars; they usually suggested to me that trouble had brewed or was brewing. Instead, I was restored to some sense of confidence by being able to walk through the neighborhood and say, "That's where Vera lives. There's Joe on the stoop. Hello, Anne."

Nonetheless, for a time the terror clearly left its mark. In our community, however, there was a more profound sense of sadness that had nothing to do with any preoccupations with our own emotional scars. We were sad at the thought of the two brothers with the gun. We thought that we had somehow failed to give them anything but money. Unlike my later experience with the knife-wielding Butch, I would have no further chance to talk with these gun-wielding robbers. Would they go on to rob again? It was not a comforting realization, but it was nevertheless true that we could not control what they were going to do; we could only hope to control what we did. We notified the neighborhood, but we did not notify the police. If we had put aside our understanding of our faith and summoned the police, would things have turned out differently? Better or worse? Neither calling the police nor contacting the neighborhood provides any guarantees that greater tragedy will be forestalled. But I do not wish to rationalize. My feeble effort to speak a word of nonviolence had been fumbling and ineffective. In our community, we could only pray that my mumbled words about not needing guns might serve as a seed — that amid all of the terror, God might provide a word: go and sin no more. And so we prayed for our assailants.

But the lesson is clear. Whether our principal concern is for personal safety or for a loving change in the lives of offenders, we cannot simply assume that if we choose not to call the police but to rely on nonviolence, then everything will turn out all right. It would be naive to assume that all attempts at nonviolence will be effective. We cannot assume that God, like the Lone Ranger, will always come to the rescue. God does not respond in such mechanical fashion. The cross informs us of that. The only assurance we have (but it is also the greatest assurance) is that wherever we may find ourselves, God will be there.

We must not yield to the temptation to look first to what will be effective. Even those who advocate the use of guns and prisons cannot be certain of the effectiveness of the tools on which they rely. As Will Campbell and James Holloway note, "if law is for the purpose of preventing crime, every wail of a siren calls out its failure."[73] With all our prisons, the victims of crime have not been protected, and the prisons have only served to create new victims. So the question we face is not what is effective but what is faithful.

Clearly, "I don't want to get involved" is *never* a good response to situations in which others are being victimized by crime or violence. The biblical admonitions not to prosecute others are *not* calls to noninvolvement; in fact, they are calls to increased personal and communal involvement. But some people maintain that a refusal to rely on the power of the police, courts, and prisons is not merely ineffective but irresponsible. What if someone is killed as a result? If the offender is not apprehended, what if he or she goes on to perpetrate greater evil in the future? By refusing to rely on the power of police and prisons, are you not responsible for that? Certainly, none of us can escape responsibility for the forms of involvement we choose, nor can any of us entirely predict or control the actions of others. But the same is true of those who continue to rely on the juridical and penal system. Surrendering personal responsibility to police, courts, and prisons is also a form of involvement that carries consequences. What if the arrival of police with guns provokes violence that might otherwise not have occurred? What violence might be done against the offender when he or she is imprisoned? What about those offenders who come out of prison embittered and more determined than ever to be the bad people they have been

---

73. Campbell and Holloway, *Up to Our Steeples in Politics*, p. 24.

told they are? If the offender *is* apprehended, what if he or she goes on to perpetrate greater crimes in the future?[74] But again, the point here is not to argue the relative effectiveness of various approaches. The cross points to criteria other than effectiveness.

Some of the stories that witness to Jesus' proclamation of liberty for the captives do not have traditional happy endings. They are not stories of events that would be judged effective by any worldly standard. And yet, they are stories of profound faith and faithfulness. William Klassen tells the story of Rene Wagler, a young woman who served the poor in inner-city Boston:

> On October 2, 1973, Rene Wagler was doused with gasoline and set on fire by a group of young men. . . . As she lay dying and the policemen were trying to get all the information from her they could, among her last words were the instructions: "If you find them, be kind to them." Her husband, Mark, when he was asked by the police whether there was anything they could do, also answered, "Yes, there is something you can do. Be kind." . . . We all knew that Rene had paid the supreme cost of love for her neighbor and that to be anything but kind to her murderers would be a denial of all that she lived for.[75]

And for Maurice "Mac" McCracken, testifying against his own kidnapers would have been a denial of all that he lived for. Mac was a preacher who ministered to prisoners in and near Cincinnati, Ohio. In November 1978, two prisoners escaped and took Mac hostage. He was later released unharmed, and in January 1979 he was called before a grand jury to testify against the two men who had kidnaped him. Mac refused, saying that he did not believe in caging people in prisons and that he could never testify against his brothers or sisters. For refusing to cooperate with a grand jury, a judge sent him to jail and said that he would remain there until he agreed to testify. So, as a consequence of having been held hostage by escaped prisoners, Mac was also held

---

74. Author Dave Jackson does not advocate totally refraining from reliance on law enforcement and penal responses, but he does anguish over "the responsibility for what might happen — to the offender in prison for years to come or to society if he is later released as a trained and angry criminal" (*Dial 911: Peaceful Christians and Urban Violence* [Scottdale, Pa.: Herald Press, 1981], p. 46).

75. Klassen, *Release to Those in Prison*, Focal Pamphlet 26 (Scottdale, Pa.: Herald Press, 1977), pp. 15-16.

hostage by the state. After four months, the court finally decided that he was not going to have a change of mind or heart, and he was released. When he got out, Mac said, "Getting out of jail is like a journey into spring. I will never testify against those men."

And for an unnamed juror, pronouncing a verdict of guilty would have been a denial of all that she lived for. Chuck Barrett relates the following true story. He writes, "I give it to you as a parable."

> A jury was trying a rape case and had been deliberating for hours over the verdict of an apparently open-and-shut case — clear-guilt — when the clerk came out of the jury room and announced in a whisper to the judge that the jury was hung by one member who refused to vote her verdict. The judge called the juror into his chambers. In came an old black woman, thin and bent and neatly dressed. The judge asked her why she couldn't reach a decision in such a simple case. The old woman looked at him out of the depth of her years and quoted him some Scripture out of Matthew. Then she said it was against her religion to render a verdict on another human. The judge fumed, shouted, reminded her of her oath, threatened her with contempt, and when the woman, obviously uneducated, refused to change her stand, he broke down and had her ushered from the courtroom and her name stricken from the rosters of eligible jurors. But the rape case had to be terminated due to mis-trial. The captive went free.[76]

Some questions need to be asked about these stories. Are these people misguided? Are they perhaps well intentioned and idealistic but ultimately unrealistic and maybe even downright dangerous? That is one option. Perhaps another option would be to say that people like Rene and Mac are saints, and while saints might be able to resist the temptation to seek revenge on those who attack them, that is not possible for common folks like you and me. And so they can be dismissed as saints — in kindly fashion to be sure, but dismissed nonetheless. That is a second option. But another option is that, even if imperfectly, stories like this and people like this witness to the love of God and the freedom God gives to all of us, not just to a few saints. This

---

76. Chuck Barrett, "One Meaning of Prison in America," in *And the Criminals with Him*, pp. 137-38.

latter option is in some ways the most frightening of the three, and it is also the one that seems closest to the Good News of the biblical proclamation.

In order to witness to Jesus' proclamation of liberty for the captives, the first and most important call is to repentance — metanoia — a turning about and resolution to travel on a different path. When believers seek to enact change, whether of a social or political or interpersonal or spiritual nature, too often we overlook repentance or hurry by it or relegate it to a position of unimportance. We are zealous to be effective, to work on new schemes and techniques, and above all to *do* something. Repentance involves a confession of sin and an acknowledgment of powerlessness. It is precisely this acknowledgment of powerlessness that modern humanity cannot abide. Of course we are not powerless over sin or over crime — if only we can concoct the proper prisons or sufficiently strict laws or an adequate police force or an ideal social environment or the right pill. Yet, until we confess our powerlessness as a first step toward repentance, we are condemned to a cycle of reforming our "criminal justice system" in its same old image. Stone dungeons are replaced by stainless steel cells, penitential silence is replaced by psychotherapy, and drawing and quartering gives way to lethal injection.

When we make a confession of our powerlessness, we will be enabled to respond in a much different way to questions about the alternatives to reliance on police and courts and prisons. We will be reoriented away from seeking to concoct institutional and technical answers. When we confess that we are powerless to offer any quick fixes (or indeed, any fixes at all), then our focus will shift away from the goals we hope to achieve and toward the way we hope to live, away from the institutions we plan to devise and toward the suffering people we hope to serve. The gospel does not issue a call to pursue utopian ends but merely to live concretely by means of discipleship and witness to the kingdom that God is already establishing among us. There is no pill, utopian or otherwise. There are no alternatives to prisons. There are only alternatives to the ways in which we victimize and cage each other.

The purpose of seeking out alternative ways of being and acting is *not* to try to achieve personal purity (as if that were possible). Due to the corporate nature of the human community, all people share complicity in both the prison system and crime, and all will remain responsible. Rather than a quest for purity, the search for alternative ways of being and acting is similar to what Mohandas Gandhi called "experiments in truth." An experiment is not an answer, but a confession that we have no pat answers, no new habits for people to adopt, no new laws for people to follow, no standard operating procedure. Unlike scientific experiments that issue forth with an answer after a time in the laboratory, Gandhi held that "experiments in truth" are lifelong endeavors. It is only in such a tentative, nondogmatic fashion that we can propose alternatives to reliance on police and prisons. But in the quest for alternatives, the renunciation of claims to ultimacy should not lead us to judge the quest itself as insignificant; we are dealing with matters of discipleship. Nor should the vocabulary of "experiment" leave the impression that we may lightly choose this or that alternative way of responding; we are dealing with matters of life and death.

If repentance is frequently ignored as irrelevant, so too is prayer. Yet the book of Acts tells us that when people were cast into prison, the response of the early Christian community was to "pray unceasingly" (Acts 12:1-5, 12). Some church members today may believe that "common criminals" are only getting what they deserve and that prayer for such prisoners would be subversive of law and social order — and indeed, it would be. Prayer for prisoners is a confession that our law and order can only inflict violence, not prevent it. Part of the subversive meaning of prayer is elucidated by biblical references to the role of prayer in exorcism (e.g., Mark 9:17-29). When we remember that the spirit of the prison is the demonic spirit of death, prayers of exorcism are appropriate responses to prisons. But this biblical understanding of the spiritual dimension of the prison points to the manner in which we are all held captive by the prison system. In terms of our ethics and our worldview, Dorothy Samuel notes that "we are what we eat,"[77] and our captivity to the prison system is being fed by a daily cultural and media regimen that extols the efficacious virtue of violence and instills a belief in a cops-and-robbers version of ethical dualism. All of this reinforces our captivity to habitual responses. Those who have guns will use them. Those who have not even thought of alternative responses will rely on habit. Those who are fed by television "entertainment" that depicts evil people as the source of our problems will find evil people (never, of

---

77. Samuel, *Safe Passage on City Streets,* pp. 88-96.

course, including themselves). It is captivity. So, in addition to praying for the freedom of prisoners, we might well pray for our own freedom from captivity to the prison system.

And we might well pray for freedom from other forms of captivity as well. Since the vast majority of crimes in America involve property and not the physical injury of people, some of our punitive inclinations are shaped by our attitudes toward material possessions. The Hasidic Jews tell the story of Rabbi Wolf of Zbarazh, whose only concern for his property was that it might tempt others to sin. One night thieves broke into his home. "From that time on, he said every evening before going to bed: 'All my possessions are common property,' so that — in case thieves came again — they would not be guilty of theft."[78] Churches could do worse than to pray that God might grant us such freedom from attachment to property.

Prayer also serves to teach us about forgiveness as it deepens our awareness of our own need to be forgiven and of God's unconditional love. As Gerald McHugh observes, "a wholesale application of 'forgiveness' would undermine the very basis of law."[79] It is in fact such an undermining of the law that is celebrated in the epistles of Paul. But people of faith must take care not to try to turn forgiveness into a new type of law. If you or I or the church community or others are called to a path of forgiveness — hallelujah and amen! But we must *never* seek to force the path of forgiveness onto other victims of crime. If we are to be of service to victims of crime, then our focus must be on them and their needs, not on our own need to preach a particular doctrine of forgiveness. It would be insensitive and cruel to approach a person who has been raped or the surviving family of a murder victim with the demand "You must forgive." For people of faith, the willingness to forgive does not derive from a demand but from an awareness of God's loving forgiveness of us. If we are to minister to victims of crime, it must be with loving service and not with doctrinal demands or with what we imagine to be quick solutions to emotional crisis.

Some believers have viewed repentance and prayer (improperly I think) as wholly private and individual matters. But any effort to witness

---

78. Martin Buber, *Tales of the Hasidim: The Early Masters* (New York: Schocken Books, 1947), p. 161.

79. McHugh, *Christian Faith and Criminal Justice*, p. 163.

to Jesus' proclamation of liberty for the captives necessarily involves us in publicly preaching the Good News.[80] Along with individuals, the principalities and powers also need to hear the proclamation that the prison has fallen. This public witness can take a variety of forms. It can take the form of opposition to new prison construction. It can take the form of going before magistrates and judges and elected officials and asking to exchange places with prisoners. It can take the form of churches reclaiming the traditional right to offer sanctuary to lawbreakers and to serve as places of refuge. It can take the form of public vigils at prisons. But at least one caution is in order: Jesus' defeat of the power of death and his proclamation of liberty to the captives stand as renunciations of *both* capital punishment and prisons. There has been an unfortunate tendency on the part of some death penalty opponents to seek life imprisonment as the alternative to executions. But the gospel is good news of life and freedom, and our witness to the gospel cannot advocate captivity.

In addition to repentance, prayer, and public witness, one alternative to reliance on the police and penal systems is nonviolent intervention. When situations of potential violence arise, it is never conscionable to say, "Since I cannot call the police and I cannot participate in violence, I must therefore stand back and let these people fight it out." A decision to avoid calling the police brings with it a responsibility to intervene personally in situations of potential violence. Examples of how some people have chosen to intervene emerge from experiences in communities such as the Catholic Worker in New York and the Community for Creative Nonviolence in Washington, D.C. At the free kitchens sponsored by these communities, the atmosphere is usually friendly and cooperative, but there have been some instances in which someone's unemployment frustrations might collide with someone's alcohol to produce situations of possible violence. When these situations erupt, members of the communities help each other to intervene by placing their own bodies as barriers between the people who are fight-

---

80. As Dale Brown notes, exclusive emphasis on the biblical call to "resist not evil" can become privatized and passive. There is also a biblical call to "overcome evil with good," and that inevitably involves us in "a mission to the structures and powers of the world" (*Biblical Pacifism: A Peace Church Perspective* [Elgin, Ill.: Brethren Press, 1986], p. 44).

ing, even though it sometimes means stepping in front of a knife or a gun. Communities such as these have produced remarkable testimonies to the power of nonviolent intervention. Although such intervention operates outside of the legal system, it is the very antithesis of the vigilante impulse. The philosophy of vigilantism maintains that the legal system fails in the administration of punishment and retribution. Nonviolent intervention starts from the premise that the legal system succeeds all too well in the administration of violent retribution. What we most lack is not law and order; in an assembly-line fashion, the machinations of the legal system are perfectly well-ordered, and we have laws sufficient to fill mountains of books. What we lack is reconciliation. While nonviolent intervention involves risks with no guarantees of success, it also holds open the possibilities for reconciliation.

Another alternative to calling the police is encouraging people to call on the community of faith for help in working through a crisis, including help in sharing financial burdens. To rely on insurance companies for recovery of losses due to theft is inevitably to involve the police, since insurance companies refuse to pay such claims unless the crime has been reported. Relying on the church instead frees us from that system. But giving money might be the easiest response to a crisis. Perhaps more difficult but also more important is being available to help people work through the sheer terror of having been victimized. The Bible makes it clear that the service of the faith community cannot be restricted to its own members. Unfortunately, part of the experience of the institutional church in America over the past few decades is that wealthier, predominantly white congregations have moved to the suburbs, while some of the lower-income people who are most heavily victimized by crime have remained in the inner city. But geographical separation does not have to prevent churches from establishing a volunteer presence in areas of need or from posting signs in "high crime areas" inviting contact from victims of crime. In fact, however, virtually all churches could begin this work without having to travel to other neighborhoods, by responding to the needs of four or five people in the immediate vicinity who have been victimized. Whether in urban, suburban, small-town, or rural environs, there would be people in need of the services the church could offer. If we are to be oriented away from chasing people and caging them and toward service to those who have suffered, this is a place to begin.

Church communities could also sponsor mediation programs patterned after the original Victim Offender Reconciliation Program started by concerned Mennonites in Canada. By bringing a victim and an offender together or sitting two disputing parties down with a third person as mediator, this model begins to respond to the admonitions presented in Matthew 18. Mediation programs strive for reconciliation. Carefully designed mediation programs need to be publicized. Programs that are easily accessible and free of charge can help to keep cases out of the judicial system.

A surprising alternative approach to lowering crime rates may actually be found in organizing community involvement in movements for justice, peace, and service. In the mid-1960s, a group of sociologists and psychologists studied fluctuations in crime rates among blacks in several cities that were the sites of intense civil rights activities. In all of the cities that were studied, crime rates dropped during periods of civil rights actions. In some cities, rates of homicide, robbery, rape, and aggravated assault dropped by one-third to one-half.[81] While this study was unfortunately limited to examining crime rates only among African Americans, Dorothy Samuel notes a similar impact on crime during periods of organizing in communities of different racial and ethnic composition.[82] Researchers offer no definitive explanation for the phenomenon. Is it that community activism brings more people out onto the streets and thus makes them safer? Or is it that struggles in pursuit of justice and peace give us an awareness of how human community should be valued and of how we need not be condemned to selfishness? Or is it simply that community activity leads us to meet other people and form friendships? It should be added that most violent crime in America is between people who know each other, so there should be no illusion that friendship (or anything else) is *the* solution. But even if it isn't a panacea, a community movement for peace, justice, and service is worthwhile in itself.

Feminist women and men have found that community organizing is a good approach to reducing rape and other violent crimes. Individualistic measures to prevent sexual assault have tended to confine women

81. See Frederic Solomon, Walter L. Walker, Garrett J. O'Connor, and Jacob R. Fishman, "Civil Rights Activity and Reduction in Crime among Negroes," in *Crime and Social Justice: Issues in Criminology* 14 (Winter 1980): 27-35. This study originally appeared in 1965 in *Archives of General Psychiatry.*

82. Samuel, *Safe Passage on City Streets,* p. 88.

and foster traditional roles by encouraging women to dress in certain ways or to avoid certain locales or to stay at home at certain times.[83] In contrast, the community-organizing approach utilizes "Take Back the Night" marches and rape crisis centers to educate the public about sexual assault. The imprisonment of men who have committed rapes provides no solution to sexual assault. One study shows that less than ten percent of convicted rape defendants are imprisoned, and, as criminal penalties become more severe, juries are less likely to convict.[84] Moreover, virtually all prisoners will eventually be released. Even those people who fully endorse the prison system need to understand that imprisonment offers no solution to this crisis. Instead of criminal sanctions, Elliott Currie has noted the manner in which informal social sanctions can be more effective in deterring violent behavior.[85] By contributing to public awareness and education, those who are involved in community organizing are helping to create the social networks and informal social sanctions that can be powerful forces in reducing sexual assault and other crimes of violence.

Joining together with others in efforts to serve people and to organize for social change provides a liberation model for responding to crime. Rather than leaving people isolated behind locked doors and barred windows, community movements for change help to empower neighborhoods and tenants in housing projects.[86] Rather than waging "war on crime," such efforts seek to make peace in the neighborhood. They represent movements away from habitual reliance on police, courts, and prisons.

But just as "law-abiding citizens" can be ensnared by habitual responses to crime and the legal system, lawbreakers can be too. Recidivism and the so-called "life of crime" can be by-products of the manner in which incarceration itself isolates and limits the horizons of the person

83. See Caringella-MacDonald and Humphries, "Sexual Assault, Women, and Community," p. 100.

84. Caringella-MacDonald and Humphries, "Sexual Assault, Women, and Community," p. 104.

85. Currie, cited by Caringella-MacDonald and Humphries in "Sexual Assault, Women, and Community," p. 111.

86. For examples, see Lloyd Klein, Joan Luxenburg, and John Gunther, "Taking a Bite out of Social Injustice: Crime-Control Ideology and Its Peacemaking Potential," in *Criminology as Peacemaking*, pp. 290-95. These authors contrast community organizing with the "paramilitarization" implicit in various media approaches to reporting crime, such as "America's Most Wanted" and the "McGruff Crime Dog" campaign.

who is imprisoned. Visions of alternatives are visions not only for the law-abiders but also for the lawbreakers. It is in this sense that alternatives to reliance on prisons necessarily involve service to prisoners and lawbreakers. Such service might include establishing bail projects, visiting prisoners, acting as their "legs" in the community, forming friendships, helping with the search for jobs, and inviting the homeless (including offenders) into our communities for hospitality. In this regard, the Catholic Worker communities are once again exemplary for the manner in which they extend hospitality to those whom some consider to be "common criminals." Realistically, some would say that inviting offenders into our homes involves risk, but it also involves promise for the birth of strong and helpful friendships. Philippe Pinel was told that emotionally and mentally disturbed people were dangerous animals who needed to be chained. When Pinel removed the chains, he was told that he was being irresponsible. And when the Flemish village of Gheel welcomed these people into their homes, they were told that they were being irresponsible. Churches and individuals who welcome former prisoners into their homes must be prepared to hear the same.

But rather than laying out elaborate plans for service to prisoners, the place to begin is with the simple act of visiting. From there, the next steps will follow quite naturally. As Will Campbell and James Holloway remind us,

> those separated from the Lord at the final judgment would have visited the prisoners had they known that *Jesus the Lord* was in jail. Yet, they didn't, and we don't, because we deny the Lord is a criminal. "Visit the prisoners" has never been taken seriously by the churches. Yet, we constantly discover men and women who have been in various types of prisons for decades without *one single visitor* having signed their record card. We have suggested on other occasions that each institutional church adopt three prisoners purely and simply for purposes of visitation — so that at least once each week every man and woman and child behind bars could have one human being with whom he could have community, to whom the prisoner could tell his story. And the visitor his. We have advocated that because we are convinced that this elementary act of charity alone would provide all the prison reform that society could tolerate.[87]

87. Campbell and Holloway, "Freedom to Prisoners," pp. 147-48.

It will be recalled that for the early church and for the Anabaptists, service to the imprisoned and opposition to the spirit of retribution flowed from biblical leadings *and also* from knowing and visiting prisoners.

It must be noted that the biblical call to visit prisoners is a call to faithfulness, but it is emphatically *not* a call to religion. Faith has to do with God coming down to us — with God revealing and establishing the kingdom among us — with God redeeming and reconciling us. Faith is a gift. Religion is the exact opposite. Religion has to do with our efforts to climb up to God. Religion has to do with apologetics and our efforts to render God's revelation irrelevant because we have somehow managed to "prove" that God exists or that Jesus is the Messiah or that the Bible is infallible or whatever else it is that we want to "prove." And above all, religion has to do with the conviction that *we* are the ones who reconcile people to God. Religion is that which inspires us to be hucksters in approaching both prisoners and victims of crime. When people are vulnerable, they are far more likely to listen to hucksters and peddlers, and people are certainly vulnerable when they are homeless, hungry, victimized by crime, or sitting in a cage. It is an opportune time for conversion. But conversion to what? Conversion to middle-class respectability? Conversion away from the illegal sin of robbing banks in favor of the perfectly legal sin of finding "financial security" in bank accounts? Conversion away from the possession of illegal weapons in favor of becoming a respectable citizen who pays taxes for weapons that are absolutely legal and absolutely genocidal? Conversion away from illegal drugs in favor of the legal but still deadly ways in which Americans are drugged with jobs and schedules and entertainments and television and all of the gimmicks the technological society has to offer? Conversion away from illegal violence against women in favor of the perfectly legal objectifications that daily reinforce a culture of violence against women?

"No," religious people might say, "we don't want to convert people to those things. We want to convert people to Jesus." If the reference is to Jesus of Nazareth (and not only to the "personal Savior" of nineteenth-century American Protestantism or the "magisterial Christ" of the medieval papacy), then why are all their efforts devoted to admonishing prisoners and the unrighteous? What about the manner in which Jesus rebuked the powerful and the righteous and those who had absolute respect for the law? In addition to "converting" the prisoners, do these religious people also propose to preach the Good News of liberty for the captives to wardens and police officers and governors? And even more, the rest of us righteous people who support these prisons with our taxes and our silence need to hear the Good News too.

We need to hear the Good News that Jesus is victor. The prison is fallen. The kingdom of God is in our very midst, and we can no longer pretend that our human warehouses serve good or restrain evil. The power of the prison is the spirit of death, and death itself has been defeated by resurrection. These imprisoned people belong to God, not Caesar. In the name of Jesus, unlock the cages!

For some people, the biblical scandal is simply the call to visit prisoners. The idea of even associating with "bad people" is scandal enough for them. But others are scandalized by the fact that Jesus only issued a call to visit and not to proselytize. Matthew 25:31-46 is not a call to proselytize the thirsty or the naked or the prisoners but simply to give drink and clothing and comfort. Once again, Jesus deflates our religious pretenses, deflates any presumptions that what makes visiting prisoners specifically "Christian" is our effort to convert them. In visiting prisoners as people of faith, we do best to leave our religion behind. We cannot proclaim Jesus as Savior and still pretend to be saving people ourselves. We must be more humble about what it is we do. If we were faithful to our calling to visit prisoners, that would be work enough without wanting to be saviors as well. Besides which, the Bible reminds us that it is not the righteous from the outside who go in to preach to prisoners; it is the prisoners who do the preaching. Visitors armed with righteousness risk being deaf to the Word of God that can be spoken through the words of prisoners at least as often as through the words of clerics.

As we consider the alternatives for addressing crime and for responding humanly to both offenders and the victims of crime, we are reminded that, biblically understood, "criminal justice" is not a separate "issue" to be addressed by some political forum. The Bible does not instruct us to segregate our lives into areas defined by the issue of crime and the issue of poverty and the issue of morality and the issue of war and peace. Biblically understood, lawlessness and the prison are both manifestations not of a political issue but of a spiritual crisis that affects us all. It is a crisis wherein we persist in choosing death even though

God has chosen life on our behalf. When we focus on this spiritual crisis, we see that violence and disrespect for life are the same no matter what the manifestation. And so we cannot talk about robbery on the streets of our cities without also talking about the robbery that takes place when we eat from full tables while one-third of the world remains malnourished. We cannot talk about violence on the streets of our cities without seeing its direct link to the fact that, as a nation, we are armed to the teeth with enough nuclear weapons to obliterate our planet. If we talk about immorality and prostitution, we must do so with an eye to the numerous ways in which we prostitute ourselves to the gods of success, respectability, and material possessions. And so efforts to address the problem of crime nonviolently will necessarily involve us in efforts to feed the hungry, resist militarism, and climb on down the social ladder.

Will any of these alternatives work? We don't know. We have no guarantees. We only have the biblical story. But what a story it is, and what things we are told! And try as we might, we can't change the story. Try as we might to pin the labels on other people — criminal, thief, murderer, monster — that won't change the story that we all have one Creator and we are all sisters and brothers. We can spend the rest of our lives inventing new handcuffs and building new prisons, but that won't change the fact that Jesus proclaims liberty for the captives and the prisons have fallen. We can buy guns and stockpile nuclear weapons until the earth sinks under their weight, but nothing we can do will ever undo the resurrection and the fact that life is chosen for us. And we can call the police as often as we wish, but let us remember the story: Jesus comes as a thief in the night.

Bibliography

This bibliography does not offer an exhaustive list of resources — only a list of those books and articles cited in this study. For purposes of the bibliography, I have arranged the resources under topical headings, but I must confess that the arrangement is somewhat artificial, and, though each source is listed only once, several of the titles could have been placed under more than one of the headings. Finally, it should be noted that reference to a particular work does not necessarily mean that I agree with that author's perspectives nor (I am sure many of these authors would want me to add) that he or she agrees with mine.

Biblical Studies

Allegro, John. *The Dead Sea Scrolls: A Reappraisal.* 2d ed. New York: Penguin, 1964.

Báez-Camargo, Gonzalo. *Archaeological Commentary on the Bible.* Garden City, N.Y.: Doubleday, 1984.

Bartchy, S. Scott. *First-Century Slavery and I Corinthians 7:21.* Society of Biblical Literature Dissertation Series, no. 11. Atlanta: Scholars Press, 1985.

Barth, Christoph F. *Introduction to the Psalms.* Translated by R. A. Wilson. New York: Scribner's, 1966.

Barth, Markus. *Ephesians 1–3.* Anchor Bible, no. 34. Garden City, N.Y.: Doubleday, 1974.

————. *Ephesians 4–6*. Anchor Bible, no. 34A. Garden City, N.Y.: Doubleday, 1974.

Batey, Richard. *Jesus and the Poor*. New York: Harper & Row, 1972.

Bauer, Walter. *A Greek-English Lexicon of the New Testament and Other Early Christian Literature*. Translated and edited by William F. Arndt and F. Wilbur Gingrich. Chicago: University of Chicago Press, 1957.

Bianchi, Herman. "Tsedeka-Justice." *Review for Philosophy and Religion*, September 1973, pp. 306-18.

Brandon, S. G. F. *Jesus and the Zealots: A Study of the Political Factor in Primitive Christianity*. New York: Scribner's, 1967.

Bright, John. *A History of Israel*. 2d ed. Philadelphia: Westminster Press, 1972.

Brown, Raymond E. *The Gospel according to John XIII–XXI*. Anchor Bible, no. 29A. Garden City, N.Y.: Doubleday, 1970.

Buber, Martin. *Moses: The Revelation and the Covenant*. New York: Harper & Row, 1958.

Caird, G. B. *The Language and Imagery of the Bible*. Philadelphia: Westminster Press, 1980.

Cassidy, Richard J. *Society and Politics in the Acts of the Apostles*. Maryknoll, N.Y.: Orbis Books, 1987.

Charlesworth, James H., ed. *The Old Testament Pseudepigrapha*. 2 vols. Garden City, N.Y.: Doubleday, 1983.

Childs, Brevard S. *The Book of Exodus: A Critical, Theological Commentary*. Old Testament Library. Philadelphia: Westminster Press, 1974.

Collins, Raymond F. *Introduction to the New Testament*. Garden City, N.Y.: Doubleday, 1983.

de Vaux, Roland. *Ancient Israel*. Vol. 1: *Social Institutions*. New York: McGraw Hill, 1965.

Eissfeldt, Otto. *The Old Testament: An Introduction*. Translated by Peter Ackroyd. New York: Harper & Row, 1965.

Friedman, Richard Elliott. *Who Wrote the Bible?* New York: Summit Books, 1987.

Frye, Northrop. *The Great Code: The Bible and Literature*. New York: Harcourt Brace Jovanovich, 1982.

Garbini, Giovanni. *History and Ideology in Ancient Israel*. Translated by John Bowden. New York: Crossroad, 1988.

Goldin, Judah. *The Living Talmud: The Wisdom of the Fathers.* New York: New American Library, 1957.

Guelich, Robert A. *The Sermon on the Mount: A Foundation for Understanding.* Waco, Tex.: Word Books, 1982.

Hengel, Martin. *Judaism and Hellenism: Studies in Their Encounter in Palestine during the Early Hellenistic Period.* Philadelphia: Fortress Press, 1981.

Heschel, Abraham J. *The Prophets.* 2 vols. New York: Harper & Row, 1962.

Hillers, Delbert R. *Covenant: The History of a Biblical Idea.* Baltimore: The Johns Hopkins University Press, 1969.

Horsley, Richard A., with John S. Hanson. *Bandits, Prophets, and Messiahs: Popular Movements at the Time of Jesus.* New Voices in Biblical Studies. New York: Harper & Row, 1985.

Houlden, J. L. *Paul's Letters from Prison: Philippians, Colossians, Philemon, and Ephesians.* Westminster Pelican Commentaries. Philadelphia: Westminster Press, 1977.

Jeremias, Joachim. *The Sermon on the Mount.* Translated by Norman Perrin. Facet Books Biblical Series. Philadelphia: Fortress Press, 1963.

Jordan, Clarence. *The Cotton Patch Version of Matthew and John.* New York: Association Press, 1970.

Käsemann, Ernst. *Commentary on Romans.* Translated and edited by Geoffrey W. Bromiley. Grand Rapids: William B. Eerdmans, 1980.

———. *Perspectives on Paul.* Philadelphia: Fortress Press, 1971.

Kee, Howard Clark. *Miracle in the Early Christian World: A Study in Sociohistorical Method.* New Haven: Yale University Press, 1983.

———. *Understanding the New Testament.* 4th ed. Englewood Cliffs, N.J.: Prentice Hall, 1983.

Keel, Othmar. *The Symbolism of the Biblical World: Ancient Near Eastern Iconography and the Book of Psalms.* Translated by Timothy J. Hallett. New York: Seabury Press, 1978.

Kugel, James L., and Rowan A. Greer. *Early Biblical Interpretation.* Library of Early Christianity, no. 3. Philadelphia: Westminster Press, 1986.

Lind, Millard C. *Transformation of Justice: From Moses to Jesus.* New Perspectives on Crime and Justice: Occasional Papers, no. 5. Akron, Pa.: Mennonite Central Committee, 1986.

Malherbe, Abraham J. *Social Aspects of Early Christianity.* 2d ed. Philadelphia: Fortress Press, 1983.

McKenzie, John L. *Second Isaiah.* Anchor Bible, no. 20. Garden City, N.Y.: Doubleday, 1968.

Meeks, Wayne A. *The First Urban Christians: The Social World of the Apostle Paul.* New Haven: Yale University Press, 1983.

————. *The Moral World of the First Christians.* Library of Early Christianity, no. 6. Philadelphia: Westminster Press, 1986.

Morrison, Clinton D. *The Powers That Be: Earthly Rulers and Demonic Powers in Romans 13.1-7.* Studies in Biblical Theology, no. 29. Naperville, Ill.: Alec R. Allenson, 1960.

Muilenburg, James. *The Way of Israel: Biblical Faith and Ethics.* New York: Harper & Row, 1965.

Munck, Johannes. *The Acts of the Apostles.* Revised by William F. Albright and C. S. Mann. Anchor Bible, no. 31. Garden City, N.Y.: Doubleday, 1967.

Myers, Ched. *Binding the Strong Man: A Political Reading of Mark's Story of Jesus.* Maryknoll, N.Y.: Orbis Books, 1988.

Neusner, Jacob. *The Mishnah: A New Translation.* New Haven: Yale University Press, 1988.

Pierce, C. A. *Conscience in the New Testament.* Studies in Biblical Theology, no. 15. London: SCM Press, 1955.

Pritchard, James B., ed. *The Ancient Near East.* Vol. 2: *A New Anthology of Texts and Pictures.* Princeton: Princeton University Press, 1975.

Reicke, Bo. *The Epistles of James, Peter and Jude.* Anchor Bible, no. 37. Garden City, N.Y.: Doubleday, 1964.

Robinson, H. Wheeler. *Corporate Personality in Ancient Israel.* Facet Books Biblical Series, no. 11. Philadelphia: Fortress Press, 1964.

Robinson, James M., ed. *The Nag Hammadi Library.* 3d ed. New York: Harper & Row, 1988.

Robinson, John A. T. *The Body: A Study in Pauline Theology.* Studies in Biblical Theology, no. 5. Chicago: Alec R. Allenson, 1952.

Romer, John. *Testament: The Bible and History.* New York: Henry Holt, 1988.

Russell, D. S. *The Method and Message of Jewish Apocalyptic.* Old Testament Library. Philadelphia: Westminster Press, 1964.

Russell, Jeffrey Burton. *The Devil: Perceptions of Evil from Antiquity to Primitive Christianity.* New York: New American Library, 1979.

Schweizer, Eduard. *The Church as the Body of Christ.* Richmond: John Knox Press, 1964.

————. *The Good News according to Luke.* Translated by David E. Green. Atlanta: John Knox Press, 1984.

Scott, Ralph. *A New Look at Biblical Crime.* New York: Dorset Press, 1987.

Sheehan, Thomas. *The First Coming: How the Kingdom of God Became Christianity.* New York: Random House, 1986.

Sloan, Robert B., Jr. *The Favorable Year of the Lord: A Study of Jubilary Theology in the Gospel of Luke.* Austin: Schola Press, 1977.

Smith, Daniel L. *The Religion of the Landless: The Social Context of the Babylonian Exile.* Bloomington, Ind.: Meyer-Stone Books, 1989.

Stambaugh, John E., and David L. Balch. *The New Testament in Its Social Environment.* Library of Early Christianity, no. 2. Philadelphia: Westminster Press, 1986.

von Rad, Gerhard. *The Message of the Prophets.* New York: Harper & Row, 1962.

History

Bainton, Roland H. *Christendom: A Short History of Christianity and Its Impact on Western Civilization.* 2 vols. New York: Harper & Row, 1966.

Bamford, Paul W. *Fighting Ships and Prisons: The Mediterranean Galleys of France in the Age of Louis XIV.* Minneapolis: University of Minnesota Press, 1973.

Barber, Malcolm. *The Trial of the Templars.* New York: Cambridge University Press, 1980.

Bellah, Robert N. "Civil Religion in America." In *American Civil Religion.* Edited by Russell E. Richey and Donald D. Jones. New York: Harper & Row, 1974.

Bellamy, John. *The Tudor Law of Treason: An Introduction.* Toronto: University of Toronto Press, 1979.

Blanc, Olivier. *Last Letters: Prisons and Prisoners of the French Revolution, 1793-1794.* Translated by Alan Sheridan. New York: Farrar, Straus & Giroux, 1989.

Blockson, Charles L. *The Underground Railroad: First-Person Narratives of Escapes to Freedom in the North.* Englewood Cliffs, N.J.: Prentice Hall, 1987.

Boswell, John. *Christianity, Social Tolerance, and Homosexuality: Gay People in Western Europe from the Beginning of the Christian Era to the Fourteenth Century.* Chicago: University of Chicago Press, 1980.

————. *The Kindness of Strangers: The Abandonment of Children in Western Europe from Late Antiquity to the Renaissance.* New York: Pantheon Books, 1988.

Bouwsma, William J. *John Calvin: A Sixteenth Century Portrait.* New York: Oxford University Press, 1988.

Brooke, Rosalind, and Christopher Brooke. *Popular Religion in the Middle Ages: Western Europe, 1000-1300.* New York: Thames & Hudson, 1984.

Brown, Peter. *The Body and Society: Men, Women and Sexual Renunciation in Early Christianity.* New York: Columbia University Press, 1988.

Calvi, Giulia. *Histories of a Plague Year: The Social and the Imaginary in Baroque Florence.* Translated by Dario Biocca and Bryant T. Ragan, Jr. Berkeley and Los Angeles: University of California Press, 1989.

Cameron, Joy. *Prisons and Punishment in Scotland from the Middle Ages to the Present.* Edinburgh: Canongate, 1983.

Cheetham, Nicolas. *Keepers of the Keys: A History of the Popes from St. Peter to John Paul II.* New York: Scribner's, 1983.

Christie-Murray, David. *A History of Heresy.* New York: Oxford University Press, 1989.

Clebsch, William A., and Charles R. Jaekle. *Pastoral Care in Historical Perspective: An Essay with Exhibits.* Englewood Cliffs, N.J.: Prentice Hall, 1964.

Cochrane, Arthur C. *The Church's Confession under Hitler.* Philadelphia: Westminster Press, 1962.

Cohn, Norman. *The Pursuit of the Millennium: Revolutionary Millenarians and Mystical Anarchists of the Middle Ages.* New York: Oxford University Press, 1970.

The Correspondence of Pope Gregory VII: Selected Letters from the Registrum. Translated by Ephraim Emerton. New York: W. W. Norton, 1969.

Cross, F. L., ed. *The Oxford Dictionary of the Christian Church.* New York: Oxford University Press, 1957.

Cross, Whitney R. *The Burned-Over District: The Social and Intellectual History of Enthusiastic Religion in Western New York, 1800-1850.* Ithaca, N.Y.: Cornell University Press, 1982.

Dalzell, George W. *Benefit of Clergy in America and Related Matters.* Winston-Salem: John F. Blair, 1955.

Dickens, A. G. *The German Nation and Martin Luther.* New York: Harper & Row, 1974.

Dörrie, Hermann. *Constantine the Great.* Translated by Roland H. Bainton. New York: Harper & Row, 1972.

Durnbaugh, Donald F. *European Origins of the Brethren.* Elgin, Ill.: Brethren Press, 1958.

————, ed. *Every Need Supplied: Mutual Aid and Christian Community in the Free Churches, 1525-1675.* Documents in Free Church History Series. Philadelphia: Temple University Press, 1974.

Estep, William R. *The Anabaptist Story.* Grand Rapids: William B. Eerdmans, 1975.

Fox, Robin Lane. *Pagans and Christians.* New York: Alfred A. Knopf, 1987.

Fox's Book of Martyrs: A History of the Lives, Sufferings and Deaths of the Early Christian and Protestant Martyrs. Edited by William Byron Forbush. Grand Rapids: Zondervan, 1967.

Friedrich, Otto. *The End of the World: A History.* New York: Fromm International, 1986.

Greven, Philip. *The Protestant Temperament: Patterns of Child-Rearing, Religious Experience, and the Self in Early America.* New York: Alfred A. Knopf, 1977.

Hall, David D. *Worlds of Wonder, Days of Judgment: Popular Religious Belief in Early New England.* New York: Alfred A. Knopf, 1989.

Harnack, Adolf. *The Mission and Expansion of Christianity in the First Three Centuries.* Translated and edited by James Moffatt. New York: Harper, 1961.

Hill, Christopher. *The World Turned Upside Down: Radical Ideas during the English Revolution.* New York: Penguin Books, 1975.

Hornus, Jean-Michel. *It Is Not Lawful for Me to Fight: Early Christian Attitudes toward War, Violence and the State.* Scottdale, Pa.: Herald Press, 1980.

Howard, D. L. *John Howard: Prison Reformer.* London: Christopher Johnson, 1958.

Hoyles, J. Arthur. *Religion in Prison.* New York: Philosophical Library, 1955.

Hughes, Robert. *The Fatal Shore.* New York: Alfred A. Knopf, 1987.

Jacoby, Susan. *Wild Justice: The Evolution of Revenge.* New York: Harper & Row, 1983.

Johnson, Paul. *A History of Christianity.* New York: Atheneum, 1979.

Johnston, Norman. "The Human Cage." In *Correctional Institutions.* 2d ed. Edited by Robert M. Carter, Daniel Glaser, and Leslie T. Wilkins. Philadelphia: J. B. Lippincott, 1977.

Jones, A. H. M. *Constantine and the Conversion of Europe.* Rev. ed. New York: Collier Books, 1962.

Josephus: Complete Works. Translated by William Whiston. Grand Rapids: Kregel Publications, 1960.

Kamen, Henry. *The Spanish Inquisition.* New York: New American Library, 1965.

Kantorowicz, Ernst H. *The King's Two Bodies: A Study in Medieval Political Theology.* Princeton: Princeton University Press, 1957.

Kelly, George Armstrong. *Politics and Religious Consciousness in America.* New Brunswick, N.J.: Transaction Books, 1984.

Kelly, J. N. D. *The Oxford Dictionary of Popes.* New York: Oxford University Press, 1988.

Kent, John. *Elizabeth Fry.* London: B. T. Batsford, 1962.

Kerr, Hugh T., ed. *Readings in Christian Thought.* New York: Abingdon Press, 1966.

Kieckhefer, Richard. *Repression of Heresy in Medieval Germany.* Middle Ages Series. Philadelphia: University of Pennsylvania Press, 1979.

Laws of the Alamans and Bavarians. Translated by Theodore John Rivers. Philadelphia: University of Pennsylvania Press, 1977.

Lewis, R. W. B. *The American Adam: Innocence, Tragedy, and Tradition in the Nineteenth Century.* Chicago: University of Chicago Press, 1955.

Lietzmann, Hans. *A History of the Early Church.* Translated by Bertram Lee Woolf. New York: Meridian Books, 1961.

Little, Lester K. *Religious Poverty and the Profit Economy in Medieval Europe.* Ithaca, N.Y.: Cornell University Press, 1983.

Lunt, William E. *Papal Revenues in the Middle Ages.* 2 vols. Records of

Civilization: Sources and Studies, no. 19. New York: Columbia University Press, 1962.

MacMaster, Richard K. *Christian Obedience in Revolutionary Times: The Peace Churches and the American Revolution.* Akron, Pa.: Mennonite Central Committee Peace Section, 1976.

MacMullen, Ramsay. *Christianizing the Roman Empire (A.D. 100-400).* New Haven: Yale University Press, 1984.

Mannix, Daniel P. *The History of Torture.* New York: Dell, 1964.

Marsden, George M. *Fundamentalism and American Culture: The Shaping of Twentieth-Century Evangelicalism, 1870-1925.* New York: Oxford University Press, 1980.

McDannell, Colleen, and Bernhard Lang. *Heaven: A History.* New Haven: Yale University Press, 1988.

McKnight, Gerald. *Verdict on Schweitzer: The Man behind the Legend of Lambaréné.* New York: John Day, 1964.

McLachlin, Noel. "Penal Reform and Penal History: Some Reflections." In *Progress in Penal Reform.* Edited by Louis Blom-Cooper. London: Oxford University Press, 1974.

Metzger, Charles H. *The Prisoner in the American Revolution.* Chicago: Loyola University Press, 1971.

Mueller, William A. *Church and State in Luther and Calvin: A Comparative Study.* Garden City, N.Y.: Doubleday, 1965.

Muldoon, James. *Popes, Lawyers, and Infidels: The Church and the Non-Christian World, 1250-1550.* Middle Ages Series. Philadelphia: University of Pennsylvania Press, 1979.

Musurillo, Herbert A. *The Fathers of the Primitive Church.* New York: New American Library, 1966.

Newhall, Richard A. *The Crusades.* Rev. ed. Berkshire Studies in European History. New York: Holt, Rinehart & Winston, 1963.

Norwood, Frederick A. *Strangers and Exiles: A History of Religious Refugees.* 2 vols. New York: Abingdon Press, 1969.

Pelikan, Jaroslav. *The Christian Tradition: A History of the Development of Doctrine.* Vol. 1: *The Emergence of the Catholic Tradition (100-600).* Chicago: University of Chicago Press, 1971.

———. *Jesus through the Centuries: His Place in the History of Culture.* New Haven: Yale University Press, 1985.

Peters, Edward. *Inquisition.* Berkeley and Los Angeles: University of California Press, 1989.

The Power of the People: Active Nonviolence in the United States. Edited by Robert Cooney and Helen Michalowski from an original text by Marty Jezer. Philadelphia: New Society Publishers, 1987.

Preston, William, Jr. *Aliens and Dissenters: Federal Suppression of Radicals, 1903-1933.* New York: Harper & Row, 1963.

Priestley, Philip. *Victorian Prison Lives: English Prison Biography, 1830-1914.* New York: Methuen, 1985.

Redondi, Pietro. *Galileo: Heretic.* Translated by Raymond Rosenthal. Princeton: Princeton University Press, 1987.

Rothman, David J. *Conscience and Convenience: The Asylum and Its Alternatives in Progressive America.* Boston: Little, Brown, 1980.

————. *The Discovery of the Asylum: Social Order and Disorder in the New Republic.* Boston: Little, Brown, 1971.

The Rule of St. Benedict. Translated by Anthony C. Meisel and M. L. del Mastro. Garden City, N.Y.: Doubleday, 1975.

Schama, Simon. *Citizens: A Chronicle of the French Revolution.* New York: Alfred A. Knopf, 1989.

Sivan, Gabriel. *The Bible and Civilization.* New York Times Library of Jewish Knowledge. New York: Quadrangle, 1973.

Smith, Timothy L. *Revivalism and Social Reform: American Protestantism on the Eve of the Civil War.* New York: Harper & Row, 1965.

Starkey, Marion L. *The Devil in Massachusetts: A Modern Enquiry into the Salem Witch Trials.* Garden City, N.Y.: Doubleday, 1969.

Strauss, Gerald, ed. and trans. *Manifestations of Discontent in Germany on the Eve of the Reformation.* Bloomington, Ind.: Indiana University Press, 1971.

Strayer, Joseph R. *Western Europe in the Middle Ages.* New York: Appleton-Century-Crofts, 1955.

Thomson, John A. F. *Popes and Princes, 1417-1517: Politics and Polity in the Late Medieval Church.* Early Modern Europe Today Series. Boston: George Allen & Unwin, 1980.

Walzer, Michael. *The Revolution of the Saints: A Study in the Origins of Radical Politics.* Cambridge: Harvard University Press, 1965.

Weber, Max. *The Protestant Ethic and the Spirit of Capitalism.* Translated by Talcott Parsons. New York: Scribner's, 1968.

Wiesenthal, Simon. *Every Day Remembrance Day: A Chronicle of Jewish Martyrdom.* New York: Henry Holt, 1987.

Wilken, Robert L. *The Christians as the Romans Saw Them*. New Haven: Yale University Press, 1984.

Williams, George H. "The Ministry of the Ante-Nicene Church (c. 125-325)." In *The Ministry in Historical Perspectives*. Edited by H. Richard Niebuhr and Daniel D. Williams. New York: Harper, 1956.

Prisons, Crime, and Punishment

Alper, Benedict S. *Prisons Inside-Out: Alternatives in Correctional Reform*. Cambridge, Mass.: Ballinger, 1974.

Archer, Dane, and Rosemary Gartner. *Violence and Crime in Cross-National Perspective*. New Haven: Yale University Press, 1984.

Bagdikian, Ben H., and Leon Dash. *The Washington Post National Report: The Shame of the Prisons*. New York: Pocket Books, 1972.

Barrett, Chuck. "One Meaning of Prison in America." In *And the Criminals with Him*. Edited by Will D. Campbell and James Y. Holloway. New York: Paulist Press, 1973.

Bayne, David Cowan. *Conscience, Obligation, and the Law: The Moral Binding Power of the Civil Law*. Chicago: Loyola University Press, 1966.

Beccaria, Cesare. *On Crimes and Punishments*. Translated by Henry Paolucci. Indianapolis: Bobbs-Merrill, 1963.

Bedau, Hugo Adam. *The Case against the Death Penalty*. New York: Capital Punishment Project, American Civil Liberties Union, 1984.

Bishop, Norman. "Aspects of European Penal Systems." In *Progress in Penal Reform*. Edited by Louis Blom-Cooper. London: Oxford University Press, 1974.

Bowers, William, and Glenn Pierce. "Deterrence or Brutalization: What Is the Effect of Executions?" *Crime and Delinquency* 26 (October 1980): 453ff.

Bradley, F. H. "Some Remarks on Punishment." In *Ethical Choice: A Case Study Approach*. Edited by Robert N. Beck and John B. Orr. New York: Free Press, 1970.

Breer, William M. "Probation Supervision of the Black Offender." In *Corrections in the Community: Alternatives to Imprisonment*,

Selected Readings. 2d ed. Edited by George G. Killinger and Paul F. Cromwell, Jr. St. Paul: West Publishing, 1978.

Burkhart, Kathryn. "Women in Prison." In *In Prison: Writings and Poems about the Prison Experience.* Edited by James E. Trupin. New York: New American Library, 1975.

Caringella-MacDonald, Susan, and Drew Humphries. "Sexual Assault, Women, and the Community: Organizing to Prevent Sexual Violence." In *Criminology as Peacemaking.* Edited by Harold E. Pepinsky and Richard Quinney. Bloomington, Ind.: Indiana University Press, 1991.

Chesney-Lind, Meda. "Girls' Crime and Woman's Place: Toward a Feminist Model of Female Delinquency." *Crime and Delinquency* 35 (January 1989): 5-29.

The Church, the State, and the Offender. Church and Society Series, no. 3. Newton, Kans.: Faith & Life Press, 1963.

Cohen, Fred. "The Law of Prisoners' Rights: An Overview." *Criminal Law Bulletin* 24 (July-August 1988): 321-49.

Colson, Charles. "Towards an Understanding of Imprisonment and Rehabilitation." In *Crime and the Responsible Community.* Edited by John Stott and Nicholas Miller. Grand Rapids: William B. Eerdmans, 1980.

Colson, Charles, and Daniel Van Ness. *Convicted: New Hope for Ending America's Crime Crisis.* Westchester, Ill.: Crossway Books, 1989.

Comfort, Alex. "Power Attracts Delinquents: A Contemporary Study." In *Patterns of Anarchy: A Collection of Writings on the Anarchist Tradition.* Edited by Leonard I. Krimerman and Lewis Perry. Garden City, N.Y.: Doubleday, 1966.

Cordella, J. Peter. "Reconciliation and the Mutualist Model of Community." In *Criminology as Peacemaking.* Edited by Harold E. Pepinsky and Richard Quinney. Bloomington, Ind.: Indiana University Press, 1991.

Currie, Elliott. *Confronting Crime: An American Challenge.* New York: Pantheon Books, 1985.

Deming, Barbara. "Prison Notes." In *Seeds of Liberation.* Edited by Paul Goodman. New York: George Braziller, 1964.

DeWolf, L. Harold. *Crime and Justice in America: A Paradox of Conscience.* New York: Harper & Row, 1975.

Durkheim, Emile. "Crime as a Normal Phenomenon." In *Crime and*

Justice. Vol. 1: *The Criminal in Society.* Edited by Leon Radzinowicz and Marvin Wolfgang. New York: Basic Books, 1971.

Elias, Robert. "Crime Control as Human Rights Enforcement." In *Criminology as Peacemaking.* Edited by Harold E. Pepinsky and Richard Quinney. Bloomington, Ind.: Indiana University Press, 1991.

Foucault, Michel. *Discipline and Punish: The Birth of the Prison.* Translated by Alan Sheridan. New York: Vintage Books, 1979.

Frank, Leonard Roy, ed. *The History of Shock Treatment.* San Francisco: Leonard Roy Frank, 1978.

Gaddis, Thomas E., and James O. Long. "Killer: A Journal of Murder." An interview with Carl Panzram. In *In Prison: Writings and Poems about the Prison Experience.* Edited by James E. Trupin. New York: New American Library, 1975.

Garfinkel, Harold. "Conditions of Successful Degradation Ceremonies." In *Deviance: The Interactionist Perspective.* 2d ed. Edited by Earl Rubington and Martin S. Weinberg. New York: Macmillan, 1973.

Goffman, Erving. "Characteristics of Total Institutions." In *Deviance: Studies in the Process of Stigmatization and Societal Reaction.* Edited by Simon Dinitz, Russell R. Dynes, and Alfred C. Clarke. New York: Oxford University Press, 1969.

Goodell, Charles. *Political Prisoners in America.* New York: Random House, 1973.

Gorelick, Steven M. "'Join Our War': The Construction of Ideology in a Newspaper Crime-Fighting Campaign." *Crime and Delinquency* 35 (July 1989): 421-36.

Gray, Ian, and Moira Stanley. *A Punishment in Search of a Crime: Americans Speak Out against the Death Penalty.* New York: Avon Books, 1989.

Greenberg, David. *The Problem of Prisons.* Philadelphia: American Friends Service Committee, 1970.

Hall, Stuart, C. Critcher, T. Jefferson, J. Clarke, and B. Roberts. *Policing the Crisis: Mugging, the State, and Law and Order.* Critical Studies Series. London: Macmillan, 1978.

Harris, M. Kay. "Moving into the New Millennium: Toward a Feminist Vision of Justice." In *Criminology as Peacemaking.* Edited by Harold E. Pepinsky and Richard Quinney. Bloomington, Ind.: Indiana University Press, 1991.

Immarigeon, Russ. "Beyond the Fear of Crime: Reconciliation as the Basis for Criminal Justice Policy." In *Criminology as Peacemaking.* Edited by Harold E. Pepinsky and Richard Quinney. Bloomington, Ind.: Indiana University Press, 1991.

Jackson, Dave. *Dial 911: Peaceful Christians and Urban Violence.* Scottdale, Pa.: Herald Press, 1981.

Jeschke, Marlin. "Toward a Christian Approach to Criminal Justice." Address to the Church and Criminal Justice Conference, sponsored by Mennonite Central Committee Offender Ministries Program, Evanston, Illinois, 18-20 September 1980.

Jolin, Annette, and Brian Stipak. "Drug Treatment and Electronically Monitored Home Confinement: An Evaluation of a Community-Based Sentencing Option." *Crime and Delinquency* 38 (April 1992): 158-70.

Klein, Lloyd, Joan Luxenburg, and John Gunther. "Taking a Bite Out of Social Injustice: Crime-Control Ideology and Its Peacemaking Potential." In *Criminology as Peacemaking.* Edited by Harold E. Pepinsky and Richard Quinney. Bloomington, Ind.: Indiana University Press, 1991.

Klofas, John M., Stan Stojkovic, and David A. Kalinich. "The Meaning of Correctional Crowding: Steps toward an Index of Severity." *Crime and Delinquency* 38 (April 1992): 171-88.

Knopp, Fay Honey. "Community Solutions to Sexual Violence: Feminist/Abolitionist Perspectives." In *Criminology as Peacemaking.* Edited by Harold E. Pepinsky and Richard Quinney. Bloomington, Ind.: Indiana University Press, 1991.

Knopp, Fay Honey, et al. *Instead of Prisons: A Handbook for Abolitionists.* Syracuse: Prison Research Education Action Project, 1976.

Kropotkin, Peter. *In Russian and French Prisons.* New York: Schocken Books, 1971.

Longabaugh, Fritz. "Problems of Valuing Violence." *Justicia* (Newsletter of Genesee Ecumenical Ministries Judicial Process Commission, Rochester, N.Y.), March 1988, pp. 4-5.

Martinson, Robert. "What Works? A Comparative Assessment." In *Crime and Justice.* Vol. 3: *The Criminal under Restraint.* 2d ed. Edited by Leon Radzinowicz and Marvin Wolfgang. New York: Basic Books, 1977.

Mathiesen, Thomas. *The Politics of Abolition.* Scandinavian Studies in Criminology, Law in Society Series. New York: John Wiley, 1974.

McCoy, John. *Concrete Mama: Prison Profiles from Wala Wala.* Columbia, Mo.: University of Missouri Press, 1981.

McHugh, Gerald Austin. *Christian Faith and Criminal Justice: Towards a Christian Response to Crime and Punishment.* New York: Paulist Press, 1978.

McShane, Marilyn D., and Frank P. Williams III. "Radical Victimology: A Critique of the Concept of Victim in Traditional Victimology." *Crime and Delinquency* 38 (April 1992): 258-71.

Melossi, Dario, and Massimo Pavarini. *The Prison and the Factory: Origins of the Penitentiary System.* Translated by Glynis Cousin. Totowa, N.J.: Barnes & Noble, 1981.

Menninger, Karl. *The Crime of Punishment.* New York: Viking Press, 1969.

Merton, Robert K. "Anomie." In *Crime and Justice.* Vol. 1: *The Criminal in Society.* Edited by Leon Radzinowicz and Marvin E. Wolfgang. New York: Basic Books, 1971.

Michaud, Stephen G. "DNA Detectives: Genetic 'Fingerprinting' May Herald a Revolution in Law Enforcement." *New York Times Magazine,* 6 November 1988, pp. 70ff.

Mitford, Jessica. *Kind and Usual Punishment: The Prison Business.* New York: Alfred A. Knopf, 1973.

Nerney, Mary. "Women Fighting Back: Commitment and Cost." *Justicia* (Newsletter of Genesee Ecumenical Ministries Judicial Process Commission, Rochester, N.Y.), November 1988, p. 9.

New York State Special Commission on Attica. "Bloody Attica." In *Social Crises: A Casebook.* Edited by Robert Hybels. New York: Thomas Y. Crowell, 1974.

Newman, Graeme. *The Punishment Response.* New York: J. B. Lippincott, 1978.

"Notes from Isolation." In *Inside: Prisons American Style.* Edited by Robert J. Minton, Jr. New York: Vintage Books, 1971.

O'Gorman, Angie, and Maggie Pharris. *Nonviolent Response to Personal Assault.* Videotape directed by Greg St. James and produced by Bill and Mary Carry. Erie, Pa.: Pax Christi USA, 1986.

Orland, Leonard. *Prisons: Houses of Darkness.* New York: Free Press, 1978.

Pepinsky, Harold E. "Peacemaking in Criminology and Criminal Justice." In *Criminology as Peacemaking.* Edited by Harold E. Pepinsky and Richard Quinney. Bloomington, Ind.: Indiana University Press, 1991.

"Prisoners as Research Subjects." Staff Paper of National Commission for the Protection of Human Subjects of Biomedical and Behavioral Research. In *Crime and Justice.* Vol. 3: *The Criminal under Restraint.* 2d ed. Edited by Leon Radzinowicz and Marvin Wolfgang. New York: Basic Books, 1977.

"Problems of Latino Prisoners Studied." *Justícia* (Newsletter of Genesee Ecumenical Ministries Judicial Process Commission, Rochester, N.Y.), January 1989, p. 6.

Regan, Clare. "Harris Cites Need for Change in Sanctions." *Justícia* (Newsletter of Genesee Ecumenical Ministries Judicial Process Commission, Rochester, N.Y.), May 1988, p. 2.

Riera, Argenis. "Latin American Radical Criminology." *Crime and Social Justice: Issues in Criminology.* Spring-Summer 1979, pp. 71-76.

Rowan, Carl T., and David M. Mazie. "The Sentencing Process Does Not Work." In *Criminal Justice: Opposing Viewpoints.* Edited by David L. Bender and Bruno Leone. Opposing Viewpoints Series. St. Paul: Greenhaven Press, 1981.

Sage, Wayne. "Crime and the Clockwork Lemon." In *In Prison: Writings and Poems about the Prison Experience.* Edited by James E. Trupin. New York: New American Library, 1975.

Salaam, Kalamu ya. "Drug Frenzy Is Nothing New in U.S." *Utne Reader,* March/April 1989, p. 78.

Samuel, Dorothy. *Safe Passage on City Streets.* New York: Abingdon Press, 1975.

Schwartz, Richard D., and Jerome H. Skolnick. "Legal Stigma." In *Deviance: The Interactionist Perspective.* 2d ed. Edited by Earl Rubington and Martin S. Weinberg. New York: Macmillan, 1973.

Solomon, Frederic, W. L. Walker, G. J. O'Connor, and J. R. Fishman. "Civil Rights Activity and Reduction in Crime among Negroes." In *Crime and Social Justice: Issues in Criminology,* Winter 1980, pp. 27-35.

Struggle for Justice: A Report on Crime and Punishment in America. Prepared for the American Friends Service Committee. New York: Hill & Wang, 1971.

Sykes, Gersham M. *The Society of Captives: A Study of a Maximum Security Prison.* New York: Atheneum, 1966.

"The Talk of the Town." *New Yorker,* 13 April 1992, pp. 27-28.

Tannenbaum, Frank. "The Dramatization of Evil." In *Deviance: The Interactionist Perspective.* 2d ed. Edited by Earl Rubington and Martin S. Weinberg. New York: Macmillan, 1973.

Van Ness, Daniel. *Crime and Its Victims.* Downers Grove, Ill.: InterVarsity Press, 1986.

Volpe, Maria R. "Mediation in the Criminal Justice System: Process, Promises, Problems." In *Criminology as Peacemaking.* Edited by Harold E. Pepinsky and Richard Quinney. Bloomington, Ind.: Indiana University Press, 1991.

Williams, David. "The Role of Prisons in Tanzania: An Historical Perspective." In *Crime and Social Justice: Issues in Criminology,* Summer 1980, pp. 27-38.

Wright, Kevin N. *The Great American Crime Myth.* New York: Praeger, 1987.

Zehr, Howard. *Changing Lenses: A New Focus for Crime and Justice.* Scottdale, Pa.: Herald Press, 1990.

Zehr, Howard, and Earl Sears. *Mediating the Victim-Offender Conflict.* Akron, Pa.: Mennonite Central Committee, 1982.

Zimbardo, Philip G. "The Psychological Power and Pathology of Imprisonment." In *Behavior Disorders: Perspectives and Trends.* 3d ed. Edited by Ohmer Milton and Robert G. Wahler. New York: J. B. Lippincott, 1973.

Theology

Althaus, Paul. *The Divine Command: A New Perspective on Law and Gospel.* Translated by Franklin Sherman. Facet Books Social Ethics Series, no. 9. Philadelphia: Fortress Press, 1966.

Aquinas, Thomas. *On the Truth of the Catholic Faith: Summa Contra Gentiles.* Translated by Charles J. O'Neil. Garden City, N.Y.: Doubleday, 1957.

Aulén, Gustaf. *Christus Victor: An Historical Study of the Three Main Types of the Idea of the Atonement.* Translated by A. G. Hebert. New York: Macmillan, 1969.

Barth, Karl. *Church Dogmatics.* Vol. 4, part 2: *The Doctrine of Reconciliation.* Translated by Geoffrey W. Bromiley and Thomas F. Torrance. Edinburgh: T. & T. Clark, 1958.

————. *Deliverance to the Captives.* New York: Harper, 1961.

————. *The Humanity of God.* Richmond: John Knox Press, 1960.

Barth, Markus. *Acquittal by Resurrection.* New York: Holt, Rinehart & Winston, 1964.

————. *Justification: Pauline Texts Interpreted in the Light of the Old and New Testaments.* Translated by A. M. Woodruff III. Grand Rapids: William B. Eerdmans, 1971.

Berkhof, Hendrikus. *Christ and the Powers.* Translated by John H. Yoder. Scottdale, Pa.: Herald Press, 1977.

Braaten, Carl E. *Christ and Counter-Christ: Apocalyptic Themes in Theology and Culture.* Philadelphia: Fortress Press, 1972.

Brown, Dale. *Biblical Pacifism: A Peace Church Perspective.* Elgin, Ill.: Brethren Press, 1986.

————. *The Christian Revolutionary.* Grand Rapids: William B. Eerdmans, 1971.

Brunner, Emil. *Justice and the Social Order.* Translated by Mary Hottinger. New York: Harper, 1945.

Bultmann, Rudolf. "New Testament and Mythology." In *Kerygma and Myth.* Edited by Hans Werner Bartsch. New York: Harper & Row, 1961.

Calvin, John. *Institutes of the Christian Religion.* 2 vols. Edited by John T. McNeill and translated by Ford Lewis Battles. Library of Christian Classics, vols. 20-21. Philadelphia: Westminster Press, 1960.

————. *Treatises against the Anabaptists and against the Libertines.* Translated and edited by Benjamin Wirt Farley. Grand Rapids: Baker Book House, 1982.

Campbell, Will D., and James Y. Holloway. "The Good News from God in Jesus Is Freedom to the Prisoners." In *And the Criminals with Him.* Edited by Will D. Campbell and James Y. Holloway. New York: Paulist Press, 1973.

Campbell, Will D., and James Y. Holloway. *Up to Our Steeples in Politics.* New York: Paulist Press, 1970.

Cullmann, Oscar. *Christ and Time: The Primitive Christian Conception of Time and History.* Rev. ed. Translated by Floyd V. Filson. Philadelphia: Westminster Press, 1964.

Ellul, Jacques. "Anarchism and Christianity." *Katallagete* 7 (Fall 1980): 14-24.

———. *Anarchy and Christianity*. Translated by Geoffrey W. Bromiley. Grand Rapids: William B. Eerdmans, 1991.

———. *The Ethics of Freedom*. Translated and edited by Geoffrey W. Bromiley. Grand Rapids: William B. Eerdmans, 1976.

———. *The Politics of God and the Politics of Man*. Translated and edited by Geoffrey W. Bromiley. Grand Rapids: William B. Eerdmans, 1972.

———. *The Theological Foundation of Law*. Translated by Marguerite Wieser. New York: Seabury Press, 1969.

———. *Violence: Reflections from a Christian Perspective*. Translated by Cecelia Gaul Kings. New York: Seabury Press, 1969.

Ferguson, Everett. "The Kingdom of God in Early Patristic Literature." In *The Kingdom of God in Twentieth-Century Interpretation*. Edited by Wendell Willis. Peabody, Mass.: Hendrickson, 1987.

Gill, Robin. *A Textbook of Christian Ethics*. Edinburgh: T. & T. Clark, 1985.

Goppelt, Leonhard. *Theology of the New Testament*. Vol. 1: *The Ministry of Jesus in Its Theological Significance*. Translated by John Alsup. Grand Rapids: William B. Eerdmans, 1981.

Gustafson, James M. *Christ and the Moral Life*. New York: Harper & Row, 1968.

Hiers, Richard H., Jr. "Pivotal Reactions to the Eschatological Interpretations: Rudolf Bultmann and C. H. Dodd." In *The Kingdom of God in Twentieth-Century Interpretation*. Edited by Wendell Willis. Peabody, Mass.: Hendrickson, 1987.

Klassen, A. J., ed. *A Bonhoeffer Legacy: Essays in Understanding*. Grand Rapids: William B. Eerdmans, 1981.

Klassen, William. *Release to Those in Prison*. Focal Pamphlet 26. Scottdale, Pa.: Herald Press, 1977.

Kraybill, Donald B. *The Upside-Down Kingdom*. Scottdale, Pa.: Herald Press, 1978.

Kümmel, Werner Georg. *The Theology of the New Testament according to Its Major Witnesses: Jesus — Paul — John*. Translated by John E. Steely. New York: Abingdon Press, 1973.

Lasserre, Jean. *War and the Gospel*. Translated by Oliver Coburn. Scottdale, Pa.: Herald Press, 1962.

Laytner, Anson. *Arguing with God: A Jewish Tradition*. Northvale, N.J.: Jason Aronson, 1990.

Lehman, Paul L. *Ethics in a Christian Context.* New York: Harper & Row, 1963.

Lewis, C. S. *God in the Dock: Essays on Theology and Ethics.* Edited by Walter Hooper. Grand Rapids: William B. Eerdmans, 1970.

Moltmann, Jürgen. *The Crucified God: The Cross of Christ as the Foundation and Criticism of Christian Theology.* Translated by R. A. Wilson and John Bowden. New York: Harper & Row, 1974.

————. *Theology of Hope: On the Grounds and the Implications of a Christian Eschatology.* New York: Harper & Row, 1967.

Moltmann, Jürgen, H. W. Richardson, J. B. Metz, W. Oelmüller, and M. D. Bryant. *Religion and Political Society.* New York: Harper & Row, 1974.

Niebuhr, H. Richard. *Christ and Culture.* New York: Harper, 1951.

Niebuhr, Reinhold. *Moral Man and Immoral Society: A Study in Ethics and Politics.* New York: Scribner's, 1960.

Olson, Mark. "The God Who Dared." *The Other Side* 26 (May-June 1990): 11-15.

Porter, J. M., ed. *Luther: Selected Political Writings.* Philadelphia: Fortress Press, 1974.

Rauschenbusch, Walter. *Christianity and the Social Crisis.* Edited by Robert D. Cross. New York: Harper & Row, 1964.

Schweitzer, Albert. *The Quest of the Historical Jesus: A Critical Study of Its Progress from Reimarus to Wrede.* New York: Macmillan, 1968.

Sölle, Dorothee. "Between Matter and Spirit: Why and in What Sense Must Theology Be Materialist?" In *God of the Lowly: Socio-Historical Interpretations of the Bible.* Edited by Willy Schottroff and Wolfgang Stegemann, and translated by Matthew J. O'Connell. Maryknoll, N.Y.: Orbis Books, 1984.

Stringfellow, William. *Conscience and Obedience: The Politics of Romans 13 and Revelation 13 in the Light of the Second Coming.* Waco, Tex.: Word Books, 1978.

————. *An Ethic for Christians and Other Aliens in a Strange Land.* Waco, Tex.: Word Books, 1973.

Trocmé, André. *Jesus and the Nonviolent Revolution.* Translated by Michael H. Shank and Marlin E. Miller. Scottdale, Pa.: Herald Press, 1973.

Wink, Walter. *The Powers.* Vol. 1: *Naming the Powers: The Language of Power in the New Testament.* Philadelphia: Fortress Press, 1984.

———. *The Powers.* Vol. 2: *Unmasking the Powers: The Invisible Forces That Determine Human Existence.* Philadelphia: Fortress Press, 1986.

Wren, Brian. *What Language Shall I Borrow? God-Talk in Worship: A Male Response to Feminist Theology.* New York: Crossroad, 1989.

Yoder, John Howard. *The Politics of Jesus.* Grand Rapids: William B. Eerdmans, 1972.

Yoder, John Howard, et al. *What Would You Do? A Serious Answer to a Standard Question.* Scottdale, Pa.: Herald Press, 1983.

Other Sources

Ansbro, John J. *Martin Luther King, Jr.: The Making of a Mind.* Maryknoll, N.Y.: Orbis Books, 1982.

Berry, Wendell. *Collected Poems, 1957-1982.* San Francisco: North Point Press, 1985.

Bienek, Horst. *The Cell.* Santa Barbara: Unicorn Press, 1972.

Buber, Martin. *Tales of the Hasidim: The Early Masters.* New York: Schocken Books, 1947.

Campbell, Will D. *Brother to a Dragonfly.* New York: Seabury Press, 1977.

Camus, Albert. *Resistance, Rebellion, and Death.* Translated by Justin O'Brien. New York: Vintage Books, 1974.

Capote, Truman. *In Cold Blood.* New York: Random House, 1965.

Cleaver, Eldridge. *Soul on Ice.* New York: McGraw-Hill, 1968.

Ellsberg, Robert, ed. *By Little and By Little: The Selected Writings of Dorothy Day.* New York: Alfred A. Knopf, 1984.

Ellul, Jacques. *The Technological Society.* Translated by John Wilkinson. New York: Vintage Books, 1964.

Faludi, Susan. *Backlash: The Undeclared War against American Women.* New York: Crown Publishers, 1991.

Foucault, Michel. *Power/Knowledge: Selected Interviews and Other Writings, 1972-1977.* Edited by Colin Gordon. New York: Pantheon Books, 1980.

Gould, Stephen Jay. *An Urchin in the Storm: Essays about Books and Ideas.* New York: W. W. Norton, 1987.

Grcić, Joseph. *Moral Choices: Ethical Theories and Problems.* New York: West Publishing, 1989.

Greene, Theodore M., ed. *Kant Selections.* New York: Scribner's, 1957.

Howton, F. William. *Functionaries.* Problems of American Society Series. Chicago: Quadrangle Books, 1971.

Mailer, Norman. *The Executioner's Song.* New York: Warner Books, 1979.

Marcuse, Herbert. *One-Dimensional Man: Studies in the Ideology of Advanced Industrial Society.* Boston: Beacon Press, 1964.

Menninger, Karl. *Whatever Became of Sin?* New York: Hawthorn Books, 1975.

Milgram, Stanley. *Obedience to Authority: An Experimental View.* New York: Harper & Row, 1974.

Miller, William D. *Dorothy Day: A Biography.* New York: Harper & Row, 1982.

Minkin, Jacob S. *The Teachings of Maimonides.* Northvale, N.J.: Jason Aronson, 1987.

Noss, David S., and John B. Noss. *Man's Religions.* 7th ed. New York: Macmillan, 1984.

Piñero, Miguel. *Short Eyes.* New York: Hill & Wang, 1975.

Piven, Frances Fox, and Richard A. Cloward. *Regulating the Poor: The Functions of Public Welfare.* New York: Vintage Books, 1971.

Plato: The Collected Dialogues. Edited by Edith Hamilton and Huntington Cairns. Bollingen Series 61. New York: Pantheon Books, 1961.

Sennett, Richard. *Authority.* New York: Vintage Books, 1981.

Sharp, Gene. *The Politics of Nonviolent Action.* Part 2: *The Methods of Nonviolent Action.* Boston: Porter Sargent, 1973.

Slater, Philip. *The Pursuit of Loneliness: American Culture at the Breaking Point.* Boston: Beacon Press, 1970.

Sontag, Susan. *Illness as Metaphor.* New York: Farrar, Straus & Giroux, 1988.

Szasz, Thomas S. *The Myth of Mental Illness: Foundations of a Theory of Personal Conduct.* Rev. ed. New York: Harper & Row, 1974.

Wachtel, Paul L. *The Poverty of Affluence: A Psychological Portrait of the American Way of Life.* Philadelphia: New Society Publishers, 1989.

Winsten, Stephen, ed. *The Wit and Wisdom of Bernard Shaw.* New York: Collier Books, 1962.

INDEX OF SCRIPTURE REFERENCES

INDEX OF NAMES AND SUBJECTS

Printed in the United States
149938LV00008B/63/A

9 780802 806703